INDIVIDUALS AND IDENTITY IN ECONOMICS

This book examines the different conceptions of the individual that have emerged in recent new approaches in economics, including behavioral economics, experimental economics, social preferences approaches, game theory, neuroeconomics, evolutionary and complexity economics, and the capability approach. These conceptions are classified according to whether they seek to revise the traditional atomist individual conception, put new emphasis on interaction and relations between individuals, account for individuals as evolving and self-organizing, and explain individuals in terms of capabilities. The method of analysis uses two identity criteria for distinguishing and re-identifying individuals to determine whether these different conceptions successfully identify individuals. Successful individual conceptions account for sub-personal and supra-personal bounds on single individual explanations. The former concerns the fragmentation of individuals into multiple selves; the latter concerns the dissolution of individuals into the social. The book develops an understanding of bounded individuality, seen as central to the defense of human rights.

John B. Davis is professor and chair of history and philosophy of economics at the University of Amsterdam; professor of economics at Marquette University, Milwaukee, Wisconsin; and Fellow at the Tinbergen Institute, the Netherlands. He is the author of *Keynes's Philosophical Development* (Cambridge University Press, 1994) and *The Theory of the Individual in Economics* (2003), which was a co-winner of the 2004 Myrdal Prize from the European Association for Evolutionary Political Economy. He is a co-editor with Wade Hands and Uskali Mäki of *The Handbook of Economic Methodology* (1998) and a co-editor with Warren Samuels and Jeff Biddle of *The Blackwell Companion to the History of Economic Thought* (2003). Professor Davis has published in journals such as the *Cambridge Journal of Economics, Economic Journal, Review of Political Economy, History of Political Economy,* and *Journal of Economic Methodology*. Professor Davis is a past president of the History of Economics Society, a past chair of the International Network for Economic Method, and a past president of the Association for Social Economics. He is a past editor of the *Review of Social Economy* and is currently co-editor with Wade Hands of the *Journal of Economic Methodology*.

Individuals and Identity in Economics

JOHN B. DAVIS

University of Amsterdam and Marquette University

CAMBRIDGE UNIVERSITY PRESS

CAMBRIDGE UNIVERSITY PRESS
Cambridge, New York, Melbourne, Madrid, Cape Town, Singapore,
São Paulo, Delhi, Dubai, Tokyo, Mexico City

Cambridge University Press
32 Avenue of the Americas, New York, NY 10013-2473, USA

www.cambridge.org
Information on this title: www.cambridge.org/9780521173537

First published 2011

Printed in the United States of America

A catalog record for this publication is available from the British Library.

Library of Congress Cataloging in Publication data
Davis, John Bryan.
Individuals and identity in economics / John B. Davis.
p.   cm.
Includes bibliographical references and index.
ISBN 978-1-107-00192-3 – ISBN 978-0-521-17353-7 (pbk.)
1. Economics – Psychological aspects.   2. Individualism.   3. Economic man.
4. Interpersonal relations.   5. Identity (Philosophical concept)   I. Title.
HB74.P8D38   2010
330.1–dc22   2010031354

ISBN 978-1-107-00192-3 Hardback
ISBN 978-0-521-17353-7 Paperback

For Zohreh

با عشق و تشکر

Contents

Acknowledgments

It is a pleasure to acknowledge my indebtedness to many people who have encouraged me and commented on and stimulated my thinking about individuals and identity at various stages of writing this book during the last several years: Richard Arena, Maarten Biermans, Ken Binmore, Mark Blaug, Larry Boland, Beatrice Boulu, Marcel Boumans, Dan Bromley, José Castro Caldas, Bruce Caldwell, Dave Colander, Annie Cot, Ricardo Crespo, Joe Daniels, Sandy Darity, Leila Davis, George DeMartino, Tyler DesRoches, Wilfred Dolfsma, Sheila Dow, Ross Emmett, Ben Fine, Nancy Folbre, Philippe Fontaine, Edward Fullbrook, Juan Carlos García-Bermejo, Rob Garnett, David George, Caroline Gerschlager, David Gindis, Nicola Giocoli, Francesco Guala, Wade Hands, Geoff Harcourt, Wendy Harcourt, Shaun Hargreaves Heap, Dan Hausman, Suzie Helburn, John Henry, Floris Heukelom, Geoff Hodgson, Hamid Hosseini, Jan de Jonge, Alan Kirman, Matthias Klaes, Judy Klein, No Knubben, Murat Kotan, Maurice Lagueux, Mike Lawlor, Tony Lawson, Fred Lee, Kyu Sang Lee, Paul Lewis, Pierre Livet, Harro Maas, Uskali Mäki, Alain Marciano, Solange Marin, Tiago Mata, Deirdre McCloskey, Robert McMaster, Steve Medema, Lanse Minkler, Phil Mirowski, Philippe Mongin, Mary Morgan, Tracy Mott, Fabienne Peter, Dick Peterson, Geert Reuten, Abu Rizvi, Ingrid Robeyns, Don Ross, Barkley Rosser, Marc von der Ruhr, Jochen Runde, Malcolm Rutherford, Warren Samuels, Ana Santos, Eric Schliesser, Bernhard Schmid, Amartya Sen, Esther-Mirjam Sent, Stefano Solari, Ron Stanfield, Irene van Staveren, Miriam Teschl, Robert Urquhart, Vela Velupillai, Jack Vromen, Tom Wells, Mark White, Stefano Zamagni, and Steve Ziliak. I am also indebted to a number of individuals who have anonymously reviewed my work at different stages and to the participants in many conference sessions where parts of this work were presented. I am also very much indebted to Scott Parris, senior editor at Cambridge University Press, for his kind support for my work and also support for work on economics and philosophy and the history of economics in general. I am grateful to Marquette University for a Way Klingler Humanities Fellowship in 2006, for a Sabbatical Fellowship Award for 2007–08, for a Miles Research Fellowship for 2004–10, and the general support of my colleagues. I am grateful to the University of Amsterdam for sabbatical support for 2007–08, and I am especially thankful for the years I have been privileged to be a member of the History and Philosophy of Economics Group. Finally, I am most indebted and most thankful to Zohreh Emami.

ONE

Introduction

The Individual in Economics

No entity without identity.
                              (Quine 1969, 23)

[A]n axiomatized theory has a mathematical form that is completely separated from its economic content.
                              (Debreu 1986, 1265)

[O]ur everyday conception of persons [is] as the basic units of thought, deliberation, and responsibility.
                              (Rawls 1993, 18, n. 20)

1.1 Individuals Count

This is a book about the conceptualization of the human individual in recent economics. Why this subject? Economics has long been seen as the social science that makes the individual central. Indeed, a leading justification for why much of our social world over the last half-century has been reinterpreted in the language and concepts of economics is that economics makes the human individual central. In this respect, economics seems in step with the world today. It is surely one of the great normative assumptions of contemporary human society – one not held in much of the past – that the human individual counts or should count, that the individual is important, and that individuals have an inherent moral value, despite all the evidence of human practices to the contrary. It is something of a mystery why people have come to believe this, considering the violent past we have inherited and the world we still have in the present; in the long record of human history, individuals have suffered and been sacrificed to "higher" causes in limitless number, often in the cruelest and most inhumane ways possible. With our history, the conclusion should be just the opposite: individuals do not count. Nonetheless, it is still ordinarily believed by vast numbers of people everywhere that individuals are important, that this is a fundamental human truth, and that human society should be constructed so that individuals are each valued as a human right. So economics' influence and power in representing the world today, it seems, is due in no small part to its being perceived as defending this deep human commitment.

There are good reasons to believe that economics operates with an inadequate conception of individuality, however, and thus does not and cannot defend this deep human commitment. Worse, a false defense of the individual, in which individuals really do not count in economics but are said to, may threaten this commitment by confusing our understanding of what is needed for saying individuals count in economic life and generally. Economics in the simplest sense is about maximizing production. Is this goal in the service of individuals, or are individuals in service to this goal? How would one know which conclusion is correct? I argued in my previous book on the theory of the individual in economics (Davis 2003) that the standard conception of the individual in economics does not explain the individual, and what people believe to be a conception of the human individual in economics is actually an abstract individual conception that represents individuals indiscriminately as single people, collections of people, parts of people, countries, organizations, animals, machines – indeed anything to which a maximizing function might be attributed. That is, though the standard view is purported to be about single human beings, or at least capable of also representing single human beings, it contains nothing to make it distinctively about human beings. Thus, basically it does not offer an account or defense of the single human being as an individual, because people have no more value in its analysis than all these other "individuals." On this view, economics is only about maximizing production, and individuals are in service to this goal.

However, economics is currently in a period of transition. It is now widely believed that important changes are under way in mainstream economics associated with the rise of a collection of new research programs and strategies of investigation, all of which can be argued to challenge fundamental assumptions in standard neoclassical economics, even if this is not necessarily the intent of those developing these new programs and strategies. Indeed there is now considerable debate about the depth and nature of the critiques that recent economics has advanced, primarily stimulated by the recognition that many of these new approaches directly challenge rationality theory, the recognized core of standard postwar economics. My view is that the recent challenges to standard economics aimed at rationality theory raise an even more fundamental challenge, namely to its assumption that rational individuals are atomistic individuals – the core idea of the abstract individual conception. Rationality theory, many seem to forget, is built around the assumption that individuals are atomistic, so that most do not see that any challenge to rationality theory is ultimately also a challenge to that conception. Thus, the new research programs in economics raise an important question: how will they reconceptualize the human individual as they seek to revise rationality theory? Will they attempt to revise rationality theory on its old atomistic individual basis, or will rethinking rationality mean rethinking individuality? Which path economists choose will say much about the continuing relevance of economics in a world in which people have already decided that individuals count.

This book thus examines the nature and different directions of development in thinking about the individual in recent economics. I treat recent economics as a heterogeneous collection of new approaches within mainstream economics that advance significant critiques of standard neoclassical economic theory, which has now undergone more than a century of development but no longer seems to be the basis on which economics is developing. The leading new research programs are: game theory, behavioral economics, experimental economics, evolutionary economics, neuroeconomics, complex adaptive systems theory, and the capability approach. I focus on these particular currents in recent economics, and not on the recent economics of non-mainstream heterodox economics, because it is the former, not the latter, that inherits the problematic legacy of the atomistic individual conception and which must accordingly determine how to address, not only what I argue is essentially a failed notion, but one that I believe is likely to be increasingly perceived as such. Of course economics as a discipline is not strongly motivated by philosophical concerns. It is a more pragmatic and applied subject, driven today especially by the exigencies of mathematical modeling and the need to explain the explosion of new market forms, and ultimately responsive to social economic policy concerns. However, this does not mean that philosophical problems do not underlie economic theorizing. They are not absent simply because most economists prefer to think on a different level. Philosophical problems are inherent in economic theorizing and thus play a role behind the scenes. Nonetheless, the recent strategies developed to re-explain the individual will be represented in this book as generally having different motivations and as being tied to the more immediate practical problems of economic theorizing. I will still argue, however, that those strategies exhibit a direction of development that raises fundamental philosophical issues, and that how they address these issues, intentionally or unintentionally, will ultimately be principal determinants of their success and social value.

Section 1.2 begins by briefly outlining the identity framework I use to discuss the individual in economics. Section 1.3 lays out why the traditional atomistic conception of the individual is deeply problematic as a conception of the individual, both in its early psychology-based form and in its postwar abstract individual form. In Section 1.4, I distinguish two main strategies for reconceptualizing individuals in recent economics, linking them to two different types of boundary problems that explanations of single individuals encounter in economics. I go on in Section 1.5 to comment on the nature of the change in recent mainstream economics in terms of the influence of other sciences and disciplines on economics. Section 1.6 addresses the issue of the normative significance of economics' view of the individual, and here I discuss the relationship between economics' individual conception and the subject of human rights, one important normative expression of the view that individuals count. Section 1.7 provides an outline of the argument of the book.

1.2　The Identity Framework

Identity is a central concept in this book, and I use a particular approach to it to organize my investigation of the individual in economics. One reason for this is that the concept is used in many different ways in contemporary social philosophy, social science, and the arts, and this profusion of senses and meanings makes it difficult to use in a systematic and coherent way (cf. Gleason 1983; Brubaker and Cooper 2000). This applies to economics as well, in which the concept has only relatively recently begun to be used, but in which it is also subject to different interpretations, relies on selective cross-field borrowings, and on the whole is poorly articulated and understood (cf. Kirman and Teschl 2004). My particular approach to identity – what I term an ontological-criterial approach to identity – involves asking whether the particular conceptions of things we employ are formulated in such a way as to be successful in identifying the things to which they are intended to refer. With respect to the individual, then, I first ask what the *concept* of an individual requires, or what fundamental criteria are involved in referring to things as individuals, and then ask whether particular *conceptions* of individuals in recent economics capture these requirements and satisfy these criteria in terms of how they are formulated. If they do not capture these requirements, my conclusion is that they fail to identify individuals, as we understand them according to our understanding of the concept of the individual. If they do capture these requirements, how they conceptualize individuals then describes the identity of the individual – or, since the subject here is specifically human individuals, that conceptualization describes the personal identity of individuals – though only, it needs to be added, in terms of what we can learn from how individuals are understood in economic life. Thus, in this type of analysis, the substantive content of what it means to be an individual comes from the conceptions economists use to characterize individuals, when those conceptions fulfill the basic requirements derived from the concept of the individual. I do not attempt to say what the identity of a person consists in but rather attempt to determine what personal identity is according to what our conceptions of individuals in economics imply when they are adequate to the concept of the individual. The method of the book, then, is to move progressively to this understanding by beginning with conceptions of the individual in recent economics that are unsuccessful in capturing what is involved in being an individual, diagnose what it is in these conceptions that makes them fall short, and then move on to conceptions that address these short-falls, exhibiting what it is about them that makes them successful.

The first of the two criteria I treat as required by the concept of the individual, one originally emphasized by Aristotle, is the *individuation criterion* (Aristotle 1924; Ross 1923). This criterion requires that for any candidate conception of an individual, if that conception indeed refers to and identifies individuals in terms of the way it is formulated, it follows that individuals in that conception are somehow successfully represented as distinct and independent beings. If this is not the case, then the candidate conception is not about individuals, despite any claims that it is. That is, it exhibits a misuse of language. The second criterion, one central to personal identity analysis in twentieth-century philosophy in connection with the idea of the self existing through time (Noonan 1991), is the *reidentification criterion*. This criterion requires that individuals that have already been shown to be distinct and independent in some conception of them can be reidentified as distinct and independent in those same terms across some process of change. That is, despite change in some or even many of an individual's characteristics, what makes that individual distinct and independent continues to be true of the individual after this change. The reidentification criterion, then, presupposes the individuation criterion, but failure of the reidentification criterion does not imply failure of the individuation criterion. We might show something to be distinct and independent on some basis at one point but not on that same basis at another, making individuality highly episodic. This point is important in this book, because I will argue that some conceptions of the individual in recent economics do succeed in showing individuals to be distinct and independent but then fail to show how they are enduringly so. Thus, the larger goal in the survey here is to locate and explain conceptions of the individual in economics that satisfy both criteria. Not all domains of investigation concerned with individuals need to have this more comprehensive goal, but I argue that economics needs to treat individuals as enduringly distinct for the following reasons.

First, economics treats intertemporal choice or choice across time as an essential part of the theory of economic behavior. Intertemporal choice assumes that people make choices they believe will affect them in the future. However, this becomes meaningless if our present selves cannot somehow be reidentified with our future selves. In economics, that is, people must be enduringly individual. Second, increasingly the most important kinds of economic activity that individuals engage in – education and training, family decisions, investment in such things as housing, saving for retirement, health care choices, and so forth – all presuppose that individuals endure through change. People's economic lives revolve around their expected survival. Indeed as income and wealth levels rise across the world, these types of long-term consumption rise as a share of all consumption, so that the character of individuals as enduring beings is becoming historically more important worldwide. Third, though it is an implicit and sometimes a suppressed premise of standard economics, individuals are thought to have an ability or capacity that they exercise in making choices. Saying people possess ability or capacity means there is something enduring about them apart from all their choices. For all three of these reasons, then, conceptions of the individual in economics need to satisfy both the individuation and reidentification criteria. In the following section, however, I argue that the standard atomistic individual conception of economics cannot satisfy either of these criteria, implying that the standard *Homo economicus* atomistic individual conception fails as a representation of human individuals.

1.3 The Atomistic Individual Conception: *Homo Economicus*

The traditional *Homo economicus* conception, as in the Robinson Crusoe fable, describes the individual as an isolated being, meaning one defined in terms of characteristics that are specific to the individual alone. These characteristics are normally taken to be preferences, but because all individuals possess preferences, they need rather to be characterized specifically as the individual's *own* preferences. Indeed Crusoe and Friday could have identical preferences over all things, but on the standard view they would still be defined as atomistic beings because they each possess those identical preferences as their own. That is, it is the ownership of preferences that matters, so what makes Crusoe an atomistic being is not simply having preferences but Crusoe having his *own* preferences. This is essentially what it means to say that preferences are exogenous. Economists can easily allow that preferences are socially influenced in terms of how people come to have them, but once individuals actually have them, they are then exogenous in the sense of being strictly their own.

However, representing an individual in terms of any set of *own* characteristics, preferences, or anything else defined as exclusively one's *own*, does not explain being individual or being an individual; it merely presupposes it in a circular way. Expanded out, it effectively says, "all things x will count as individuals, we will then give these x's such-and-such a characterization, and we will then say x is an individual in virtue of that characterization." Or, if you were to operationalize this procedure by claiming, say, that it enabled you to pick out distinct and independent individuals, this would be equivalent to first picking out what you want to call individuals, then ascribing to each of them some set of distinguishing characteristics, and then saying that they can be individuated in terms of those characteristics. In contrast, in a noncircular individuation procedure, you need to be able to refer to a set of features in the world without presupposing that they belong to a certain kind of thing already taken to be an individual and then show that those features of the world delimit and individuate something that you will say is to be taken as a certain kind of individual. For example, in Ronald Coase's theory of the firm (Coase 1937), in terms of features of the world, we distinguish nonmarket exchange from market exchange, and then we define the firm as an individual thing as a domain of nonmarket exchange. That is, we successfully individuate firms in terms of a particular type of exchange without at the same time referring to firms as independent entities; nonmarket exchange thus functions as a noncircular individuation criterion for firms.[1]

So the traditional atomistic individual conception does not explain individuality but merely stipulates a certain use of the term "individual." Remarkably, postwar neoclassicism has embraced this conclusion, while at the same time denying it to be a criticism by making circularity with

---

[1] I interpret Coase's analysis here as not making essential reference to the entrepreneur who distinguishes between contracting out and internally provided services. If the individuality of the firm depends on the individuality of the entrepreneur defined in terms of a set of own subjective preferences, then the firm fails to be individuated as a distinct and independent agent in a noncircular way.

respect to the individual a logical virtue in its now standard axiomatic representation of *Homo economicus*. Thus, individuals are identical to their utility functions because the formal conditions imposed on preferences – that preferences are complete, reflexive, transitive, continuous, and strongly monotonic – jointly guarantee that there exists a continuous utility function that represents those preferences. Individuals are assured of having their *own* preferences, then, not because the preference behavior we observe in the world in fact delimits and individuates people. Indeed there is much evidence in the form of patterns of shared tastes that the preference behavior we observe in the world fails to individuate people. Rather, individuals have their *own* preferences because "preferences" are axiomatically required to be "well-behaved" in order to represent the single individual to whom they are logically ascribed. People are consequently individuated as single individuals formally, not empirically. This state of affairs, of course, reflects the half-century-long flight of neoclassical economics from psychology – from early marginalism and cardinal utility theory to ordinalism and indifference analysis to Paul Samuelson and revealed preference to the formal and axiomatic representation of individuals in the postwar period. As Nicola Giocoli puts it,

We started from the classic notion of a rational agent inherited from the early marginalist writers, who viewed the agent as a relentless maximizer who aimed at pursuing his/her own goals and desires, and ended with the shrinking of rationality to a formal requirement of consistency, where the notion of agency was so stripped down of its human peculiarities as to become an all-purpose concept valid for real individuals as well as for groups or machines. (Giocoli 2003b, 3)

Economists of course still speak informally of preferences as if they were psychological phenomena, but what they really mean by the term is a formal ordering relation constructed so as to allow equilibrium market analysis. "Preferences" need to be "well-behaved" so that "choices" are rational, meaning that they support a functional representation of individuals that guarantees down-sloping demand and up-sloping supply curves when prices are parametrically varied. In this abstract individual *Homo economicus* conception that has replaced the old prewar psychological *Homo economicus* conception, rationality and individuality are co-defined, not in connection with human behavior, but by reference to the logical-mathematical properties of equilibrium analysis. As Gerhard Debreu says, "An axiomatized theory has a mathematical form that is completely separated from its economic content" (Debreu 1986, 1265). On this view, it follows, we could say that anything can be an "individual" in contemporary neoclassical economics as long as it fulfills the requirements of supply-and-demand equilibrium analysis. But actually, the correct implication for Debreu is that abstract individual conception really refers to nothing in the world whatsoever.

Yet, as hermetically secure as abstract Crusoe is in formal space, there are now widespread doubts regarding the applicability of the standard account of rational behavior to the real world as the result of an increasing volume of evidence produced by psychologists that people do not behave as they "rationally" should. This has had a significant impact on the direction of development of recent economics, but I believe what will be even more important in the long run for creating doubt about economics' rationality paradigm than the evidence regarding "anomalies" in choice theory is the wide-ranging debate and research outside economics throughout science regarding the nature of rationality, especially in mathematics, computational science, physics, engineering, communications sciences, and artificial intelligence studies, all of which regard a key test of what is rational as what computational processes can be engineered into physical mechanisms. Here, ironically, war and the design of armaments historically have had the lead, as rocketry, "smart" engineering systems, computable processes of all kinds, information science, and multiple forms of created or artificial intelligence have increasingly commanded the interpretation of what gets counted as rational (Clark 1998; Mirowski 2002; Klein 1998, 1999). One important conclusion that this approach to rationality produces is that rationality is always bounded by the historical state of scientific development with regard to how computational processes can be technically implemented and embedded in engineered hardware. Applied to economic behavior, if people are a kind of hardware, then their rationality is similarly bounded in terms of the computational or cognitive processes they are able to exercise at any point in time, where this reflects the historical state of development of a range of kinds of institutions, many sorts of computational tools and devices, education and training, social organization, and so forth.

What I draw from this is that if human rationality is materially bounded because of the way it is embedded in the world, then it seems fair to say that individuality is also bounded in virtue of the way it is embedded in the world. In this book I interpret the boundedness of individuality in terms of the space in which our explanations of individuals as enduringly distinct successfully operate. I argue that generally speaking this space is bounded in two directions reflecting the two identity criteria presupposed by the concept of an individual. The individuation criterion requires that individuals be distinct and independent. For individuals to be distinct and independent, they must hold together as single whole beings and cannot fragment or break up into multiple selves. Thus, one bound on successful single-individual explanations lies in how our representations of individuals enable us to say why they do not fragment into collections of sub-personal multiple selves. The reidentification criterion requires that individuals maintain their individual distinctness across change, especially when this change causes them to share many of their characteristics with others. They do not dissolve or disappear into the mass of people or society generally but can be reidentified as enduringly distinct individuals. Thus, the second bound on successful single-individual explanations lies in how our representations of individuals allow us to say why they do not become part of the supra-personal social world.

Nathaniel Wilcox has distinguished these sub-personal and supra-personal bounds in an especially clear way with respect to his explanation of what single agents are. The sub-personal bound concerns the "*fission* of agency," whereas the supra-personal bound concerns the many "*fusions* of agency" possible in social life (Wilcox 2008, 527). His view is not motivated by identity criteria but shares with my view the idea that our explanations of what individuals are break down where our discourse shifts to the sub-personal and supra-personal world. In those domains we have different explanatory goals tied to concerns we have with different types of entities, for example, cognitive structures that operate "within" individuals and social groups that operate "above" them. Single individuals or agents effectively drop out of these types of explanations. They concern coordinate domains of human explanation that share boundaries with single-individual types of explanations where they leave off and we return to the domain of single-individual explanations. The task for the latter, then, is to mark off and map out the explanatory space in which single individuals are our object, framing this in terms of the sub-personal and supra-personal bounds that structure it. Moreover, given that human knowledge is in a continual state of development, this marking off and accounting for where the bounds on single-individual explanations lie requires continual interpretation and reinterpretation. This book's examination of recent economics confines this interpretive process to new thinking about individuals in economics and how it addresses the bounds on their explanation as enduringly distinct.

1.4 Two Strategies and Two Problems for Reconceptualizing Individuals in Recent Economics

Whereas an important motivation for much of the new research in mainstream economics is the belief that standard rationality theory does not adequately explain choice behavior, I will argue that there are two broadly different views about what is wrong with rationality theory in recent economics, and that these views can be distinguished according to how they address one or the other of the two boundaries on single-individual explanations. What are the two broad views regarding what is wrong with traditional rationality theory? One emphasizes the interdependence of individuals' choices and sees the failure to take this into account as the main problem. This concern gave rise to game theory in the 1980s, which produced the first major diversification of mainstream economics away from the purely price-theoretic supply-and-demand neoclassical model. The second emphasizes the extensive evidence on choice anomalies and sees a lack of realism as the problem in standard choice theory. This concern gave rise to both an "old" and "new" behavioral economics, though it has only been the latter, since the 1990s, that has had an impact on mainstream economics. Other new research programs in economics seem to have more diffuse motivations, and in some cases share both concerns. Whether the concern is choice interdependence or realism or both, the focus has largely been on rationality, not on individuality. This means that conclusions about how individuality is being reconceptualized depend on drawing out the implications of how rationality is being reconceptualized. Consider the implications, then, that each of these two concerns about rationality has for the explanation of individuality.

First, if interdependence of choice is considered essential to explaining rational behavior, and choice interdependence is a kind of social interaction, then the further implication of this concern is that our explanation of individuality needs to include social interaction. Social interaction, of course, can mean many things, and game theory clearly limits its meaning to how one person's choices depend on another's. At the same time, game theory assumes that how one person's choices depend on another's can be explained without significantly revising the traditional *Homo economicus* conception. Thus, with respect to both rationality and individuality, the larger goal of game theory can be interpreted as being to demonstrate that the explanation of choice can be improved by incorporating social interaction understood as choice interdependence in a way compatible with standard thinking about individuality.

Consider, however, what is involved in combining social interaction thus understood and the *Homo economicus* conception. Given that the *Homo economicus* simply presupposes that people are distinct and independent and does not actually allow us to show that they are, there is no clear reason to think that treating social interaction as choice interdependence will provide a very substantial account of the former, nor significantly improve the explanation of rational choice by including the effects of social interaction on choice. Indeed the protracted and seemingly endless discussion of the paradoxical prisoner's dilemma – which shows rationality to be inefficient – seems to show this. Why, then, have game theorists not given more serious attention to stronger interpretations of social interaction than choice interdependence? I suggest that the answer is that with their attachment to the *Homo economicus* conception, they have no way of theorizing the supra-personal bound on single-individual explanations that separates the domains of individuality and sociality, and so they cannot begin to show how stronger forms of social interaction might be compatible with people still being individuals. Part 2 and the last chapter in Part 1 are accordingly devoted to how this issue is addressed in recent economics in connection with attention to the supra-bound issue and the nature of interaction between individuals.

Second, if the other main concern in recent economics about rational choice theory is that it is insufficiently realistic – specifically, insufficiently psychologically realistic – and if the way to address this shortcoming is to explain how individuals employ various empirically observed choice mechanisms, then the further implication of this concern is that our explanation of individuality needs to incorporate these various choice mechanisms. By choice mechanisms, the new behavioral economists mean the many ways psychologists have shown that the choices people make reflect the character of the contexts in which choices are made. This strategy is also thought to be essentially compatible with maintaining the traditional *Homo economicus* conception, and so we may interpret the larger explanatory goal here as showing that a more psychologically realistic account of choice can be built up around standard thinking about individuality.

However, again, since the traditional *Homo economicus* conception does not actually allow us to explain individuality, it cannot provide grounds for saying that all the different empirically identified choice mechanisms psychologists have studied work at the level of the single individual or rather function sub-personally. Do single individuals make choices across time, or are their choices somehow a function of the changing contexts in which they make them? If the latter, then they may fragment into a series of multiple selves who each make their own choices according to their specific circumstances. That this is seen to be a significant problem in behavioral economics is the considerable discussion of the evidence showing that individuals behave time-inconsistently and constantly abandon their past choices, selves, and commitments as their circumstances change. Behavioral economists nonetheless have stuck by the *Homo economicus* conception, and assume that time-inconsistent preferences can somehow be explained away within the standard individual framework. Their attachment to the *Homo economicus* conception, I suggest, consequently prevents them from fully recognizing the nature of the sub-personal bound on single-individual explanations, and thus prevents them from recognizing the problem of explaining how people can have multiple selves and yet somehow still be single individuals. The first two chapters of Part 1 especially are devoted to how this issue is addressed in connection with psychologically more realistic accounts of choice behavior.

Thus, one thing I will argue in this book is that whereas much of the new research in recent mainstream economics challenges the neoclassical paradigm by aiming to improve on standard rationality theory, when those strategies operate within the scope of the traditional *Homo economicus* conception, they fail to address the associated and linked issues involved in representing and explaining individuals. They thus fail to explain how both rationality and individuality are bounded in virtue of their being embedded in the world. The book's second conclusion is that those strategies that depart from the traditional *Homo economicus*, and which have sought to explain the ways in which individuality is bounded just as rationality is bounded, have indeed made progress in explaining both in economic life. Yet there is no great reason for optimism here. Because the question of what individuality is lies mostly in the shadow of mainstream economists' chief interest in the nature of rationality in economics, discourse on the question remains unfocused, and many contributors do not even appear to recognize the positions they have implicitly taken about individuals (so great, it seems, is the hold of the *Homo economicus* conception on economists' imaginations). Accordingly, how economics will sort itself out on this issue in the future remains generally unclear.

1.5 Economics' Embeddedness

The discussion in the preceding sections may make it seem that economics as a subject develops according to its own internal logic and is little influenced by other disciplines and sciences. Yet historically economics has not developed in isolation, but has rather regularly borrowed and appropriated the concepts, ideas, principles, and methods of other sciences. Indeed, one of the key facts about the collection of new research strategies that have emerged in recent mainstream economics is that they all have their origins largely outside of economics. Somewhat oversimplifying, we can say that game theory comes from mathematics, behavioral economics comes from psychology, experimentalism is standard throughout science, neuroeconomics was first conceived of by neuroscientists, complexity modeling in economics was stimulated by physics, evolutionary thinking comes from biology, and the capabilities approach shows the influence of philosophy. There are also indigenous sources of change in recent economics, such as those resulting from the export of neoclassical principles into nonmarket social domains (the family, law, religion, and government), often referred to as economics imperialism (Lazear 2000; Fine and Milonakis 2009). However, the more transformative effects on economics, not surprisingly, have come from research programs that have imported quite different conceptual frameworks and methodologies of investigation employed in other fields but not in economics (Colander, Holt, and Rosser 2004; Davis 2008c). We distinguish sciences and disciplines from one another because they are different in fundamental ways. Thus, cross-science movements of concepts and strategies of investigation have a special potential for redirecting the course of what goes on in any given science or discipline. This is no less the case with economics than other fields.[2]

There are also distinctive features of economics' recent pattern of borrowing, however, in that it has been relatively one-sided and disproportionately a mathematics and natural science borrowing. This is fairly obvious with respect to the game theory, evolutionary economics, experimentalism, complexity economics, and neuroeconomics. Behavioral economics might be thought an exception on the grounds that psychology is a social science, but the psychology that underlies behavioral economics is its most naturalistic branch, and social psychology has had at best a modest influence on recent economics. Only the capabilities approach really does not fit this story and indeed its hold on the mainstream is tenuous. Thus natural science and a naturalist vision of what science should accomplish seem dominant in the current reorientation of economics, so that the new general view of economic behavior is basically that it is a phenomenon that can be investigated with natural science methods. Indeed, this is especially clear when we record some of the sciences and disciplines that have not had much recent influence on economics but did have influence in the nineteenth century when the field was called moral science or political economy and also more recently in the twentieth-century interwar period in connection with American institutionalist economics: political science and statecraft,

---

[2] On the subject of boundaries between disciplines, see Abbott (1988), Bourdieu (1988), Galison and Stump (1996), Bowker and Starr (1999), Collins (1998), Geiryn (1993, 1999), and Lamont and Molnár (2002).

history, sociology, social psychology, anthropology, cultural studies, business studies, philosophy, ethics, theology, and law. Economics, then, may be more open today than it has been for many years in the sense that it has freely engaged in appropriating and accommodating developments from other sciences, but it is also doing so in a highly selective manner. I will not discuss what is methodologically problematic about a social science modeling itself on natural science, because this would involve a lengthy discussion, but I will simply comment on what this might imply for future thinking about the individual in economics.

Thus, one thing it seems fair to say about the natural sciences versus the social sciences and the humanities with respect to the subject of the individual is that the former have a relatively weak commitment, if any at all, to the idea that the human individual is a fundamentally important object of investigation. The natural sciences, that is, tend to look past single individuals to natural forces operating on individuals (should they even recognize individuals as distinguishable phenomena), whereas the social sciences and the humanities tend to build their explanations around the idea that individuals are agents, indeed key agents in the world, as reflects social opinion generally. Thus, it is conceivable that a continuing development of economics along natural science lines will ultimately eliminate individuals as significant actors from economics discourse. Indeed, one interpretation of economics' movement over the last century from its early view of the individual as "a relentless maximizer who aimed at pursuing his/her own goals and desires" to its postwar abstract individual conception "so stripped down of its human peculiarities as to become an all-purpose concept valid for real individuals as well as for groups or machines" (Giocoli 2003b, 3) is that this was a century in which a natural science vision of economics came to dominate the field (and some would say to dehumanize it). Yet one must wonder, given that economics is in fact a social science, whether this trend is sustainable. In particular, if economics ceases to be about human individuals, can it ultimately maintain its standing as a policy science? Does economic policy that cannot be formulated in terms of its impact on individuals because it cannot identify them actually make sense from the point of view of the consumers of economics? That economics has long been assumed to be about human individuals may be partly responsible for this question infrequently being posed. Perhaps, then, the apparent return of psychology to economics in the form of behavioral economics (cf. Hands 2006) may signal a beginning realization that mainstream economics is in need of being regrounded in an understanding of the human individual. However, as argued in the chapters to follow, that this return to psychology is mostly based on updating *Homo economicus* leaves many questions about how much it will accomplish.

Yet there is no doubt that how economics develops in the future will also depend heavily on what occurs in the world beyond the science community. Economics is also embedded in a system or set of systems of human social organization that are the product of a history associated with accelerating technological change, complex worldwide problems of social adjustment, and increasing environmental fragility. Indeed, the two boundary problems I distinguished in Section 1.3 to define the space of single-individual explanations are real problems for individuals themselves in the world today. What significance individuality has as social interaction becomes more dense and many-sided and how people sustain their identities as their circumstances exhibit more frequent and more unexpected change are ordinary issues in contemporary life. The idea of identity has not become a more common subject of discussion simply because people write more about it today than they did in the past. People write about it more today because it has become more of a concern than it was in the past. I attribute this to the sense many have that the rate of social change is increasing. If this is indeed true about the world we live in, it seems reasonable to ask: What is likely to become of individuality? What will economics have to say about it?

1.6 The Normative Significance of Economics' View of the Individual

Don Ross criticized my previous book on the individual (Davis 2003) for being humanist; by this he meant that I treat the individual as an object of normative rather than scientific concern and let "normative considerations trump scientific-behavioral ones" (Ross 2005, 269, 270). He regards his own approach to the individual, which he characterizes as "scientism," to be methodologically superior in defending an "antianthropocentric view, uniting core insights of neoclassical economics with evolutionary cognitive and behavioral science" (ibid., 16, 19). I accept the label he gives me, and I believe that the individual is indeed an object of normative concern. Like John Rawls, I hold a normative conception of the person that "begins from our everyday conception of persons as the basic units of thought, deliberation, and responsibility" and values people as individuals (Rawls 1993, 18, n. 20). The opposition Ross creates between us is unfair to both of us, because as a self-proclaimed political liberal he also defends a kind of normative individualism (Ross 2005, 16ff.), whereas I do not, as he says, make normative values "trump" my analysis of the individual in economics, which is rather based on an identity analysis of individual conceptions as we find them in economics. Moreover, the idea that there exists some kind of value-neutral approach to the individual in economics employing a natural science vision of economics in my view altogether misses the way in which social values operate throughout economics and science. That economics has worked with a circular conception of the individual for so long in part explains why so many economists are at fault in this regard, because when you presuppose individuality in your analysis, you tend to think that individuals are natural objects; that is, naturally occurring collections of preferences that can be scientifically investigated as if there were no value assumptions underlying this view. However, individuals are in fact central to economics, not because economists have determined that individuals are scientifically relevant, but because the social world we live in values individuals and thus makes them an object of normative and scientific concern. The lesson in this for economics is that it has both scientific and normative responsibility with respect to how it addresses the individual. Most of this book is concerned with the former in the analysis I offer of how economists have sought to represent individuals in terms of their behavior, but in this section I briefly discuss why individuals also ought to be seen as objects of normative concern for economics.[3]

There are many ways in which economics' view of the individual can be normatively significant, but I will emphasize the central role it plays in determining the scope and nature of economic rights seen as crucially important human rights. Economic rights, along with political, social, and cultural rights, have been widely regarded as human rights for more than a half-century since the 1948 United Nations Declaration of Human Rights.[4] However, in terms of their relation to overall individual well-being, economic rights are easily seen to be especially important human rights. Consider the following facts (Hertel and Minkler 2007, 1). From 1998 to

---

[3]　In Chapter 10, I return to the normative dimensions of economics and discuss how the individual conception one employs determines the nature of economic policy and also has repercussions for one's view of democracy and justice.

[4]　In the United Nations Universal Declaration of Human Rights (http://www.un.org/en/documents/udhr/), as originally adopted in 1948, individuals' economic rights are represented as what is needed to secure an ordinary livelihood – thus existence itself. The Declaration lists as economic rights the rights to (a) property (Article 17), (b) employment, including fair compensation and freedom from discrimination (Articles 23 and 24), (c) an adequate standard of living, including food, clothing, housing, medical care, and security against unemployment, sickness, disability, and old age (Article 25), and (d) basic education (Article 26). These economic rights are further explained and expanded on in the United Nations International Covenant on Economic, Social, and Cultural Rights (http://www2.ohchr.org/english/law/cescr.htm), as subsequently adopted in 1966.

2005, it has been estimated that terrorism killed twenty thousand people globally – a violation of individual political rights. Yet in 2001 alone, twenty-two million people died preventable deaths due to poverty and deprivation – a violation of individual economic rights. Moreover, in that same year, 2.7 billion people lived on two dollars a day or less, implying inadequate nutrition, shelter, employment, and medical care – a further violation of individual economic rights. Thus, human rights are very much a matter of economic rights. However, there is a problem in making the case that human and economic rights ought to matter that reflects how they differ from the more familiar political rights. The defense of political rights has historically gone hand in hand with the defense of national democratic structures, so that political rights have a comparatively secure basis in citizenship rights. However, human rights as the rights of individuals per se are by definition supranational rights and thus have historically had a markedly thinner set of justifications.

Here, then, economics finds itself in a historically central position, because the conception of the individual it employs potentially has important consequences for the defensibility of economic rights and thus, given their importance, the defensibility of human rights. That is, because economic rights concern individuals' most fundamental economic requirements, and because economics makes claims about what individuals are, what economics ultimately says about individuals plays a central role in determining the status of economic (and human) rights in the world today. Unfortunately, economics' current *Homo economicus* conception of the individual has little to offer in this regard. Indeed, the standard view of the individual is more closely associated with the traditional economics doctrine of consumer sovereignty, or the idea that individuals each know their own economic interest better than anyone else, which is largely an extension of the classical liberal view of political rights that treats each individual as sovereign with respect to speech, religion, and political participation. Moreover, the privacy idea that preferences are individuals' "own" preferences underlies much classical liberal doctrine long deployed in defense of political rights, not human rights. Thus, the standard conception of the individual in economics really does not support the idea of individuals having economic rights seen as human rights in the United Nations Declaration.

What conception of the individual economics will employ in the future is an open question. The method of analysis employed in this book, then, is not only meant to determine whether the individual conceptions under development in recent economics are adequate as single-individual explanations. It is also meant to tell us something about what being an individual requires in economic life. That is, if we can use identity analysis to say what it is for people to be enduringly distinct individuals, then we ought also have some understanding of what is needed in the form of economic policy should society seek to ensure this. Thus, an investigation that is scientific in nature can also be normatively significant. Indeed, normative concerns are an important motivation for this book, though at the same time they do not exhaust what it is about.

1.7 Outline of the Argument of the Book

The book is divided into three parts with Part 1 (Chapters 2, 3, and 4) examining strategies in recent economics that are closest to standard economics' atomistic individual view, Part 2 (Chapters 5, 6, and 7) turning to accounts that make a departure from it by making social interaction central to the explanation of the individual, and Part 3 (Chapters 8, 9, and 10) explaining individuals in both a relational and evolutionary way as socially embedded. Parts 1 and 2 discuss strategies that are really alternative to one another; Part 3 extends and further develops the successful strategies of Part 2. Generally the argument of the book moves from what I regard as basically unsuccessful strategies for explaining individuals to increasingly successful ones. Part 1 also sets the stage for the arguments that follow; I show how the general strategy of revising the atomistic individual view by making it psychologically more realistic runs aground on one of the two main boundary problems single-individual explanations face: fragmentation and dissolution of the individual into multiple selves. Parts 2 and 3 then show how both this problem and the second boundary problem are addressed more or less successfully in the different strategies examined there, thus as a whole setting out the space in which single-individual explanations work in economics.

Part 1 begins in Chapter 2 with a discussion of one of two reactions on the part of early postwar psychology to economics' rational choice theory – that associated with psychologist Ward Edwards' influential Behavioral Decision Research (BDR) program at the University of Michigan. Two different strategies emerged for Michigan BDR psychologists, one associated with Daniel Kahneman and Amos Tversky's collaboration to produce prospect theory and one associated with the idea that preferences are socially constructed. These two views are each associated with a different interpretation of the nature of rationality. Both views had a subsequent impact on economics, prospect theory on the "new" behavioral economics and preference construction thinking in a more indirect manner on market experimentalism. Chapter 2 goes on to focus on prospect theory, and Chapters 3 and 4 discuss two further main developments in behavioral economics. (Discussion of market experimentalism comes later in connection with interaction in Part 2.) In Chapter 2, I argue that prospect theory seeks to revise the atomistic individual conception by making it psychologically more realistic, but its attachment to atomism compromises its conception of the individual by generating multiple selves problems, particularly inter-temporal ones. Chapter 3 is then devoted to a leading view in behavioral economics regarding how the multiple selves problem can be explained away within the framework of *Homo economicus*, and also to the dilemmas in welfare policy associated with "libertarian paternalism" that result from how time-inconsistent behavior produces multiple selves. One of the main conclusions Chapter 3 advances is that behavioral strategies developed to deal with multiple selves fail because they fail to adequately integrate interaction into the analysis of individuals with multiple selves. Chapter 4 accordingly then looks at strategies in behavioral economics that might address this failing by introducing interaction directly into the individual utility function in the form of social preferences. However, this strategy for revising atomism, an internalizing sociality strategy, only produces more complicated multiple selves problems, particularly as connected to individuals having social identities. Thus, the general conclusion of Part 1 is that maintaining an attachment to the atomistic individual conception, even when made psychologically more realistic, ultimately generates intractable multiple selves problems. Not only are people then not individuated as distinct and independent whole beings, but it follows that they cannot be reidentified as such either. I suggest that this is the conclusion one would expect given the circular character of the traditional atomistic individual conception. In any event, I claim that economics redeveloped in this way does not offer a way forward for thinking about what individuals are.

The premise of Part 2 is that explaining individuals in terms of social interaction constitutes a potential means of escaping the limits of atomism. Game theory, discussed in Chapter 5, assumes individuals interact directly, but I argue that classical game theory is unable to develop this intuition on account of its commitment to the atomistic individual conception. At the opposite extreme, experimental game theory, when indefinitely repeated play is assumed, raises a whole host of issues regarding the effects inter-action has on individuals, which threaten to dissolve individuality into sociality altogether – the second boundary problem for single-individual explanations. Chapter 6 then turns a positive corner in the book's argument and looks at two recent game theory views that assume individuals have multiple selves, but then shows how individuals can nonetheless be thought to be distinct and independent whole beings because of how they interact with others. One case draws on social identity theory and the other involves neuroeconomics, but both deal directly with the sub-personal bound on single-individual explanations and derive individuality from interaction. They are what I characterize as relational individual conceptions. They satisfy the individuation criterion, but they do not succeed in also showing how individuals can be reidentified as enduringly distinct and independent, and thus they do not successfully address the supra-personal bound on single-individual explanations. Thus, in order to explain relational individuality through time, Chapter 7 turns back to early postwar psychology and the second main reaction to economics' rational choice theory, that associated with Herbert Simon and his way of explaining ecologically rational individuals as adaptive and self-organizing. This chapter then sets out a combined relational-evolutionary individual conception that plays a role in Vernon Smith's market experimentalism and in Ken Binmore's evolutionary game theory reasoning. In principle, this individual conception successfully addresses both the individuation and reidentification issues. Key to it is the assumption that people have certain fundamental human capacities. However, on a genuinely evolutionary view of the world, people's human capacities should also be seen as evolving. That is, they ought to be seen as capabilities people develop that co-evolve with their forms of social interaction.

This introduces the discussion of Part 3, which treats individuals as collections of capabilities in contrast to the traditional view of them as collections of preferences. The shift from capacities to capabilities that people are always developing makes the relational-evolutionary individual type of conception from Part 2 a fully social conception, because we cannot talk about individuals' capabilities except in social settings where those capabilities have their meaning in interaction with others. Chapter 8 thus discusses what individuals are when seen as collections of capabilities, and emphasizes the special importance of complex capabilities. I argue that social psychology explains individuals in this way in terms of how they continually order and reorder their self-conceptions – a working self-concept idea. I interpret this as a matter of having a personal identity self-narrative and regard this as a key human capability. Chapter 9 returns to social identity seen as a special kind of capability and the "economics of identity," and discusses how we understand individuality when personal identity is seen as endogenous to the dynamics of social groups. Here I distinguish two different kinds of social identities and the different ways individuals relate to them as entire social identity structures. As self-organizing beings, individuals are said to manage these structures of social identity as they construct their personal identity self-narratives in developing their capabilities. Part 3 and the book then conclude with Chapter 10. There I turn to the normative implications of this analysis of the individual and argue that as economic policy is ultimately designed to promote the aims of individuals, it needs to be reconfigured to accommodate a capabilities rather than preferences conception of the individual. This entails we take seriously normative values that currently do not play a role in economics. I argue that as there are many such values, and that value pluralism characterizes the world, how society is organized becomes relevant to the formulation of economic policy. The chapter closes with a discussion of how we should understand democracy and justice when value pluralism is embraced and we regard individuals as collections of capabilities.

PART 1

ATOMISM REVISED

TWO

Psychology's Challenge to Economics

Rationality and the Individual

Though the field's scientists may begin to lose faith and consider alternatives, they are unlikely to renounce the paradigm that has led them into crisis. Once it has achieved the status of a paradigm, a scientific theory is declared invalid only if an alternative candidate emerges to take its place.
(Boumans and Davis 2010, 100)

2.1 Psychology's Behavioral Decision Research: Two Origins

It is widely held that psychology's postwar critique of rationality theory constitutes a fundamental challenge to economics. I argue that this challenge must ultimately be understood in terms of the connection between rationality theory and its underlying *Homo economicus* conception of the individual. In fact, psychology offers two different critiques of standard rationality theory associated with two different underlying conceptions of the individual, one that largely takes over and revises economics' atomistic individual conception and one that clearly rejects it. This chapter is devoted to the first of these critiques; Chapter 7 discusses the second. Both arise with the emergence of the postwar psychology field of Behavioral Decision Research (BDR) that produced first an "old" and then later a "new" behavioral economics (Sent 2004; Angner and Loewenstein, forthcoming). The "old" behavioral economics, associated with Herbert Simon, Reinhard Selten, and Gerd Gigerenzer, takes the stronger position, develops a view of rationality as bounded, and rejects economics' atomistic individual conception, offering in its place a more evolutionary type of view that effectively supports an ecological conception of rationality combined with what can be characterized as an ecological conception of individuality. The "new" behavioral economics, associated with Daniel Kahneman and Amos Tversky, also essentially develops a view of rationality as bounded but basically retains economics' atomistic individual conception, revising it in ways that lightly embed individuals in the world in an essentially ahistorical nondevelopmental way. Most commentators have focused on the differences between these two behavioral economics in terms of their differences regarding the critique of rationality theory, but my view is that these differences need to be understood in terms of their differences regarding the nature of individuality and how it is bounded as well. This chapter begins to defend this conclusion by examining the individual conceptions that underlie the two currents in postwar BDR, one of which lays the individual foundations for the "new" behavioral economics.

BDR is a subfield in psychology that investigates the psychological characteristics of individual decision making in circumstances of risk, which is understood as probabilistic uncertainty. It arose in the 1950s when psychologists first began to systematically investigate expected utility theory (EUT), first developed by John von Neumann and Oskar Morgenstern (1944) and subsequently as subjective expected utility analysis by Leonard Savage (1954). There were two main views regarding the meaning and significance of EUT within BDR. First, Ward Edwards, a psychologist at the University of Michigan, who knew economics well and whose father was an economist, saw EUT as basically correct but in need of modest changes to make it more realistic psychologically. He thus took on the task of introducing psychologists to economists' expected utility reasoning with the goal of refining that theory psychologically, early on producing two highly influential papers that are generally regarded as foundational for the field (Edwards 1954, 1961; cf. Edwards, Miles, and von Winterfeldt 2007). He also helped bring Savage to Michigan and trained many of the individuals who later made key contributions to the emerging field of BDR, including Amos Tversky, Sarah Lichtenstein, and Paul Slovic (Phillips and von Winterfeldt 2007; Fryback 2005).

Second, a quite different take on EUT also central to the postwar emergence of BDR came from Herbert Simon at Carnegie-Mellon, who from early in his career argued forcefully against the standard view of rationality as utility maximization and posed an alternative in two also highly influential papers that argued individual decision making needed to be understood in terms of the cognitive capacities of human decision makers relative to the environments they occupy (Simon 1955, 1956; cf. Payne and Bettman 1992). Simon and his colleagues at Carnegie-Mellon were subsequently instrumental in developing the new field of Administrative Science, which trained many researchers in the theory of decision making in organizations. However, as we will see in Chapter 7, Simon, despite his differences from

Edwards, also influenced a number of people trained in the latter's program, thus helping produce a current in Edwards' program that gave up the strategy of revising *Homo economicus*, did not contribute to the psychology that led to the "new" behavioral economics, and which ultimately rather had an impact on market experimentalism in economics.

The combination of Edwards' dissemination and Simon's critique of EUT made the theory accessible to psychologists in the new field of BDR, but it also created a split regarding research strategies. The strategy Edwards preferred was to treat standard rationality theory as normatively correct but to regard behavior descriptively inconsistent with it as a deviation from rationality – a position now central to the "new" behavioral economics (Thaler 2000; Heukelom 2009). This involved adopting modified "utility" functions as individual objective functions so as to make them more realistic, and also implied there were no significant implications in the revision of EUT for the atomistic individual conception. However, this strategy was inherently problematic for psychologists, which in part explains why Simon's approach had influence at Michigan. A psychologically more realistic approach had to allow for factors that influenced preferences – a subject psychologists had long studied – and the idea that preferences might be socially constructed in some way undermined the idea that individuals had well-defined utility functions. This became an increasing concern for two of Edwards' Michigan students, Lichtenstein and Slovic, whose experiments on gambling behavior later produced the first widely accepted critiques of standard rationality theory in connection with preference reversals. They were thus really closer to Simon than Edwards in recognizing the weight of environmental influences on individual decision making; but in contrast to Simon, their Edwards-inspired modified "utility" function entry point with preferences as the central construct, once questioned, essentially left them without any conception of the individual whatsoever. In a world in which preferences are constructed, individuals are somehow constructed as well, thus erasing the boundaries on individuality. Simon, as we will see in Chapter 7, did not build on the preferences view of individuals, but began with an alternative conception of the individual, a dynamic ecological conception relying on individuality-reinforcing feedback principles. However, this alternative research strategy fell outside the Edwards program at Michigan of upgrading EUT and the preference approach generally.

This chapter examines the two currents within the Edwards-inspired BDR program: Tversky and Kahneman's heuristics and biases program and prospect theory, which led to the "new" behavioral economics, and Lichtenstein and Slovic's alternative preference construction program, whose preferences reversal analysis was an important stimulus to the emergence of market experimentalism in economics. Both psychological approaches, I will argue, fail to develop an adequate conception of the individual, because their entry point is the traditional atomistic conception and because of the weak connection they assume between rationality and individuality. In the two chapters that follow this one, I examine strategies later adopted in "new" behavioral economics that attempt to address the fundamental problems the Tversky-Kahneman current encounters with its revised atomistic individual conception. This chapter is my only discussion of the alternative preference construction approach, and when I return to the Simon current in BDR in Chapter 7, preference construction gets reconfigured by experimental economists who emphasize learning and adaptation as a means to explaining equilibration in markets. There, however, it is more the direct influence of Simon (and Gigerenzer) on Vernon Smith that will provide the segue when postwar BDR's second track comes back into play, as psychology's preference construction program as it has arisen out of the work of Lichtenstein and Slovic has not had much impact on economics beyond the illustration of preference reversals. Broadly speaking, then, the historical narrative presented here is one of multiple, cross-cutting disciplinary boundary crossings between economics and psychology. EUT was first imported from economics into psychology in the 1950s and redeveloped. Then new views of decision making and individuals were exported back to economics, first by Simon and his followers in the form of the "old" behavioral economics, then later by the followers of Kahneman and Tversky in the form of the "new" behavioral economics, and then even later in Smith's more recent grounding of his experimental approach in Simon's ecological rationality idea.

Section 2.2 begins with the rationality-individuality connection in standard theory, arguing that the atomistic individual conception is tied to rationality in two different ways in postwar standard economics as reflect its two main views of rationality. This means that as there are two broad ways in which rationality breaks down, so there are two broad ways in which individuality breaks down. One of these two views of rationality and individuality is targeted in Kahneman and Tversky's prospect theory, and the second is targeted in Lichtenstein and Slovic's preference reversal analysis. Section 2.3 focuses on Kahneman and Tversky's prospect theory and argues that their alternative account of decision making and individuals leads to the problem of multiple selves across time. Section 2.4 focuses on Lichtenstein and Slovic's preference reversal analysis and argues that its alternative preference construction account of decision making and individuals altogether undermines the idea that the individual is a single being. These two BDR strategies, then, either fragment individuals into multiple selves or produce so many multiple selves as to entirely eliminate them. They thus each fail in explaining the sub-personal bound on single-individual conceptions. Section 2.5 turns back from psychology to economics and to behavioral economics and market experimentalism, associates the former with the first line and the latter (at least early on) with the second line of thinking.

2.2 The Two Rationality-Individuality Connections in Standard Economics

Here I argue that as standard rationality theory in economics and the atomistic *Homo economicus* individual conception go hand in hand, challenges to standard rationality theory are ultimately also challenges to the atomistic individual conception. I make this argument with respect to each of the two broad approaches to rationality I distinguish in mainstream economic theory: preference maximization and consistency in choice.[1] Rationality as preference maximization, or utility maximization, presupposes the objective being pursued and treats rational choice as optimal behavior in achieving it. Consistency in choice, on the other hand, makes no reference to the objectives of choice; it simply compares choices themselves and derives principally from Samuelson's revealed preference theory proposal to free the theory of economic behavior "from any vestigial traces of the utility concept" (1938, 71). The approaches are often not distinguished and are similar in that both rely on a well-known set of axiomatic assumptions regarding the nature of preferences whose violation produces irrational choice behavior. More interesting from my perspective is that both also treat violations of rational behavior as disrupting the associated conception of the individual, but they are different with regard to how these violations disrupt that conception.

The preference maximization approach to rationality focuses on the relation between the axioms governing preferences and the representation of individuals in terms of individual utility functions. When those axioms are violated, that utility function representation of the individual also fails. In particular, when the continuity assumption is violated (such as when

---

[1] Consistency in choice has become the dominant view of rationality, but many economists continue to reason in terms of preference maximization. For accounts of each, see Sen (1997); for the rise of the consistency view and the "escape from psychology" at the expense of the more traditional preferences maximization view, see Giocoli (2003b); for an historical overview of rationality choice theory, see Sugden (1991).

individuals exhibit lexicographic preferences), the utility function is discontinuous, and a given set of preferences cannot then be shown to belong to a single maximizing individual, or alternatively a given set of preferences can support more than one utility function. Because utility functions represent the single individual, if preferences do not support a single utility function, the individual fragments into multiple selves. In contrast, the consistency-in-choice approach to rationality focuses on the relations between the choices themselves, particularly as they reflect the transitive preferences axiom. Should this axiom be violated and individuals have intransitive preferences, they can then make choices that cause them to function as money pumps. This allows them to be arbitraged out of existence by having their resources eliminated, leaves them then unable to make further choices, and implies that they thereby cease to exist as decision makers.[2]

The different ways in which the two views explain the breakdown of the atomistic individual conception can also be explained in terms of their different strategies for individuating preference-maximizing individuals or consistent decision makers as distinct and independent beings. For the preference maximization approach, should preferences support utility functions, preference-maximizing individuals are then individuated by their utility functions, which are understood atomistically as being constituted out of their own or individual-specific preferences. That is, appropriately structured preferences and their associated utility functions individuate preference-maximizing individuals. For the consistency-in-choice approach, should choices be consistent, choosers are individuated as rational decision makers, where this essentially means their resources cannot be invaded by others. In this case, appropriately structured sequences of choices manifest themselves in resource sets under full control of the decision maker, thereby individuating the decision maker as a consistent resource manager. In both approaches, then, rationality requirements individuate atomistic beings, or individuals understood solely in terms of features that apply to them as individuals. Thus, any critique of the standard foundations of rationality also threatens the basis for individuating atomistic individuals because rationality requirements are also individuation requirements.

We should nonetheless ask how serious the problems with rationality need to be if they are to be thought to jeopardize the associated atomistic individual conception. Might there be deviations from rationality that yet leave the atomistic individual conception largely intact? If such problems

---

[2] "If most agents are irrational, then a rational individual can make a lot of money; eventually, therefore, the rational individual will take over all the wealth" (Arrow 1982, 7).

are seen more as anomalies rather than as challenges to rationality per se, then a revised view of rationality might still be consistent with the atomistic individual conception, perhaps itself appropriately revised. Indeed Chris Starmer (2000) explains that as the result of the evidence accumulated since the early 1950s contradicting the independence axiom, there has emerged a whole variety of theories exhibiting "well behaved" preferences that permit violations of the independence axiom, retain the principle of monotonicity, and assume that agents behave "as if" optimizing some underlying preference function (where "as if" refers to an instrumental rather than a realistic type of explanation). Because these "as if" underlying preference functions replace the standard utility function, they might serve as an alternative basis for individuating preference-maximizing individuals as atomistic beings, because individuals would still be defined in terms of their own ("as if") preferences. Starmer labels revised rationality theories of this kind conventional theories. However, he also goes on to label theories with more serious violations of rationality that cannot be "reduced to, or expressed purely in terms of a, single preference function" nonconventional theories (Starmer 2000, 339). These theories would not support traditional atomistic individual conceptions, because the absence of a single preference function means individuals cannot be explained solely in terms of even "as if" preferences. Other presumably nonsubjective factors also somehow enter into the constitution of the individual, raising the issue of how individuals who are not purely subjective are to be individuated as single individuals (if they can be at all). Kahneman and Tversky's prospect theory is taken as representative of nonconventional theories.

To follow up on this issue with respect to both views of rationality, in the following Sections 2.3 and 2.4, I will respectively explain how the two different currents in Edwards' BDR program each target one of the two different views of rationality, and how they accordingly each encounter one of the two different associated problems regarding the breakdown of individuality. In Section 2.3, I argue that the line of thinking that sees rationality theory as normatively meaningful and behavior descriptively not consistent with it as a deviation from rationality, and which accordingly works with a revised conception of the atomistic individual on alternative decision-making foundations, targets the preference maximization approach to rationality. Here prospect theory (Kahneman and Tversky 1979) will be taken as the paradigm case. Then in Section 2.3, I argue that the line of thinking that emphasizes the construction of preferences, and which investigates how different possible cognitive mechanisms operate on individual preferences, targets the consistent choice approach to rationality. Here my paradigm case will be the literature stemming from the empirical demonstration of preference reversals (Lichtenstein and Slovic 1971). In both sections, my goal is to diagnose the consequences of their critiques of rationality for their two associated individual conceptions.

2.3 Prospect Theory: The Atomistic Individual Revised

Kahneman and Tversky's original version of prospect theory (Kahneman and Tversky 1979; cf. Tversky and Kahneman 1992) offers a model of individual decision making under risk they regard as being psychologically more realistic than the standard expected utility theory model. It models individual choice as if it were a two-phase process, where in the first phase decision prospects with monetary outcomes and probabilities are edited to simplify and organize them for subsequent evaluation and choice, whereas in the second phase these prospects are evaluated so that the highest value prospect is chosen according to an individual value function V expressed in terms of two scales, π and v. The π scale associates decision weights with probabilities and assumes people tend to overreact to small probability events and underreact to medium- and large-probability events. The v scale reflects the subjective value of outcomes defined relative to a reference point taken to be the individual's current asset position, so that outcomes are defined in terms of gains and losses rather than as final states of wealth. The individual value function V is also concave for gains and convex for losses, and steeper for losses than for gains – later emphasized as respectively capturing diminishing sensitivity and loss aversion (Tversky and Kahneman 1992).

Given the discussion in the last section, how are we to understand the individual value function V as compared to a standard utility function? On the one hand, Kahneman and Tversky regard V as being like a utility function: "As in utility theory, V is defined on prospects, while v is defined on outcomes" (Kahneman and Tversky 1979, 276). Indeed they say that V simply "generalizes expected utility theory by relaxing the expectation principle" (ibid.). On the other hand, V is different from the standard utility function in that the v scale in V expresses the subjective value individuals place on outcomes defined relative to some reference point. Thus:

An essential feature of the present theory is that carriers of value are changes in wealth or welfare, rather than final states. This assumption is compatible with basic principles of perception and judgment. Our perceptual apparatus is attuned to the evaluation of changes or differences rather than to the evaluation of absolute magnitude. When we respond to attributes such as brightness, loudness, or temperature, the past and present context of experience defines an adaptation level, or reference point, and stimuli are perceived in relation to this reference point. (Kahneman and Tversky 1979, 277)

Reference points give a role for context, and context is extrasubjective in the sense that it allows the world to contribute something to how individuals value. As Kahneman and Tversky explain, in general the "preference order between prospects need not be invariant across contexts, because the same prospect could be edited in different ways depending on the context in which it appears" (Kahneman and Tversky 1979, 275). Thus, whereas on the standard view preferences are truly exogenous and fully cut off from the world as purely subjective phenomena, because for V changes in context influence preferences, subjective preferences become in some fashion also endogenous to the world and can consequently no longer be considered purely subjective phenomena.

That Starmer classifies Kahneman and Tversky's prospect theory as a nonconventional theory thus seems best explained in terms of the role they create for context. In his words, their account cannot be "reduced to, or expressed purely in terms of a, single preference function" (Starmer 2000, 339). At the same time, preferences are still basically subjective for Kahneman and Tversky, because they clearly treat context as influencing rather than fully determining the ways people value. Individuals are still seen as having stable, well-defined individual value functions by which they themselves determine – given the context – how they value prospects. Thus, nonconventional though their theory may be, the introduction of the simple principle that "context matters" weakens rather than overturns the standard atomistic individual view; we might say it only contextualizes subjectivity, implying that Kahneman and Tversky continue to work with a utility function analogue providing the basis for a revised *Homo economicus* atomistic individual conception.

Does this produce a satisfactory conception of the individual? Consider the ambiguity surrounding the idea of a reference point. The simple idea of a reference point by itself is quite open-ended, and although Kahneman and Tversky use it rather narrowly in their prospect theory model by restricting it to the individual's level of wealth or welfare – something that requires no essential reference to other individuals – it is fair to say that individual value functions are also likely contextualized by various types of characteristically social phenomena, such as social group membership, social identities, and social norms – all well established topics of investigation in psychology – which rather act as "social reference points" underlying the prospect editing process. The concept of a social group as specifically a "reference group" dates from early postwar social psychology (Merton and Kitt 1950) and has been widely employed since. Henri Tajfel's influential "minimal group paradigm" idea, based on experimental evidence that grouping individuals by arbitrary categories produces group loyalties, also shows that social groups can create social identities that function as reference points for individuals (e.g., Tajfel 1973; Tajfel et al. 1971). The further idea and evidence that a sense of social identity can create a basis for cooperation additionally shows that reference points may override individuals' sense of their own self-interest, and by extension individually specific reference points (e.g., Orbell, van de Kragt, and Dawes 1988; Dawes, van de Kragt, and Orbell 1990). Cristina Bicchieri further extends this thinking by arguing that social norms can function as means by which individuals settle on points of agreement in order to achieve common interests (Bicchieri 2002).[3]

Note, then, that what is at issue here is not whether preferences are somehow socially constructed (the issue that arises for Lichtenstein and Slovic), because for Kahneman and Tversky the v scale or their equivalent of preferences is still thought to express the subjective value individuals place on outcomes, now relative to some reference point. The problem is that when we include social reference points alongside their more naturalistic individually specific ones, we change the constitution of the individual from being a relatively homogeneous collection of preference-reference point combinations that can be seen as individually specific to being an essentially heterogeneous collection of preference-reference point combinations that are ambiguous with respect to whether they are individually and/or socially specific. In principle there is nothing wrong with seeing individuals as made up of these different types of materials or contents if one can still set out some principle of unity that holds these disparate materials together and explains how we individuate them as single individuals. This involves a departure, of course, from the standard *Homo economicus* view, in which we individuate the single individual as a homogeneous collection of preferences (albeit by using circular reasoning). Kahneman and Tversky amend this view by anchoring their V function by contextual nonsubjective reference points, and as long as these reference points are clearly individually specific as in the case of the ones they emphasize, their V function might still be seen as subjective. However, it is hard to believe that social group reference points should be seen as subjective, at least in the same way, particularly in light of arguments such as Tajfel's that social groups effectively contribute to a prospect editing process when they influence individuals' perception of their what their social identities are. Following

---

[3]   See Brewer (2001) and Brown (2000) for general surveys of social identity theory.

Edwards and economics, however, Kahneman and Tversky assume that they are still operating with a subjective individual conception, and so they are committed to its method of individuation that attempts to make individuals a unity of subjective contents. At the same time, they undermine this type of explanation by opening the door to the multisided principle of context. If we suppose, then, that social reference points are as important to choice as individually specific ones, individuals become heterogeneous collections of materials lacking any obvious principle of unity, and consequently can no longer be individuated as single beings. Prospect theory, it seems, has no way of excluding this expanded view of context.[4]

A second problem with Kahneman and Tversky's framework regarding the individual concerns the reidentification problem and derives from their assumption that reference points are liable to shift (Kahneman and Tversky 1979, 266). We reidentify individuals as enduring when we can repeatedly individuate them on some given basis. Thus, suppose for the moment that Kahneman and Tversky's individual value function might somehow successfully individuate individuals as "subjective" beings. Now consider changes in reference points. Kahneman and Tversky say that a "change of reference point alters the preference order for prospects" (Kahneman and Tversky 1979, 286). Because sets of preferences are only distinguishable according to their order or organization, it follows that changes in reference points produce different collections of preferences. Note that on the standard view, individual preferences are exogenous both in the sense that they are private and in the sense that their structure is unchanging, meaning that if individuals could be individuated in terms of their own ordered preferences (in a noncircular way), then they could be reidentified across change in terms of those same well-ordered preferences. When reference points change preference orders, however, this is no longer possible. Changes in context, that is, disconnect the different stages of individuals from one another and prevent us from saying that those stages all belong to the same individual. This leaves Kahneman and Tversky's individual with multiple unconnected individual value functions, a new version of standard theory's multiple utility functions problem (cf. Davis 2003, ch. 4). There, as individuals are distinguished from one another by their having their own sets of preferences,

---

[4] I make a parallel criticism of Stigler and Becker's (1977) music appreciation example, though in a dynamic context (Davis 2003, 55–58). They allow accumulations of music human capital to change individuals' choices, and thus depart from a pure subjectivist view of the individual. The resulting "hybrid structure of preferences and embodied endowments" similarly undermines individuating single individuals on a subjective basis.

if those preferences change, they effectively become different individuals; here, similarly changes in reference points produce different individuals.

This general problem of reference points changing, it should be noted, is well recognized in behavioral economics in connection with time-inconsistent or hyperbolic preferences. Time-inconsistent preferences reflect individuals' present bias, which involves continually using the perspective of the present as one's reference point in intertemporal decision making. Individuals exhibit time-inconsistent preferences – and there is considerable evidence that they do (Frederick, Loewenstein, and O'Donoghue 2002) – when they repeatedly re-anchor themselves in each successive present, overturning past decisions that pertain to futures that have become present, and essentially disowning their former selves in the form of their past preferences regarding the future. Efforts to solve this problem within the framework of prospect theory require a behavioralist intertemporal utility function analysis somehow able to reunify the multiple selves that present-bias anchoring produces in the form of a single individual. That there is now a considerable literature devoted to this particular problem is one confirmation that the difficulties in Kahneman and Tversky's individual conception are serious. I turn to one of the most important efforts to work out this problem in the next chapter but continue this section with further discussion of Kahneman and Tversky's individual conception.

Consider, then, how the reidentification problem also reverberates back on the previous individuation problem. The suggestion that individuals might still be individuated as "subjective" beings in some loose sense depends on supposing that extrasubjective context does not undermine the subjective nature of individual preferences – a contextualizing of subjectivity rather than a full construction of subjectivity. It cannot be easily said, however, that changes in reference points have minor and modest effects on preferences if entire preference orders can change. Rather it seems more reasonable to say that, in general, extrasubjective context has significant effects on preferences, and consequently that the idea that individuals might be individuated as "subjective" beings in even a loose sense has little basis. Changes in references points, that is, also bring prospect theory's subjectivist individuation into question. This is not to say, however, that for Kahneman and Tversky subjectivity is constructed by context, but it shows how little there is that distinguishes contextualizing and constructing subjectivity, and thus puts considerable burden of clarifying the concepts of context and reference points that in their account are quite general. Indeed, there is nothing in their analysis that determines the relative weights of the extrasubjective and the subjective in individual value functions, and so their conception of the individual at best ends up being ambiguous.

Their problem, it seems fair to say, is that their critique of rationality takes the standard view of the individual as given but undermines it at the same time. Like many critics of rationality theory, they assume strong separability between rationality and individuality. This reflects, oddly for empirical psychologists such as Kahneman and Tversky, an underlying belief that cognition can be understood largely independently of how it is embedded in the world and apart from an understanding of what exercises it – what I called the light embedding thesis. I can only speculate, of course, on why this view might seem attractive. One possibility that accords with the ahistorical nondevelopmental perspective they take on reference points is that they have a very naturalistic understanding of human beings, so that their biological constitution always broadly explains their psychological behavior. Evidence for this interpretation lies in Kahneman's research in the psychophysics of vision perception and its subsequent impact on his collaboration with Tversky (Kahneman 2003; Heukelom 2009). Another related possibility is that Kahneman and Tversky shared twentieth-century economics' commitment to the idea that a strong dichotomy exists between subjectivity and the objective world, a traditional Cartesian view reinforced by classical liberal political thinking in the Anglophone world.

I put these questions aside, however, and close this section with a comment on framing, an important concept in behavioral economics related to prospect theory's phase-one editing process and the broader heuristics and biases program. Unlike prospect theory, the program of investigating heuristics and biases (cf. Gilovich, Griffin, and Kahneman 2002) – essentially a list of experimentally observed deviations from rational behavior loosely theorized in terms of anchoring – is not bound up with developing a new representation of the individual, utility function-like or otherwise, and thus by itself does not tell us much about behavioral economics' strategies for revising *Homo economicus*. Indeed, the heuristics and biases program seems to have run more or less parallel to the development of prospect theory, rather than either constituting a development of the other (Gilovich and Griffin 2002). Nonetheless, Kahneman and Tversky appear to have thought that there was one important way in which the two projects were linked, and this link tells us something about what might ultimately be said about the role of subjectivity in their analysis.

For them, the key insight of prospect theory was that the individual value function V is concave for gains and convex for losses relative to some reference point. Kahneman (ibid.) asserts that he and Tversky had noticed early on in their work on the theory that for a wide range of observed behavior "the preference between negative prospects is the mirror image of the preference between positive prospects" – something they appropriately termed "the reflection effect" (Kahneman and Tversky 1979, 268) – so that changing the signs of outcomes in gambles almost always caused preferences to flip from risk-averse to risk-seeking and vice versa. They went on to explore this phenomenon more generally with their famous "Asian disease" example (in which the choice is alternatively framed either in terms of the language of lives "lost" or "saved") and used the idea of a "decision frame" to characterize the decision maker's conception of the choice being faced (Tversky and Kahneman 1981, 1986). Though they likened alternative frames in decision problems to visual perspectives, what is important in the Asian disease example is that it is really more a matter of the decision maker interpreting language and social states of affairs. In contrast to many of their more naturalistic examples of heuristics and biases in which the vision analogy might be persuasive, in this case what mattered were the conceptions decision makers employ about the nature of the world, including normative views about the value of human life. Perception in this case, in effect, is socially loaded.

Indeed, this interpretation gains weight in the heuristics and biases program in connection with the subsequent collaboration of Kahneman and Tversky with Richard Thaler and his emphasis on how framing effects involve systems of mental accounting (Thaler 1985) – a collaboration Kahneman put much weight on (Kahneman 2003). Thaler's mental accounts view of framing, though also explained in terms of individual subjectivity, additionally makes use of social categories, as his own research from early in his career had examined the effects of marketing strategies on individual choice. Marketing of course targets subjective factors that may influence individual choices, and, like social group effects on individuals' perceptions of their social identities, does so by taking over more of the framing process, making it difficult to say whether individuals' mental accounts ought to be understood in subjective or extrasubjective terms. Perhaps the key consideration, however, is that the mental accounting interpretation of framing tells us that decision makers operate with conceptual representations of their choices, not with uninterpreted objects of preference. This is quite at odds with the subjectivism of standard utility theory, because the emphasis on the manner in which choices are conceptualized presupposes some role for language, and language is intersubjective in nature.[5]

---

[5]   That Harsanyi's proposal to treat preferences as informed (Harsanyi 1982, 1997) has gone largely ignored further suggests that departures from the subjectivist understanding of preferences are not seen as consistent with the standard view.

Thus Kahneman and Tversky's contextualizing subjectivity approach to the individual cannot be said to succeed in revising the standard *Homo economicus* conception. Whereas that conception attempts to put clear boundaries on what single individuals are (if unsuccessfully), prospect theory only muddies those boundaries, makes it unclear what subjectivity is, and thereby brings into question the entire strategy of explaining individuals in subjective terms. One accordingly gets the sense that psychology's challenge to economics, meant to add realism to EUT, rather has as an unintended outcome exposing the uncertain basis on which rationality is grounded in individuality in standard theory, because the attempt to provide some grounding via reference points makes it unclear just what individuals are. In this regard, we will see that the outcome of the second current within the Edwards-inspired BDR approach to bringing psychology into economics – the constructing subjectivity current – is even worse. Whereas the particular problem prospect theory encounters is the break-up of single individuals into multiple selves, the Lichtenstein-Slovic constructing subjectivity current, which rather targets the consistency conception of rationality plus the idea that individuals cannot be money pumps, encounters a quite different problem: the elimination of single individuals altogether.

2.4 The Construction of Preference: Revelation Versus Elicitation

The main assumption in the second current of thinking in Edwards' BDR program is that people do not have given, unchanging preferences, but rather that their preferences are constructed to fit the situation they face (cf. Lichtenstein and Slovic 2006). People of course have histories of expressing preferences, and these expressed preferences are an important starting point in the determination of their current preferences. However, past preferences are also often poor guides to what preferences will be in new decision-making environments. Moreover, as new environments can be quite varied, strategies for mobilizing past preferences may need to vary, so that there is no single way of saying how past preferences apply to the future. Indeed, there is no obvious way of saying just how past preferences provide a basis for future preferences. The BDR preference construction approach accordingly investigates how individuals use many different techniques in constructing preferences according to the context of decision making, and the heart of the approach is an active research program generating multiple theories of preference construction, seen to concern the core of human decision making.

Economists, not surprisingly, are largely ignorant of the program, and what they know of it, namely Lichtenstein and Slovic's demonstration of preference reversals (Lichtenstein and Slovic 1971), might be regarded as a relatively minor early step in the program's development. Preference reversals, of course, violate something of genuine concern to economists, the transitivity assumption of rationality theory, perhaps the least dispensable of the standard axioms. For most economists it seems intuitively certain, and on the money pump arbitrage argument its regular violation seems impossible in an economic world with any kind of agents. Indeed, the money pump argument is the closest thing in economics to what philosophers call an ontological argument; that is, an argument that proves the existence of something in virtue of its definition, in this case one proving the existence of rational individuals. Thus, individuals are defined as rational; but then money pumps are impossible; therefore rational individuals necessarily exist.[6] For Lichtenstein and Slovic, however, demonstrating that preference reversals occur was only a means of convincingly showing that individuals do not have stable preference orders – something psychologists had already long believed for a variety of other reasons. At the same time, Lichtenstein and Slovic directly addressed the money pump argument by their exhibition of preference reversals in gambling experiments at the Four Queens Casino in Las Vegas where individuals literally functioned as money pumps (cf. Lichtenstein and Slovic 2006, Figure 1.2).

Choosing to demonstrate that preference reversals occur may have been something of an historical accident. When Lichtenstein and Slovic got their Ph.D.'s under Edwards, he was intent on applying Bayesianism to psychology, especially after Savage arrived at Michigan (e.g., Edwards, Lindman, and Savage 1963). This involved trying to show how the subjective expected utility model worked in practice, and so many of Edwards' students concentrated on experimentally investigating its descriptive violations with the goal of determining how they might be explained in keeping with EUT. This was the route Tversky pursued in many experiments before beginning his collaboration with Kahneman. As it turned out, however, preference reversals was a fertile subject of investigation in itself and soon generated multiple theories of preference reversals whose differences appeared to be due to the different circumstances in which preferences could be constructed. As Lichtenstein and Slovic later put it, "The idea of preference

---

[6]   The more familiar ontological argument for the existence of God is that the definition of God includes perfection, and perfection implies existence. Philosophers generally agree that the argument is invalid.

construction implies the *necessity* of multiple theories [of preference reversals]" (Lichtenstein and Slovic 2006, 20). This proliferation of theories then ultimately led to the umbrella idea of preference construction as an alternative to Edwards' Bayesian project. Thus, Edwards succeeded in introducing psychologists to EUT; but without their having any special attachment to economists' commitment to the assumption of stable preference orders, many were rather inspired instead to link violations of the standard model to concerns more traditional to psychology and a subject altogether foreign to standard economics, preference construction.

This path of development was also facilitated by the early work of Simon – said to have an "enormous influence" on the development of the preference construction approach (Lichtenstein and Slovic 2006, 23; also cf. Payne and Bettman 1992, 88). Simon was interested in information processing and the cognitive capacities of the decision maker relative to its environment, and he argued that when the decision-making agent's environment is perceived as complex the agent relies on "very simple perceptual and *choice mechanisms to satisfy* its several needs," and that "no 'utility function' needs to be postulated" to explain this (Simon 1956, 137–8). As his Carnegie Mellon colleague and co-author James March later summarized it, "Human beings have unstable, inconsistent, incompletely invoked, and imprecise goals at least in part because human abilities limit preference orderliness" (March 1978, 598). Simon's recommendation to abandon the standard utility function framework was not influential in economics, but Lichtenstein and Slovic's demonstration of preference reversals was. Most economists initially dismissed it on a priori grounds, but David Grether and Charles Plott believed that they could go farther and demonstrate that preference reversals could not possibly exist. They identified thirteen potential errors in psychologists' preference reversal experimental methodology and accordingly set out to show that preference reversals were only an artifact of experimental design. Nonetheless, they ended up confirming their existence as well as Simon's judgment of utility functions.

Taken at face value the data are simply inconsistent with preference theory and have broad implications about research priorities in economics. The inconsistency is deeper than the mere lack of transitivity or even stochastic transitivity. It suggests that *no optimization principles of any sort* lie behind the simplest of human choices and that the uniformities in human choice behavior which lie behind market behavior may result from principles which are of a completely different sort from those generally accepted. (Grether and Plott 1979, 623; emphasis added)

Published in the *American Economic Review*, this was a momentous admission for economists. However, for many psychologists the debate was already long over, and research had moved on to which theories best explained preference construction. James Bettman published what is regarded as the first theory of preference construction in the same year Grether and Plott's paper appeared (Bettman 1979), a major review of preference construction theories appeared in 1992 (Payne and Bettman 1992), and Lichtenstein and Slovic's retrospective volume appeared in 2006 (Lichtenstein and Slovic 2006). As Slovic put it in 1995, "It is now generally recognized among psychologists that utility maximization provides only limited insight into the processes by which decisions are made" (Slovic 1995, 365). Grether and Plott, interestingly, extended their own critique of standard rationality to Kahneman and Tversky's proposed prospect theory replacement, implicitly highlighting the difference between the two currents in Edwards' BDR program.

> We need to emphasize that the phenomenon causes problems for preference theory in general, and not for just the expected utility theory. Prospect theory as a special type of preference theory cannot account for the results. (Grether and Plott 1982, 575)

Here, however, I do not attempt to review the vast preference construction literature itself, but instead I focus on what this literature implies about the nature of the individual in virtue of its particular critique of standard rationality theory.

The preference construction approach targets the consistency-in-choice view of rationality. At first, preference reversals were thought to arise from violations of both the independence and the transitivity axioms, but the consensus view now is that they cannot be due to violations of the independence axiom, and that violations of the transitivity axiom explain only a small percent of preference reversals (Tversky, Slovic, and Kahneman 1990). Rather it seems that the main causes of preference reversals are violations of description invariance (or framing effects) and procedure invariance (or elicitation effects). Framing effects, we saw in Section 2.3, were illustrated by Kahneman and Tversky with their Asian disease example. Elicitation effects occur when the experimental procedure for eliciting a preference changes, causing the preference to change as well. On the standard view, originally termed extensionality (Arrow 1982), neither framing nor elicitation effects should exist as individuals' choices should solely reflect their preference orderings. With preference reversals, however, the evidence is that people's choices are not only influenced by how the world is represented (framing effects), but also how they interact with it (elicitation effects).

At issue here is not just whether individuals can be represented by utility functions, as in the preference maximization view of rationality, but how individuals' choices cohere, as in the consistency-in-choice view of rationality. In revealed preference theory, choices cohere in the sense that if one bundle of goods is preferred to another that is affordable, that first bundle is revealed preferred to the second. There is nothing here about maximization of anything; all that is at issue is the relationship between choices over bundles of goods as exhibited in an individual's choice. However, with framing and elicitation effects, individuals can make intransitive choices, and the weak axiom of revealed preference does not hold. Elicitation effects are particularly interesting in this regard. The "revealed preferred" idea tells us that preferences can be discovered without being influenced by the discovery process. In contrast, elicitation is the idea that the discovery process influences preferences. Thus, whereas framing effects make extrasubjective interpretation and language essential to "subjective" preferences, elicitation effects make interaction with the world, and presumably with other people, essential to "subjective" preferences. Combined they tell us that individuals cannot be defined as subjective beings in the standard way, and thus invite us to ask how individuals are to be defined.

In the discussion in the last section, I emphasized the need to establish clear boundary conditions between individuals, understood in terms of individuation and reidentification criteria, to be able to explain individuality in prospect theory. Those same arguments apply to the preference construction approach as well, because framing and elicitation effects blur the lines between individuals, and consequently make it unclear what makes individuals distinct from one another. The preference construction approach raises an additional issue, however. The term "preference construction," clearly, is ambiguous regarding what does the constructing. Individuals might construct their preferences, or circumstances might construct individuals' preferences, or individuals and circumstances together might construct their preferences. The term "construct" is an agency term referring to a power to bring something about, and the attribution of agency is one way of developing an understanding of individuality. However, the preference construction approach does not systematically develop the concept of agency. Not only is this avenue not exploited, but ambiguity in the idea of how preferences are constructed allows for the possibility that agency resides elsewhere, and preferences get constructed *for* individuals.

In fairness to those involved in this research program, they have not been concerned with this philosophical issue, but rather with explaining the preference construction process – an investigation that might put aside the difficult question of what actually carries out preference construction to focus instead on the character of preferences as constructed. At the same time, the fact that the preference construction approach, like prospect theory, entails a critique of standard rationality theory with implications for its associated theory of individuality leaves open the question of what might occupy the vacuum thus created. In the case of prospect theory, the upshot was a multiplication of selves whose number the theory appears unable to determine or limit. In the case of the preference construction approach, there is simply the vacuum. That is, there appears to be no obvious basis for talking about individuals as distinct beings whatsoever, much less reidentifying them in any way. This is due to this approach's target of consistency in choice in rationality theory. Minus a utility function to represent the individual, the consistency-in-choice approach simply rests individuality on a strong counterfactual: if individuals are not rational, they can be arbitraged out of existence. Thus, having shown individuals are not revealed preferred rational type beings, their nonexistence follows. It follows that individuality has to be somehow constructed, and yet there is no basis on which this can be done within the framework of the atomistic individual conception.

2.5 Behavioral Economics and Experimental Economics

In closing this chapter, let me return to the larger picture with which I began of the two programs of thinking in psychology's postwar BDR program – Edwards' and Simon's – and begin to sketch out how they have influenced thinking about the individual in recent economics. First, consider the new behavioral economics, a direct descendent of Edward's program. Broadly speaking, new behavioral economists follow the revised utility function pathway created by Kahneman and Tversky's prospect theory, and see one of the main advantages of prospect theory as its potential for redeveloping the individual "utility" function framework for economics in ways consistent with behavioral evidence from psychology (cf. Kahneman, Slovic, and Tversky 1982; Rabin 1998; Kahneman and Tversky 2000; Camerer, Loewenstein, and Rabin 2003). Indeed, as Matthew Rabin puts it, Kahneman and Tversky's success was due to the fact that they were "able and willing to address economists in standard economic language and venues" (Rabin 1996, 111). Or, as Colin Camerer and George Loewenstein see it, by increasing the realism of the psychological foundations of choice theory in economics, behavioral economics seeks to improve economics essentially on its own terms (Camerer and Loewenstein 2003). However, this greater realism, we have seen, also creates the problem of individuals having multiple selves. I turn to this in the next chapter and look at how behavioral economists seek to explain the unity of the individual in connection with hyperbolic preferences and present bias in the positive theory of individual behavior. I then also look at how behavioral economists have relatedly sought to address the normative implications of these phenomena in welfare theory in connection with the doctrine of libertarian or asymmetric paternalism. This involves an alternative type of multiple selves problem whereby we ask: If individuals often behave irrationally, are rational experts needed to act paternalistically as surrogate rational selves?

Second, consider experimentalists in economics who have accepted Grether and Plott's conclusions and who also have been influenced by Vernon Smith's market experiments research program (cf. Lee 2004; Guala 2005; Santos 2010). They assume that even a revised standard utility function approach for explaining individuals is no longer feasible, but they resist the negative implications of this conclusion associated with psychology's preference construction approach by arguing that individuals operating in the institutional context of markets, especially competitive ones, ultimately "discover" their underlying preferences after a period of trial-and-error learning and adaptation – a view that has been referred to as the discovered preferences hypothesis (Smith 1989; Harrison 1994; Plott 1996; Binmore 1999; though also cf. Cubitt, Starmer, and Sugden 2001). As Smith explains, "economic agents do not solve decision problems by thinking about them and calculating in the same way as economists," as if they possessed pre-given sets of well-ordered preferences, yet at the same time "it should not be presumed that economic agents will fail to get the 'right' answers in the context of markets" (Smith 1989, 162–3). On this view, interaction between individuals somehow produces or reinforces individuality. This conclusion both accepts and rejects the logic of the preference construction current in Edwards' program. It accepts it in giving up the idea that preferences are per se well-ordered, but rejects it in supposing they may become so in market interaction. That is, it replaces the idea that preference construction eliminates individuality with the idea that well-ordered preferences and individuality ultimately emerge through interaction.

Thus, the influence of psychology's BDR program on economics has given rise to two new strategies for reconceptualizing individuals. The Edwards-inspired prospect theory strategy manifest in the new behavioral economics involves a light embedding of individuals in the world through the idea of choice reference points. In effect, whereas rationality is bounded, individuality is not in that allowing for reference points does not change the understanding of the individual in any important way. In contrast, the preference reversals or Simon-inspired strategy manifest in experimental economics (especially as we will see later) involves a stronger embedding of individuals in the world that relies on the idea of choice having an institutional (market) context. Rationality is bounded, and individuality is bounded as well in that how individuals interact with the world determines, not just what their rationality involves, but also what is involved in being an individual. Both strategies, nonetheless, depart in important ways from the traditional fully disembedded, purely subjectivist *Homo economicus* conception and create new agendas for explaining the relationship between rationality and individuality. Prospect theory's more modest departure from the traditional conception, I suggest, reflects a stronger attachment to economics' postwar formalism and the untenable view that one can adequately understand economic behavior apart from an understanding of what exercises it. Experimental economics following Smith makes a stronger challenge to economics' postwar consensus, contextualizing individuals in a more significant way that in some respects recalls prewar institutionalist economic theorizing.

To close this chapter, note how the particular problems that the two Edwards-inspired BDR approaches respectively encounter in conceptualizing individuals – the multiple selves and no self problems – exhibit the particular problems of explaining the sub-personal bound on single-individual explanations. Prospect theory generates multiple selves problems, meaning it fails to say how a person can have multiple selves and yet still be a single individual. That is, it fails to adequately address the sub-personal bound by saying what holds an individual with multiple selves together. Essentially, the revised *Homo economicus* conception it employs prevents it from doing so, because it presupposes the individual remains intact as a unity despite the evidence the individual fragments into multiple selves. The preference construction approach is a more complicated case. On the one hand, it also fragments the individual into multiple selves, so much so that individuality ceases to exist altogether, thus indicating an inability to deal with the sub-personal bound. On the other hand, the cause of fragmentation is the many factors in the world that influence preference construction. Thus, in this case it is specifically social interaction that produces the break-up of the individual, implying that this approach fails to address both the sub-personal and also the supra-personal bound operating on single-individual explanations. This points us toward the discussion of market experimentalism in Chapter 7 in which the discussion returns to Simon and the supra-personal bound is the focus.

THREE

Multiple Selves and Self-Control

Contextualizing Individuality

[A]n important class of intertemporal markets shows systematic deviations from individual rational behavior and ... these deviations are consonant with evidence from very different sources collected by psychologists
(Arrow 1982, 8)

3.1 From *Homo economicus* to *Homo sapiens*

Behavioral economics has become an active and well-established research program in economics that makes a wide-ranging critique of standard rationality thinking. Yet why has the "new" behavioral economics become successful so quickly when bounded rationality thinking as developed in the now "old" behavioral economics had relatively little impact on economics? One possible reason is that economists are now convinced that the introduction of more realistic psychological assumptions into economics is likely to improve prediction, and they take prediction more seriously. Behavioral economists have consistently argued that their models have solid empirical foundations that produce better results, and instrumentalist economic methodology emphasizing prediction has been influential in economics since the case made for it by Milton Friedman (Friedman 1953). A second and related possible reason is the unexpected impact of laboratory experiments on economics. Having long denied laboratory experiments are possible in economics, economists have been arguably caught off balance in judging their value, and as a result they have been perhaps overinclined to accept the evidence from the lab and thereby the arguments of behavioral economists. However, I will emphasize a third possible reason, namely, that the adjustment involved in introducing psychological assumptions into economics appears to many economists, at least thus far, to be compatible with much of standard theory. Individual economic agents are still the focus, they interact in markets, and whereas they are boundedly rational, they still aim to optimize, if only somewhat less successfully. Simon's program, in contrast, proposed a quite different view of the economic process as well as an individual conception that abandoned optimization for satisficing. In effect it demanded revolution rather than reform, and too much would have had to go from standard theory for Simon's program to have attracted many adherents.

However, the view that the behavioral economics program is compatible with much of standard economics may not be accurate if the ways in which behavioral economics revises the standard *Homo economicus* conception undermines the idea that economics is essentially about individuals' interaction in markets. We saw in the last chapter that prospect theory produces a multiple selves account of the individual, an important manifestation of which is a present-bias type of choice anchoring in intertemporal decision making. As we will see in this chapter, one response to this is to recommend that benevolent rational experts design decision contexts and choice architectures for irrational decision makers – the "libertarian paternalism" of Richard Thaler and Cass Sunstein. Such a strategy emphasizes interaction between individuals outside of markets, and thus makes it unclear whether economics is still primarily about individuals' interaction in markets, and whether behavioral economics' introduction of psychological assumptions into economics is as compatible with standard economics as some may believe. What, then, does behavioral economics' revised utility function conception of the individual actually involve? As good an answer as any to this question comes from Richard Thaler, whose *Journal of Economic Perspectives* "anomalies" series has done much to popularize behavioral economics, and who gives a concise and clearly motivated view of how the individual conception of behavioral economics is different from the traditional conception. For him, behavioral economics should be seen as replacing the traditional *Homo economicus* conception with a *Homo sapiens* conception of the individual, in which the latter exercises ordinary human rationality in real world settings (Thaler 2000). His argument is that the thrust of postwar economics was to increasingly populate economic models with hyperrational economic agents, whose capacities were only limited by "the IQ of the smartest economic theorist;" but with greater emphasis on realism he believes we can expect that "this trend will be reversed in favor of an approach in which the degree of rationality bestowed to the agents depends on the context being studied" (ibid., 134). Thus, if Kahneman and Tversky's prospect theory is seen as "contextualizing subjectivity," Thaler might be said to see behavioral economics' bounded rationality *Homo sapiens* conception as "contextualizing individuality."

More specifically, "the context being studied" is the economic context, meaning the circumstances of ordinary economic life that determine the kinds of choices that individuals need to make. Intertemporal decision making, for example, arises out of the particular circumstance that in economic life individuals' consumption and income levels generally do not coincide in time, so that they need to make decisions at one point in time that apply to future periods, as in connection with such things as pensions, education, health plans, and so forth. Indeed, how people make intertemporal choices is one of the most extensively researched subjects in behavioral economics. Further, though the standard *Homo economicus* view is that rational individuals place the same weight on all time periods and use constant rates of time discount (Samuelson 1937), considerable empirical evidence demonstrates that individuals regularly exhibit present bias and employ declining or hyperbolic time discount rates – relatively high discount rates over short horizons and relatively low discount rates over long horizons (Frederick, Loewenstein, and O'Donoghue 2002).[1] *Homo sapiens*, then, regularly exhibits what is known as weakness of will when people's current selves plan for the future and are later overruled by their future current selves who reject earlier plans. Jon Elster previously brought the concept of weakness of will to economists' attention but left many questions unanswered regarding how human will and the associated idea of self-control can be integrated into a preferences conception of the individual (Elster 1983).[2] Whether individuals can address weakness of will and overcome present bias is an important part of what is involved in behavioral economics' attempts to revise the *Homo economicus* conception. This chapter is devoted to assessing the two main avenues adopted in behavioral economics for addressing the problem.

The first, carried out with considerable sophistication in a succession of articles by Roland Bénabou and Jean Tirole, seeks to simultaneously solve the weakness of will and multiple selves problems by redeveloping *Homo sapiens* as the conception of a being able to exercise self-control. Indeed Bénabou and Tirole make the issue of the individual's identity explicit and aim to show that the more realistic *Homo sapiens* is a boundedly rational single individual despite having multiple selves in virtue of weakness of will. The second avenue, pursued by Thaler and Sunstein under the banner of "libertarian paternalism," alternatively abandons the unity of the

---

[1] Samuelson regarded the constant rate of discount assumption as convenient for modeling intertemporal choice but did not make a case for it as a realistic assumption.

[2] Much earlier, weakness of will or *akrasia* is discussed in Plato's dialogue *Protagoras*.

individual, differentiates between normative and descriptive theories of choice, and argues that as people generally exhibit time-inconsistent preferences, rational experts motivated by efficiency and benevolence ought to design markets and social contexts in such a way as to encourage individuals to make rational choices. To the extent that the design of markets and social contexts successfully reduces individuals' present bias, they can then be said to behave "as if" they are single individuals.

This chapter discusses and evaluates these two strategies for dealing with behavioral economics' multiple selves problem. Section 3.2 discusses Bénabou and Tirole's identity analysis of the individual, which is based on the idea that individuals exercise self-control to maintain personal assets of self-confidence and self-reputation. Section 3.3 evaluates their analysis in connection with their ambition of advancing a general equilibrium-type unified approach to social psychology, arguing that it is not successful in developing a *Homo sapiens* conception based on the principle of con-textualizing individuality. Section 3.4 examines and evaluates Thaler and Sunstein's strategy of differentiating normative and descriptive theories as a means to justifying the role of experts who understand the principle of rationality and are motivated by "libertarian paternalism." Section 3.5 compares the two strategies and looks at them as responses to Elster's treatment of weakness of will. Neither strategy solves Elster's multiple selves problem, because despite their added psychological realism, they are still essentially bound to a preferences conception of the individual.

3.2 Self-confidence and Self-regulation: Bénabou and Tirole

Bénabou and Tirole accept the behavioral economics research agenda associated by Thaler with replacing *Homo economicus* with *Homo sapiens*, and make their principal focus the relationship between self-confidence – alternatively self-esteem – and self-regulation – alternatively self-monitoring (Bénabou and Tirole 2002, 2003b). *Homo sapiens* lack the hyperrationality of *Homo economicus* in three ways: imperfect self-knowledge, imperfect willpower, and imperfect recall. Incorporating these behavioral character-istics, they say, increases the realism of their analysis, though it requires important departures from standard theory. First, assuming imperfect self-knowledge goes significantly beyond standard information econom-ics, which concerns how individuals signal to one another regarding their privately known characteristics but supposes that individuals face no uncertainty about their own abilities and preferences (that is, about their own identities). When individuals are uncertain about their own abilities, however, they do not know what they will be able to achieve; and because with present bias (or weakness of will) their future selves are biased toward instant gratification, they do not know whether their future selves will abide by the plans of their current selves. Individual traits such as self-confidence and personal motivation then become crucial. Second, standard theory also assumes that individuals always act in their own best interest, so that imperfect willpower and self-control problems do not arise. Because individuals employ hyperbolic discounting, however, there can be conflicts of interest between individuals' successive temporal selves and also ex ante suboptimal behavior associated with their subsequent preference reversals. Third, if present bias is state-dependent and imperfectly known, the individual's self-view and associated capacity for self-monitoring then become important. However, self-monitoring encounters the cognitive weakness of imperfect recall, also overlooked by standard theory. Worse, not only is memory imperfect, but empirical research in psychology also indicates it may be self-serving (a motivated cognition) and undercaptures the intensity of feeling of past experiences.[3]

For Bénabou and Tirole, then, *Homo sapiens* is less rational than *Homo economicus*, but not entirely irrational either. Individuals at any point in time (their different temporal selves) try to do the best they can for themselves and are not altogether ignorant about the information biases affecting their self-knowledge regarding their abilities, preferences, and memories. Any individual's temporal self, that is, is both optimizing and Bayesian, though all the individual's temporal selves put together – the person as a whole – is neither optimizing nor Bayesian on account of time-inconsistent behavior and the possibility of self-deception. The adjustment involved in introducing these psychological assumptions into the standard model of the individual, it is fair to say, might still be largely compatible with standard thinking about the individual. At the same time, injecting greater realism into the analysis in this way builds the problem of multiple selves directly into the analysis, because the assumptions that individuals are optimizing and Bayesian can only be ascribed to individuals' temporal selves. This puts a real burden on the analysis to successfully show that somehow people are still single individuals. How, then, does Bénabou and Tirole's identity analysis of the individual work? There are two key elements in their explanation: self-confidence and personal rules.

---

[3] Failure to recall the intensity of experience is explained in terms of "hot-cold empathy gaps" (Loewenstein 1996) and divergences between experienced utility and decision utility (Kahneman 2000).

3.2.1 Self-Confidence

Self-confidence is treated as having both a demand side and a supply side. On the demand side, people are said to value self-confidence as a personal asset, because it increases individual effort in the face of imperfect willpower and thus increases the probability of success on projects that extend into the future. As much of our behavior has this through-time character, people accordingly want to protect their self-confidence and consider how their actions may increase it in their future selves. At the same time, however, people have imperfect knowledge about their own abilities in regard to the likelihood of their achieving future goals; rather than risk weakening their future self-confidence, they may prefer to limit what they undertake and the consequent effort they undertake and expect of their future selves. One way they may accomplish this is by allowing themselves to remain ignorant about the extent of their abilities (Carrillo and Mariotti 2000); another is to engage in a variety of self-handicapping activities to reduce their possibilities for failure in the future. The problem individuals face, then, is created by the trade-off between setting high effort levels and high expectations for future selves in anticipation of the resulting gains to self-confidence and the risk of overconfidently setting effort levels too high when it is better to expect less of future selves, thus risking losses to self-confidence.

The supply side of self-confidence is determined by the "reality constraints" individuals face that limit the extent to which they are able to engage in wishful thinking. Their propensity to engage in wishful thinking stems from, inter alia, that they tend to recall successes more than failures, that they have self-serving memories, and that they often overestimate their abilities – all classified as self-deception phenomena commonly studied by psychologists. Yet people are not perfect self-deceivers. The meaning of self-deception, Bénabou and Tirole argue, is that the individual somehow "must simultaneously know and not know the same information," implying that it is "more realistic to view people as *imperfect Bayesians* who do not fully internalize the fact that their recollections may be self serving" (Bénabou and Tirole 2002, 885, 898; their emphasis). They reason that the "intertemporal model allows us to unbundle the 'self that knows' from the 'self that doesn't know,' and thereby reconcile the motivation ('hot') and cognition ('cold') aspects of self-deception within a standard information-theoretic framework" (ibid., 885–6).

The basic idea is that the individual can, within limits and possibly at a cost, *affect the probability of remembering* a given piece of data. At the same time, we maintain rational inference, so people realize (at least to some extent) that they have selective memory or attention. (Bénabou and Tirole 2002, 874–5; their emphasis)

Here, then, we clearly go beyond the preferences-only standard conception of the individual in that people are explicitly represented as active beings able to evaluate and control their own propensities toward self-deception. Moreover, by selectively determining how they remember and attend to their past experiences, people are able to address the problem of maintaining self-confidence while also avoiding overconfidence, thus bringing together the demand and supply sides of the self-confidence problem.

To explain how this might happen, Bénabou and Tirole then provide a multi-self game-theoretic model of a person's endogenous memory or awareness management, whereby the person's self tomorrow is able to discount at a cost the positive reports of that person's self yesterday by increasing the probability of correctly recalling any given information about the past.

The resulting structure is that of a game of strategic communication between the individual's temporal selves. In deciding whether to try to repress bad news, the individual weighs the benefits from preserving his effort motivation against the risk of becoming overconfident. Later on, however, he appropriately discounts the reliability of rosy recollections and rationalizations. (Bénabou and Tirole 2002, 875)

The degree to which individuals discount "the reliability of rosy recollections and rationalizations," that is, sets the level of self-confidence the individual's later self will allow regarding its earlier self's long-term plans. Individuals accordingly function collectively as single individuals who self-regulate themselves across their temporal selves by continually evaluating their successive selves' efforts to maintain and increase self-confidence.

This dynamic view of the self, it should be emphasized, is compatible with there being multiple possible equilibria for any given individual at any one time, reflecting the individual's degree of time inconsistency (or particular tendency toward instant gratification) and memory repression costs as the demand and supply parameters respectively of the model. Indeed, Bénabou and Tirole allow that individuals may fall into a spectrum of different types of inferior equilibrium "self-traps" associated with how they regard their past self-evaluations of ability that range from systematic denial to complete self-honesty. This, they add, often creates a role for families, friends, therapists, and others in helping individuals escape such "self-traps," as reflected in the practice of psychology therapy aimed at assisting individuals to alter their views of themselves and their abilities and improve their self-confidence. However, these therapeutic strategies may also have undesirable or insignificant effects, and thus Bénabou and Tirole extend their self-regulation view to allow for individuals' recourse to personal rules as private strategies of self-control.

3.2.2 Personal Rules

Personal rules, or internal commitments, are examined by Bénabou and Tirole in connection with their model of self-reputation with respect to willpower (Bénabou and Tirole 2004). In contrast to Elster's emphasis on external commitment devices associated with assistance from others, as well as such things an individual can do in interaction with others such as signing binding contracts, making side bets, holding illiquid assets, and so forth (cf. Elster 1983), internal commitments take the form of personal rules (diets, exercise regimens, personal resolutions, moral and religious precepts, etc.) that are self-imposed and are consequently by definition a source of self-control. The main idea (following Ainslie 1992) is that because people have imperfect knowledge of their willpower, they must infer it from their past choices, and consequently then see their choices as determining their reputations as to what kinds of people they are. From this it is inferred that when individuals are weak of will, or suffer lapses in will, they fear they are creating precedents that will undermine their self-reputations. This then creates incentives to resist weakness of will that can lead to their adoption of personal rules meant to counteract it. Self-reputation, therefore, acquires a hold of sorts over individuals, which supports their adoption of personal rules.

Once personal rules are in place, sustaining them depends on individuals correctly seeing their lapses as weakness of will rather than in their rationalizing those lapses or forgetting them. This in turn means that, not only must individuals overcome imperfect self-knowledge about their abilities, but they must also reliably recall their past preferences and overcome imperfect recall. What influences their ability to do this? Again, self-confidence is important, because self-control is easier for self-confident individuals, who perceive there to be reputational capital at stake in their decisions and are accordingly more likely to exercise selective recall and pay attention to their lapses. External controls associated with supervisory roles for parents and others are also influential on whether individuals recognize their lapses. These have mixed effects, however, sometimes producing benefits and sometimes costing individuals in terms of lost autonomy (Bénabou and Tirole 2003b). Finally, the better the "technology" of an individual's memory (using personal rules with good mnemonic properties and adopting such practices as rehearsing rules), the better an individual's self-monitoring, and the more difficult it becomes to rationalize or forget past lapses.

Bénabou and Tirole's personal rules analysis, then, provides a second means for addressing individuals' multiple selves. Not only do individuals' multiple selves manage their self-confidence, and thus their present bias by managing their imperfect self-knowledge and imperfect recall, but they also adopt personal rules strategies for doing so through their concern with self-reputation regarding their willpower and vulnerability to weakness of will. Put in terms of the personal asset concept, Bénabou and Tirole's account of individuals as multiple selves depends, not only on regarding self-confidence as a personal asset, but also on regarding self-reputation as one as well. Indeed, they are clear that individuals' concern with these two personal assets is interconnected in virtue of their mutual influences on one another. Self-confidence strengthens personal rules that build self-reputation, whereas a strong self-reputation helps combat weakness of will and present bias, thus making it easier for individuals to enjoy gains from self-confidence.

Thus, Bénabou and Tirole's analysis of self-control and self-regulation involves seeing individuals as portfolios of personal assets that need to be managed in a risky world under the limitations of the three human imperfections (and departures from standard theory) they incorporate in their models. Portfolios in standard capital theory, of course, are more than the sum of their individual elements, because they are structured according to a variety of balancing and trade-off principles that link their elements together. The same can be said for treating the individual as a portfolio of personal assets; and though the nature of the assets is obviously different in this case, the portfolio concept is appropriate because Bénabou and Tirole rely on the same economic logic of investment and return and gains and losses. Thus, individuals can be said to exercise self-control in virtue of their commitment to the logic of maintaining themselves as portfolios of personal assets. This might seem to mean that management of these personal assets passes from one of an individual's multiple selves to the next, leaving us again with multiple selves. However, a slight change in emphasis puts the situation in a different light: individuals are portfolios of personal assets there to be managed by whichever self happens to be currently responsible for the program of doing so. That is, if one invokes the concept of (fiduciary) responsibility to properly capture the asset management process, one thereby makes reference to a single management or self-control practice, because responsibility implies some single thing for which responsibility is exercised. This emphasis on responsibility, it seems fair to say, adds another idea to Bénabou and Tirole's individual conception idea of the individual being an active being, namely, the idea of the individual being a reflexive being. Both ideas represent potentially important extensions and departures from the standard *Homo economicus* conception.

For Bénabou and Tirole, then, individuals are single beings, not just collections of multiple selves without a principle of unity. Moreover, because individuals clearly differ according to how good their portfolios are, with some having higher quality self-confidence and self-reputation assets than others, differences in their individuality can be understood in terms of differences between them as distinct portfolios. This, however, invites us to ask how interaction between individuals is to be understood, particularly as they sustain the traditional view that economics is about individuals interacting in markets. Bénabou and Tirole accordingly extend their analysis of within-individual multiple selves "social" interaction to between-individual social interaction in connection with their goal of ultimately producing a "unified approach to social psychology" for behavioral economics.

3.2.3 A Unified Approach to Social Psychology

Though the entry point to their analysis, as we have seen, is the single individual, Bénabou and Tirole properly say that their theory remains incomplete without attention to social interactions between individuals. At the same time, they do not believe that a more complete account substantially changes any of their conclusions reached with respect to how single individuals manage themselves.

A unified approach to social psychology should start from a single view of the individual's preferences, cognitive machinery, and basic problem-solving strategies. While incentives and feedback, and therefore behavior, are highly context-dependent, the underlying "fundamentals" are the same whether the individual is engaged in self-regulation or interacting with others. (Bénabou and Tirole 2003b, 159)

They then go on to summarize how an expanded framework includes social interaction.

The common thread running through a wide variety of social situations is that one agent (or more) is trying to get another one (or more) to perform a certain task: study, work, buy or sell, consent to a relationships, etc. Conversely, the other party is interested in determining, and if possible maximizing, "what is in it" for them. In such settings, which economists refer to as principal-agent relationships, psychologists have studied two types of interactions (going in opposite directions) between an individual's self-view and his social environment. (ibid.)

Of these two types of interactions, one is termed self-presentation; the second is termed the "looking glass self," an idea derived from Charles Cooley (1902). Self-presentation is where an individual (or rather one temporal self of the individual) tries to influence another individual (or another individual's temporal self) by conveying information about itself through signaling. Signaling is possible because an individual has private (if imperfect) knowledge regarding its own abilities via its memories (though imperfect). Putting this in principal-agent terms, the principal wishes to determine the attractiveness of an offer to an agent, and in doing so makes an assessment of that agent's motivation, apparent self-confidence, and likely ability to perform any agreed-upon tasks. Accordingly, the agent has an incentive to self-present itself strategically by, say, signaling high self-confidence when hoping to signal to the principal the commitment it has to a planned project. In contrast, the "looking glass self" concerns situations in which others try to influence the self-view of an individual (or rather one temporal self of the individual), such as when parents attempt to boost children's self-confidence (a case of altruism). Here, the principal (the parents) holds information that is not available to the agent (the child), such as about the long-term benefits of education when trying to instill confidence regarding performance in school. Similarly, the agent (the child) holds information not available to the principal regarding self-confidence, and so forth.

"A unified approach to social psychology," then, in which the "underlying 'fundamentals' are the same," whether we focus on individuals interacting with others or separately engaged in self-regulation across their multiple selves (Bénabou and Tirole 2003, 159), is simply one that applies principal-agent theory both interpersonally across individuals and intrapersonally across individuals' multiple selves. Further, in a world of imperfect and privately held information, signaling proper explains principal-agent relationships across individuals, whereas self-signaling explains principal-agent relationships across individuals' multiple selves.[4] As their entire analysis of interaction is game-theoretic, a complete game-theoretic account consequently examines signaling-based principal-agent relationships between individuals whose multiple selves exhibit self-signaling principal-agent relationships among themselves. Thus, one temporal self of an individual may enter into a game-theoretic principal-agent interaction with the temporal self of another individual, in which both individuals' temporal selves are simultaneously involved in game-theoretic principal-agent relationships with their other respective temporal selves. Moreover, these

---

[4] Bénabou and Tirole link their use of the self-signaling idea to work in psychology as follows: "The idea that people learn about themselves by observing their own actions, and conversely make choices in ways designated to achieve or preserve favorable self-conceptions, is quite prevalent in psychology and well supported empirically" (Bénabou and Tirole 2004, 852). They compare their analysis to that of Bodner and Prelec (e.g., 2003).

"temporal selves games" do not need to be temporally coincident, as one individual's current self might enter into a game with another individual's past self. Indeed, this might represent a more complete statement of what many traditional principal-agent games involve as when, for example, the self-confidence an owner of some business has created in the past is a factor in negotiations with a manager hired to run that business today.

3.3 "Self"-control?

There are a number of things in Bénabou and Tirole's analysis that might appear objectionable to some, but which arguably do not really involve significant problems. For example, one objection might be that likening individuals to portfolios of capital assets misconceives in a most fundamental way what human beings are. Yet if one puts aside the capital concept connotations and thinks only of individuals inheriting and possessing such psychological traits as self-confidence and concern with self-reputation, the matter is less problematic, because traits are indeed kinds of stocks. It might then be objected that whereas such traits are indisputably human, it is a mistake to understand their operation in individuals in terms of the economic logic of investment and return and gains and losses. However, it seems that the issue is not the economics vocabulary itself, because it can be taken metaphorically, and indeed the idea of gains and losses is more primitive than economics itself. Another possible objection might be to treating individuals' intrapersonal equilibria in terms of noncooperative games rather than coordination games. Somehow it seems counterintuitive to regard an individual's multiple selves as independent and self-interested if we want to ultimately show they all belong to one person. However, the rationale for seeing a person's intrapersonal games as noncooperative is that this seems to capture the nature of present bias and weakness of will through the idea of an individual's different selves being at odds with one another. In Chapter 6, I discuss Don Ross's account of intrapersonal multiple selves equilibrium as a coordination game, and thus I will postpone further discussion of this issue until then.

A serious problem does seem to arise, however, when we consider how Bénabou and Tirole seek to go beyond their original entry point of single individuals, and turn to their larger account that includes social interaction in their explanation of a unified approach to social psychology. As we have seen, that they are in the first instance concerned to explain how individuals address weakness of will – the problem that adding more realism to the standard model generates – means that they first show how single individuals are able to exercise self-control vis-à-vis their different temporal selves, in which this becomes a matter of managing a personal asset portfolio made up of stocks of self-confidence and self-reputation. This thus constitutes a kind of partial equilibrium analysis because one individual's temporal self interaction with other individuals' temporal selves is held to the side in order to first explain self-control. However, their unified approach to social psychology combining between-individual signaling and self-signaling involves a general type of equilibrium analysis, and so we cannot say that individuals work out self-control problems in abstraction from their inter-action with one another. Indeed, this is precisely what Bénabou and Tirole say in connection with their "looking glass self" treatment of influence between the temporal self of one person on another, as in the parents and child case. In contrast to self-control, we might label interpersonal influence "other-control." But then, that their unified approach to social psychology involves a general game-theoretic equilibrium means that self-control and other-control are inextricably intertwined, and it makes no sense to say in their analysis that individuals exclusively exercise "self"-control. More gen-erally, with the world made up of many temporal selves ever influencing one another across time, it is simply not possible to say that single individu-als are engaged in "self"-control, nor indeed is it possible to say that there even exist single individuals made up of multiple selves. That is, the general game-theoretic world they envision is just a world of many mutually influ-encing temporal selves. In this respect, their modeling the *Homo sapiens* conception as an asset portfolio is telling, because in the financial world any given agent's asset portfolio is influenced by many investors and there is nothing in the nature of the asset portfolio by itself that assigns it to one agent. That is the job of private property law.

This negative result, I suggest, is what one might have expected as an outcome in a strategy that aims to revise the standard conception of the individual as a collection of preferences by using the concept of self-control to reinterpret that collection. Self-control is an agency concept and here implies that individuals are active, reflexive beings. When we think of individuals as active and reflexive, however, we must attribute abili-ties (alternatively, capacities or capabilities) to them to do things and take themselves into account in the process. In contrast, the idea of preferring as an affective concept offers little foundation for this sort of characteriza-tion, and accordingly Bénabou and Tirole's introduction of these concepts within the framework of the standard preferences conception of the indi-vidual simply has insufficient theoretical structure to explain self-control. The multiple selves problem involved thus ends up being finessed rather than solved. Ability, of course, is a complex concept whose understanding requires deeper consideration than given to it by Bénabou and Tirole. Absent that, it is easy to make the mistake of supposing that ability can first be uniquely associated with individuals, and then imagine that this prior ability is somehow influenced or perhaps modified at most by interaction with others, as, say, through "informational spillovers" (Battaglini, Bénabou, and Tirole 2005). However, in their interpersonal-intrapersonal game-theoretic framework, the individual's abilities – or more accurately the abilities of one of an individual's temporal selves – likely reflect social interaction. We thus seem to somehow have our individual abilities in part because of social interaction. It is difficult to make any progress in sorting out this issue, as well as the question of self-control, however, when operating with a basic assumption that individuals are simply collections of preferences.

Bénabou and Tirole, then, do not solve the multiple selves problem produced by the evidence that individuals discount hyperbolically. The "individual" consequently remains fragmented as a collection of episodic selves, and the purportedly more realistic *Homo sapiens* conception remains but a promise. This in turn raises questions about the compatibility of behavioral economics with standard theory. If the greater realism intended only shows there is no apparent way to explain individuals in the utility framework, then the unintended consequence is that behavioral economics is ultimately disruptive of the goals of standard theory, as is evident now in its failure to explain how individuals are able to successfully engage in intertemporal decision making. Another way of looking at this is in terms of a critical assessment of the "light" embedding of individuals in context – Thaler's motivating principle. In Bénabou and Tirole's general game-theoretic equilibrium, individuals' temporal selves can be influenced by so many other individuals' temporal selves that they are really too heavily embedded, as it were, to even be single individuals. In effect, the principle of "lightly" embedding individuals in context is a slippery slope, collapsing into a full embedding. Its introduction fails, then, as a strategy for addressing the sub-personal in single-individual explanations that concerns how people can be both single individuals and possess multiple selves.

In the balance of this chapter, I turn to a second behavioral economics response to present bias and time-inconsistent behavior that is essentially the opposite of Bénabou and Tirole's. This is Thaler and Sunstein's libertarian paternalism view that essentially assumes we cannot solve the multiple selves problem with a theory of self-control, so that rational experts are needed as surrogates to individuals to help them solve their weakness of will problems, "as if" they were single individuals. Bénabou and Tirole are to be commended for expanding our thinking about individuals to include self-confidence and self-reputation in a world of imperfect self-knowledge, imperfect willpower, and imperfect recall, because these concepts are clearly part of any realistic understanding of individuals; but the next two sections look at what behavioral economics ought to say when individuals cannot be expected to exercise self-control.

3.4 "As if" Individuals: Libertarian Paternalism

Libertarian paternalism, also "soft" paternalism and asymmetric paternalism, is different from a "hard" paternalism in that the latter mandates behaviors whereas the former only encourages individuals to act as they would if acting rationally. This encouragement operates through institutional redesign of choice settings (or the "choice architecture") that is the work of rational experts who benevolently take the best interest of others in the interests of efficiency and as a general normative goal. The idea that soft paternalism is an asymmetric paternalism derives from the idea that institutional redesign ought to be carried out in such a way as to selectively affect irrational individuals and have no effect on rational individuals. Thaler and Sunstein's libertarian paternalism label has attracted the most attention in connection with its seemingly problematic juxtaposition of the concepts of libertarianism and paternalism, as reflected in the title of their "Libertarian Paternalism is Not an Oxymoron" article (Sunstein and Thaler 2003). Their goal, in fact, was to dispel the notion that a soft paternalist approach to public policy abridges individual freedom. Their argument for this conclusion is that individuals who are weak of will are not free, and that policies that allow them to overcome present bias (or, more generally, status quo bias) enable them to act as they themselves would freely wish to act. That is, rationality implies freedom. Similarly, the title of their later book *Nudge* (Thaler and Sunstein 2008) suggests influence without interference.

However, the issue that seems most immediate here – whether individual freedom and paternalism are compatible – cannot be separated from another of deeper significance, namely, how a paternalism aimed at assisting people in gaining self-control really aims at constructing individuals by causing their fragmented multiple selves to act as if they were single individuals. Thus, the underlying assumption of the argument should be enlarged to say that, not only does *Homo sapiens* generally not act rationally, but *Homo sapiens* also does not generally act as a single individual. As people regularly reverse past plans for the future to which they were committed, they continually reject their past selves as not themselves, and are thus ever a prey to circumstance, especially by comparison with unified rational individuals of standard theory whose plans are represented as consistent across time. In contrast to Bénabou and Tirole's positive analysis that seeks to show how people are single individuals able to exercise self-control, Thaler and Sunstein emphasize the empirical evidence that they fail to do so and consequently adopt a normative stance in favor of – not just promoting rational behavior in the interest of efficiency –promoting individuality itself. Moreover, as this individuality is modeled on standard rationality theory, this implies that rational experts ought to help make *Homo sapiens* behave as much as possible as *Homo economicus* would, thus reflecting behavioral economics' strategy of revising *Homo economicus* rather than replacing it.

An important though relatively unexamined dimension of Thaler and Sunstein's account is how a particular kind of social interaction becomes a central focus, namely that between rational experts and those people whose identities are constructed as single individuals. Essentially what they argue is that because the latter's identities are constructed in the image of the former, the identities of rational experts come to play a larger role in the identities of the individuals they construct. Because people remain weak of will, it cannot be said that their identities are fully constructed as those of rational individuals. This means that the individual identities created are complex; they are made up of elements that naturally belong to individuals themselves and elements that are created by the inhabitation of rational experts. This combination of elements – the individual's "own" and third-party ones of others – recalls prospect theory's mixing of subjective preferences and extrasubjective reference points in the constitution of the individual. Here as well, Thaler and Sunstein fail to show that the individual that rational experts construct is a single unity, because the boundary crossing this involves makes the boundaries on being a single individual unclear. In contrast to prospect theory, the problem now arises out of human intervention and the social interaction between rational experts and the weak of will, rather than from simply psychologists' evidence that people rely on extrasubjective reference points. This reflects economists' interest in social interaction; and indeed how social interaction underlies individual identity turns out to be an increasingly important theme in behavioral economics, as we will continue to explore in the next chapter in connection with how behavioral economics treats social identities and social preferences. The following two Sections 3.4.1 and 3.4.2 give one account of the role that social interaction plays in thinking about identity by explaining Thaler and Sunstein's account, first, in terms of the how it derives from the view that rationality or economics ought to correct people's present-bias behavior, and second, in terms of the logic of surrogates they embrace in the role assigned to rational experts or economists.

3.4.1 Multiple Selves and Normative Versus Descriptive Theories

On the standard view, individuals do not always behave rationally, but departures from rationality are seen as anomalous, infrequent, usually self-correcting, and thus not a reason for giving up the view that markets are generally efficient. Rational choice theory is descriptive of behavior, and laissez faire frames and circumscribes economic policy. Behavioral economists, however, distinguish between normative and descriptive theories of choice, in which the former "characterize rational choice" and the latter "characterize actual choices" (Thaler 2000, 138; cf. Heukelom 2009). A normative rational choice theory characterizes what individuals ought to do to behave rationally, recognizing that they must be described as frequently acting otherwise. Applied to the traditional doctrine of consumer sovereignty, this means people are generally not sovereign over what they regard as being best for themselves; so that to maintain this doctrine, one needs to make what they would rationally believe best for themselves possible for them to achieve. Consumer sovereignty is then sustained through intervention in markets and is cut free of its traditional laissez faire foundation. If the main justification for laissez faire is a utilitarian defense of consumer sovereignty, securing people's own best interests requires giving up laissez faire. Economic theory, driven by research in psychology regarding human choice behavior, then becomes a fundamentally normative enterprise. Rather than a positive account of how individuals interact in markets, it is an investigation of what measures ought to be taken by policy makers, given people's actual behavior, to bring about what they would like to be the case, on the assumption that utilitarian ethical reasoning provides the best basis for policy.

Consider the application of this logic to decisions people make that have long-term consequences, in which "in the context of intertemporal choice, people exhibit dynamic inconsistency, valuing present consumption much more than future consumption ... [and so] have self-control problems" (Thaler and Sunstein 2003, 176). This phenomenon has been studied extensively in connection with people's savings behavior, in which status quo bias causes individuals to undersave, as in connection with the level of contributions they make to employee pension programs. That it is undersaving rather than low levels of desired saving is inferred from individuals' later expressed desire to have saved more when confronted with the consequences of their past savings decisions (Samuelson and Zeckhauser 1988; Madrian and Shea 2001). Given this expressed desire, the new doctrine of consumer sovereignty tells us that individuals' choices should be structured for them so as to enable them to maintain the levels of savings they would prefer. The particular policy measure that has generally been recommended to combat status quo bias is to design the enrolment forms of employer pension plans in such a way that the default option in the sign-up gives a desired level of savings. The default mechanism constitutes the "nudge" in the choice architecture that enables individuals to act as they would prefer.

That this strategy depends on identifying the choices people wish they would like to make might be seen as a problem of their having insufficient information about the consequences of their choices, especially in a world in which long-term choices are often complicated. This interpretation cannot be sustained, however, because status quo bias is, broadly speaking, a problem of people making plans with foresight and then abandoning them. People can be well-informed about the consequences of their decisions and yet still exhibit weakness of will in maintaining them. Indeed, in the case of employer contribution pension plans, people generally understand that they ought to commit themselves to long-term savings plans even when they do not do so. The problem is not an information one, but rather one of the stability of their preferences, which present bias causes to change across time. This means that the goal of a libertarian paternalist social policy is to stabilize people's preferences in such a way as to guarantee that their "preferred" preferences prevail. But what are "preferred" preferences? On the standard view, individuals' preferences are exogenous, and this expression exhibits redundancy. For behavioral economics, however, it is meaningful, but not just because a distinction can be made between what people prefer on any given occasion and what they rationally ought to prefer. The program of ensuring people act on one set of preferences also works to preclude such social dilemmas as widespread insufficient savings behavior (especially an issue with aging populations). When behavioralist economists rule out nonintervention, then, they also rule out simply letting people make sovereign savings choices that might leave them destitute in old age. Therefore, efficiency is not the only motivation for libertarian paternalism. The benevolence of the policy maker toward individuals and concern with societywide good are also involved in determining what people ought to prefer. "Preferred" preferences, then, are preferences endogenized by social goals, such as in this instance that people ought to take individual responsibility for certain lifetime needs like old-age income by means of personal savings plans. Note also that if we suppose that people are generally concerned with their own day-to-day circumstances and with societywide dilemmas in only a limited way, then the determination of social goals also falls largely within the province of rational experts.

3.4.2 Rational Experts

Given this understanding of the basis for social policy, how do rational experts implement policy? Thaler and Sunstein (2003) offer a two-track approach. Rational experts (or sensible planners as they prefer to call them) should ordinarily use cost-benefit analysis to determine the best choices for individuals, but when this is infeasible due to information on costs and benefits being unavailable or because the cost of analysis is too large, indirect proxies for determining what promotes individual welfare can be adopted. The three proxies recommended are: selecting strategies that the majority would choose if explicit choices were required and revealed, forcing people to make their choices explicit, and selecting strategies that minimize the number of opt-outs. These indirect strategies might suggest that the goal is to get people to "reveal" their preferences, but what they rather argue is that "the starting point" (or reference point) for every choice situation has "preference-shaping effects."

> When paternalism seems absent, it is usually because the starting point appears so natural and obvious that its preference-shaping effects are invisible to most observers. But those effects are nonetheless there. Of course it is usually good not to block choices, and we do not mean to defend non-utilitarianism here. But in an important respect, the anti-paternalistic position is incoherent. (ibid., 177)

Thus, if preferences are always being shaped and if anti-paternalism is incoherent, there is no neutral vantage point for evaluating people's choices, and policy makers ought to use cost-benefit analysis and the indirect means listed above to judge preferences as they interpret them to formulate desirable policy. Of course, the difference between "interpret" and "construct" is not clear. Moreover, when we think about policy implementation more concretely, we recognize that more is involved than simply developing techniques to make people's choices explicit. There is also the give-and-take sort of real-world process whereby policy itself gets adjusted to people's preferences while it also influences those preferences. Policy makers, that is, hardly set policy from some neutral location. This, however, points us to the paradox involved in claiming that economists – or anyone else for that matter – can be considered rational experts free of the characteristics psychologists attribute to all people. Because status quo bias and weakness of will go to the heart of rational choice theory, how can rational experts who rely on that theory claim to occupy a higher ground from which to make policy?

Some people, of course, may simply have the authority to create policy for choice architectures, namely, those "sensible planners" who "include anyone who must design plans for others, from human-resource directors to bureaucrats to kings" (ibid., 178) to doctors, to tax specialists, to travel planners, to religious counselors, and on and on in an almost endless list reflecting the array of specializations that characterize society today. But what this ultimately implies is that people's preferences (their "preferred" preferences) are determined by disparate and often conflicting patterns of social interaction. They first reflect inherited starting points and default settings and then, given the multitude of kinds of "sensible planners" in the world, are subject to analysis and interpretation by a range of rational experts with different interests, domains of specialization and concern, and thus views of what is right. That is, contrary to Thaler and Sunstein's narrow focus on economists, there are as many varieties of social policy targeting individuals' preferences as there are different kinds of experts. Further, because Thaler and Sunstein's sensible planners are really just people with authority to influence others, there is no special reason to suppose that they are necessarily motivated by benevolence rather than malevolence. We are left accordingly with individuals fragmented over many possible multiple selves and thus considerable ambiguity regarding what the identity of people consists in. Though Thaler and Sunstein's revised utility function entry point separates their program from psychology's preference construction school, their embedding of preferences in complex social processes all but produces the same outcome: there is no apparent basis for saying what an individual is.

Suppose, nonetheless, we take libertarian paternalism at face value in order to see it as Thaler and Sunstein see it, namely, as a development of the standard view whereby benevolent experts with higher degrees of rationality can design choice settings that individuals would discover elicit choices they believe are in their own best interest. Then it still follows that a social process causes people to behave as if they are relatively autonomous single individuals, and individuality is a product of social interaction, not a presupposition of it as on the standard view. If this then is how behavioral economics revises the traditional *Homo economicus* conception, its departure from that standard conception is quite dramatic because atomism is abandoned rather than revised. Moreover, if some of the support that behavioral economics has received in the economics profession is due to the perception that it is largely compatible with standard theory, that perception seems to be mistaken, though understandably so as Thaler in particular has made every effort to liken *Homo sapiens* to *Homo economicus* – an ambition that is reinforced by Bénabou and Tirole's parallel project of rebuilding the atomist conception. In closing this chapter, then, let us look at how these two behavioral economic strategies relate to one another.

3.5 Self-control and Social Control

Time-inconsistent behavior produces a multiple selves problem, but the two strategies for addressing it examined in this chapter are opposite of one another. Whereas Bénabou and Tirole seek to solve it intrapersonally as a self-control problem at the level of the individual, Thaler and Sunstein seek to solve it interpersonally as a policy problem at the level of society. Not surprisingly, the difficulties they respectively encounter are obverse of one another. Bénabou and Tirole take the individual as their entry point and make arguments for the unity of the individual, but when they extend their game-theoretic analysis to social interaction, they undermine their unity argument. Thaler and Sunstein take social interaction as their entry point and interpret this in terms of how rational experts ought to correct people's status quo bias, but the resulting account of individuals as constructed opens the door to all sorts of influences on individuals, transforming the meaning of social interaction from what they had hoped it to be. Both strategies, then, are unsuccessful in mapping out the relationship between what it means to be a single individual and social interaction, despite coming at this from different directions. More importantly, both arguments fail to solve the multiple selves problem.

Both strategies can also be seen as two different responses to Elster's earlier attempt to explain how people act as single individuals through the exercise of self-control. Elster (1983) argued that individuals exercise self-control in social settings through various types of precommitments they make to others (signing binding contracts, holding illiquid assets, making public side bets, etc.) in advance of occasions when they may find themselves weak of will (like the mythical Ulysses who had his crew bind him to the mast of his ship in anticipation of hearing the Sirens). From Bénabou and Tirole's perspective, Elster's argument lacks an account of how individuals internally practice self-control. If the constraints one places on oneself are external and always depend on others, then in themselves individuals really remain multiple selves and indeed may be taken advantage of by others who are able to manipulate their precommitment devices. However, Bénabou and Tirole's general equilibrium game-theoretic account also puts "other" control on a par with "self" control, and consequently fails to improve on Elster. Thaler and Sunstein, on the other hand, directly embrace Elster's logic of external constraints; but rather than explain them as being self-imposed as he does, they relocate them in the choices of rational experts acting as surrogates for weak-of-will individuals. For them, Elster fails to properly locate where individual control mechanisms reside, as the evidence indicates that individuals are unable to constrain themselves per se. However, their "experts" can only be understood as constructing "as if" individuals' preferences rather than enabling people to practice self-control, so Elster's multiple selves problem is really abandoned altogether rather than solved.

Why, then, is Elster's problem so seemingly intractable? Bénabou and Tirole and Thaler and Sunstein arguably make progress on Elster by emphasizing conceptual apparatus he does not. The former emphasize reflexive behavior as central to their account of the individual by developing the concepts of self-regulation and self-reputation as key to understanding self-control, whereas the latter emphasize social interaction in their account of the individual by showing how others can help individuals avoid weakness of will. Neither of these concepts is really developed by Elster, because he restricts his conception of the individual to the idea of simply being a collection of preferences. Bénabou and Tirole enrich individuals' preference structures by giving them a reflexive dimension; Thaler and Sunstein enrich the account of what preferences are by recognizing the role that others play in determining individual preferences. Neither of these strategies really goes much beyond the preference framework itself in reconceptualizing individuals, however, and this appears to be the limiting factor operating on each. Specifically, if one is to argue individuals are *able* to overcome such multiple selves problems as weakness of will, either on their own or in interaction with others, it seems one's individual conception needs to include some concept of ability, capacity, or capability, a concept quite different from the concept of preferring. Put differently, if individuals are agents, our conception of them needs to include some account of how they bring things about, not just what they prefer to come about. This type of thinking is missing in the two strategies discussed in this chapter, which thus ultimately remain true to standard *Homo economicus* view that individuals are essentially just bundles of preferences.

In the chapter that follows, I look at two further behavioral economics strategies for advancing the standard individual conception: Akerlof and Kranton's inclusion of social identities in individuals' utility functions and a number of different accounts of how individuals' utility functions include social preferences. These strategies have the merit of offering new ways of thinking about the relationship between individuality and sociality. I will examine them in terms of whether they provide adequate conceptions of single individuals.

FOUR

Social Identity and Social Preferences
in the Utility Function

4.1 Internalizing Sociality

The previous chapter examined two strategies that combine the traditional atomistic individual conception with accounts of social interaction: Bénabou and Tirole by moving from their model of the self-regulating individual to their unified psychology general game-theoretic analysis and Thaler and Sunstein by explaining how rational experts seek to make *Homo sapiens* act like *Homo economicus*. This chapter examines two further behavioral economics approaches that proceed quite differently in that they inject social content and social interaction directly into the standard utility function representation of the individual: George Akerlof and Rachel Kranton's social groups social identity analysis and the social preferences approach developed by James Andreoni, Matthew Rabin, Ernst Fehr, Klaus Schmidt, and many others. That is, rather than contextualize individuality (and subjectivity) by placing individuals in a world in which they interact with others, they internalize sociality by giving the utility function an unmistakably social dimension. Their general strategy, then, is more radical in that it contests the traditional understanding of atomism itself. How can people be atomistic individuals if they are in some fashion also social individuals? At the same time, it remains a traditional kind of strategy in that the analysis is developed within the utility function framework in which individuals' preferences, whatever their nature, are still their own preferences.

Neither of the approaches discussed in this chapter, however, is formulated as a response to the multiple selves problem, presumably because in behavioral economics that problem is generally associated with present bias and time inconsistency, and neither of these approaches is specifically concerned with that issue. However, present bias causes only one kind of multiple selves problem, specifically an intertemporal one, and this chapter will accordingly investigate how multiple selves problems resurface in two additional forms in connection with these different strategies for explaining individuals. In particular, in the Akerlof-Kranton analysis the multiple selves problem reappears in connection with individuals having multiple social group identities, whereas in social preferences analysis it arises in connection with uncertainty over whose preferences individuals serve, their own or those of others. In both cases, that is, individuals' multiple selves are their multiple social selves. Thus, the strategy of internalizing social relationships within the utility function locates different social selves directly within individuals. The question these approaches consequently face is whether it still makes sense to say the utility function constitutes a single individual unity.

The two approaches discussed here also fall within the new behavioral economics in virtue of the kinds of departures they make from the standard axiomatic account of individuals. Akerlof and Kranton emphasize that social psychology has valuable resources to offer to economics, and the proponents of social preferences draw on extensive experimental evidence to reject the idea that individuals act only out of self-interest (e.g., Kahneman, Knetsch, and Thaler 1986a, 1986b). Thus, they agree that economics needs to become more realistic, where this means greater psychological realism. In contrast to what we saw in the previous two chapters greater psychological realism now means greater social psychological realism, and the evidence being drawn upon concerns what psychologists and others believe they know about the nature of social interaction. Indeed, whereas prospect theory arises out of the field of behavioral decision research, the views examined in this chapter draw more on social psychology, which has a quite different home in psychology (itself a more decentralized discipline than economics) from BDR. Yet one should not assume too quickly that what social psychologists and other noneconomists believe to be the case about social interaction can or has entered smoothly into behavioral economics without interpretation and selection. Disciplinary boundaries in the form of different structures of concepts and organizing principles act as filters in all fields, and they tend to re-form adopted nondisciplinary contents to suit the receiving field. In this chapter, we look at how social identity and social preferences have been accommodated in behavioral economics' revised *Homo economicus* conception, but in connection with Akerlof and Kranton's analysis we also look at a set of social psychology concepts regarding individuals' social identities that have failed to cross the disciplinary boundary between economics and psychology on account of the constraints the utility framework imposes.

Section 4.2 summarizes Akerlof and Kranton's main argument regarding how social identities operate in the utility function from their influential first paper on identity in economics. After a general introduction, I describe the tradition in psychology from which they draw, and set out their utility function model. Section 4.3 evaluates their analysis, particularly in light of the two different traditions in thinking about social identity in social psychology.[1] Section 4.4 turns to the social preferences approach, distinguishes four different strategies and kinds of social preferences, and then differentiates this approach from the social identity approach. Section 4.5 evaluates the social preference approach by interpreting it as relying on empathy as an extended form of sympathy. Section 4.6 draws conclusions about both strategies examined in the chapter, as well as about the others discussed in Part 1, and then points toward a different way of rethinking what individuals are, which is the subject of Part 2.

4.2 Akerlof and Kranton on Identity as Self-image

Akerlof and Kranton's "Economics and Identity" paper is not the first discussion of identity in economics, but it represents a significant innovation in modeling identity as an argument in the individual utility function seen as "a new type of externality" (2000, 717).[2] Their motivation for introducing identity into economics is that the concept of identity is a powerful tool in social science, and thus likely to be illuminating in economics as well. If this is the case, why has the concept had almost no application in economics until recently? Akerlof and Kranton's answer is that it has been unclear just how the concept could be applied in economics.

> Because of its explanatory power, numerous scholars in psychology, sociology, political science, anthropology, and history have adopted identity as a central concept. This paper shows *how* identity can be brought into economic analysis, allowing a new view of many economic problems. (Akerlof and Kranton 2000, 716; emphasis added)

Modeling identity as "a new type of externality" not only represents an extension of standard thinking about individuals, thus addressing the problem of what economics can accommodate from the other social sciences, but

---

[1] In both sections, I draw on Davis (2007a).

[2] Earlier contributions include Sen (1985a, 1999b), Folbre (1994), and Davis (1995). Akerlof and Kranton have extended their analysis to identity in organizations (2002, 2005) and have brought all their arguments together in a single account of how identity affects people generally (2010), but their modeling strategy is essentially the same, and thus I restrict my discussion to their original paper. See Fine (2009) for a critique of their approach.

is also central to the strategy of revising the standard individual conception by internalizing sociality within individuality. If a central complaint against the atomistic *Homo economicus* is that it leaves the individual outside the world of social interaction looking in, then the "new type of externality" way of introducing identity and sociality into economics offers a clever twist on a traditional view. How, then, exactly do Akerlof and Kranton incorporate identity into the individual utility function?

First, the specific concept of identity they employ is that of social identity or social group identity, which they understand from the individual's point of view as the person's "sense of self" or "self-image." More accurately, a person's self-image is a set of self-images corresponding to all the different social categories (ethnicity, gender, religion, occupation, neighborhood, nationality, etc.) that are assignable to the individual as social group identities. Social categories are broad social science classifications used in academic research, government agencies, and the popular media to describe widely recognized social aggregates. An individual's "sense of self" or "self-image," then, is an individual's identity because, as Akerlof and Kranton put it, "identity is bound to social categories; and individuals *identify with* people in some categories and differentiate themselves from those in others" (Akerlof and Kranton 2000, 720; emphasis added). The idea of "identifying with" others is the main content of the idea of social identity. However, there are other identity concepts. In particular, Akerlof and Kranton are silent about the concept of personal identity, or the idea of an individual's "identity apart from" others. Note also that their particular view of social identity, namely, that individuals identify with others in terms of established social categories, is different from the idea that individuals identify with others through social structural phenomena such as participation in groups, institutions, and interpersonal relationships, as will later be discussed in connection with the sociological approach to identity.

Second, to explain the relationship between social identity and the individual, Akerlof and Kranton draw on Kerry Thomas' fairly standard account of the psychodynamics of personality and personality disorders (Thomas 1996).

This model can be expressed by ideas central to the psychodynamic theory of personality, found in almost any psychology text. In personality development, psychologists agree on the importance of *internalization* of rules for behavior. Freud called this process the development of the *superego*. Modern scholars disagree with Freud on the importance of psychosexual factors in an individual's development, but they agree on the importance of *anxiety* that a person experiences when she violates her internalized rules. One's *identity*, or *ego*, or *self*, must be constantly "defended against anxiety in order to limit disruption and maintain a sense of unity." (Akerlof and Kranton 2000, 728; their emphasis)[3]

Social categories, then, are associated with various rules of behavior appropriate to people to whom those categories apply, and individuals internalize these rules in such a way as to constitute an individual identity or sense of self with respect to each category. Should individuals violate these internalized rules (as Akerlof and Kranton model in a game-theoretic way), this generates a sense of anxiety on the part of the individual, or "cognitive dissonance," leading the individual to undertake actions intended to reduce this anxiety and thereby restore the individual's "sense of unity." Akerlof and Kranton model this all in terms of utility maximization. Part of utility maximization, they thus argue, is cognitive dissonance minimization. Moreover, because cognitive dissonance is disruptive of the individual's sense of self, their model is one in which utility maximization or cognitive dissonance minimization works to maintain individuals' unity as single individuals.

Note that the concepts of "personality," "ego," "self," and "sense of unity" from the previous passage are used in essentially the same way as the concepts of "sense of self" and "self-image" in that all refer to the identity of the individual understood in social identity terms. Yet the first three terms really refer to the individual as a whole, whereas the latter two terms must refer to multiple senses of self or self-images according to all the different social categories that apply to individuals. This is important because the association of multiple senses of self and the self opens the door to the possibility that individuals can have multiple egos and senses of unity. We should also note that, whereas the first four concepts in Thomas' theory are labels for psychodynamic mechanisms (for restoring a sense of unity in response to anxiety), the latter two concepts refer to the various social category contents of an individual's identity (in which the individual's entire self-image has as its content all the different social group identifications with others that the individual has). Akerlof and Kranton of course want to explain choice where identity matters, and they want to accomplish this task with greater psychological realism. Thomas' psychodynamic theory as an account of a unity-restoring mechanism serves these two objectives, though because it is conceived as an internal mechanism that is by nature inaccessible to individuals, they emphasize that they do not use the verb "choose" in the literal sense when they refer to individuals' unity-restoring

---

[3]   The quoted passage is from Thomas (1996, 284).

responses to anxiety. "We do not presume one way or another that people are aware of their own motivations, as in standard utility theory which is agnostic as to whether an individual shopper is aware or not of the reasons for her choices" (Akerlof and Kranton 2000, 719).

4.2.1 Psychology's Social Identity Approach

Social psychology is a hybrid field that includes approaches originating in both psychology and sociology. Often these approaches are quite different in nature, as one would expect according to the differences between psychology and sociology. Akerlof and Kranton adopt what is known as the "social identity" approach that comes from psychology. The "social identity" approach dates from the 1970s and the work of Henri Tajfel, whose thinking continues to be highly influential (cf. Abrams and Hogg 1999). Tajfel defined social identity as "the individual's knowledge that he belongs to certain social groups together with some emotional and value significance to him of his group membership" (Tajfel 1972, 292). Though a great deal has been published on social identity in the three-plus decades since Tajfel's initial work, those following Tajfel continue to explain social identity in terms of pre-given social identities understood via the different socially constructed group categories to which individuals may be assigned. The principal extension of the social identity approach is "self-categorization theory" developed by John Turner first in 1985, which elaborates a process whereby individuals come to see themselves, or categorize themselves, in terms of certain social categories (Turner 1985; Turner et al. 1987). Akerlof and Kranton follow this particular development in their explanation of social identity. They depart modestly from the social identity literature in emphasizing psychodynamic personality theory and the role of anxiety in individual behavior, neither of which figures per se as a theoretical construct for current proponents of the Tajfel-Turner approach. However, whereas the main emphasis in self-categorization theory is on cognitive processes and individuals' beliefs about themselves and social groups, there is also emphasis on "uncertainty reduction" as a core motivation (Hogg 2001). As Akerlof and Kranton use both anxiety reduction and cognitive dissonance reduction as mechanisms to explain behavior, their recourse to psychodynamic personality theory seems consistent with the main arguments of psychology's social identity theory.

It is worth noting that from the outset the literature on social identity theory has largely set aside the difference between the concept of social identity and the concept of personal identity, though many contributors recognize the distinction. The former refers to commonalities between people within social categories as well as to differences between individuals in different social categories, whereas the latter refers to the self as distinct from other people in general. According to Tajfel and others, the reason for this is that social identity theory originated in postwar European traditions in social psychology that were at odds with American views that social psychology explanations of collective phenomena needed to be formulated in individualist terms (Tajfel, Jaspars, and Fraser 1984). A consequence of this for social identity theory research is that contributors have generally neglected how individuals' social and personal identities might relate to one another. Thus, effectively the only concept of the self that social identity theory employs is that of the collective or social self in which individuals are seen as collections of different social identities. Though this is a multiple selves idea, as personal identity has not been a concern for most social identity theorists in psychology, so neither is multiple selves seen as a problem that needs to be addressed.

Relatedly, Turner's self-categorization theory has as a central mechanism that people are "depersonalized" in their adoption of social identities in that they come to see themselves as simply embodiments of group prototypes. Turner does not take depersonalization to imply, as it might appear, that individuals are "dehumanized" or "deindividuated," meaning that they cease to act as human individuals when identifying with others, but simply supposes that they set aside their status as independent beings when engaged in self-categorization. If individuals depersonalize themselves in identifying with others, however, we are left with very little to say about how they differ from one another as individuals in the ways that they identify with others. Clearly, even individuals who have similar characteristics do not always self-categorize themselves in the same ways, as they may emphasize and order their social identities differently from one another. This suggests that individuals have personal identities as well as social identities. Akerlof and Kranton do not make depersonalization a part of their argument, but they follow the literature in leaving aside the problem of how individuals with the same group identities may self-categorize themselves differently. I return to this issue at the end of Section 4.3.

4.2.2 Self-Image as an Argument in the Utility Function

To model the effects of social identity on behavior, then, Akerlof and Kranton treat self-image as a new type of argument in the individual utility function (here symbols in bold are vectors):

(1) $\quad U_j = U_j \left(\boldsymbol{a}_j, \boldsymbol{a}_{-j}, \boldsymbol{I}_j \right).$

The utility of person j depends on j's identity or self-image I_j and also on j's actions a_j and the actions of others a_{-j}. Identity or self-image itself is defined as:

(2) $I_j = I_j (a_j, a_{-j}; c_j, \epsilon_j, P)$.

The identity or self-image of person j depends again on j's actions and the actions of others, on j's assignable social categories c_j, on j's own character-istics ϵ_j, and on the extent to which j's own given characteristics match the social ideals of j's categories, as indicated by recognized social prescriptions **P**. Maximizing utility, then, is interpreted to mean that the individual acts to reduce anxiety-creating cognitive dissonance created by the behavior of others whose actions may or may not fit recognized social prescriptions associated with the social categories assignable to them and the individual. In interactive terms, if something is prescribed behavior for a given group, but others within the group behave inappropriately, the individual plays a "game" with them aimed at securing prescribed behavior appropriate for individuals with the characteristics of that group, in order to reduce the anxiety their behavior generates.

This analysis applies to any given self-image an individual has in I_j. Thus, individuals at any one time can find themselves in multiple games with others in which more than one of their self-images in I_j is in ques-tion. How are all these different games related, and how do people know which game to play? Akerlof and Kranton close off this issue and simply say, "When an individual's identity is associated with multiple social cat-egories, the 'situation' could determine, for example, which categories are most salient" (Akerlof and Kranton 2000, 731n.). The concept of salience, of course, has long been used as one way to provide solutions to single games with multiple equilibria (cf. Schelling 1960), and indeed it essentially works by making context or the "situation" a determining factor. This is the same principle that underlies prospect theory seen as a means of adding realism to choice analysis. For Akerlof and Kranton, it provides a further way of grounding individuals' social identity behavior. Individuals' choices inter-nalize social identities with their associated prescriptive character, yet they know how to act on these identities according to the situation or context. Sociality is internalized *and* contextualized. The effect is that, whereas on the standard view individuals know how to rank their preferences, here individuals know how to rank the games they play with others and thus their social identities.

Recall that for Akerlof and Kranton sociality is not introduced after the explanation of the individual is complete, as with Bénabou and Tirole, but instead at the beginning directly into the account of the individual. At the same time, for Akerlof and Kranton individuals are still clearly understood to be independent agents in that they each operate with their own separate utility functions. One effect this combination has is to give self-image a particular interpretation. For Bénabou and Tirole, self-image in the form of self-reputation constitutes an image of the self per se or of the self as a whole; but for Akerlof and Kranton the self as a whole is the utility function itself, and self-image reflects matching relationships between particular characteristics of the individual and the ideal characteristics of certain social categories. As such, it concerns an aspect (or collection of aspects) of the self rather than the self per se. Another way of putting this is to say that, despite the ordinary meaning of the term, self-image in the Akerlof-Kranton model is not a reflexive relationship, as it is with Bénabou and Tirole. In a reflexive relationship, the subject takes a stance toward the subject itself or the subject makes the entire subject its object. For Akerlof and Kranton, however, the subject not only takes no such stance, but self-image is determined in terms of third-party observable relationships between the individual and certain social characteristics that the individual monitors. Thus I_j might better be labeled a "social" self-image assigned to the individual.

The Akerlof-Kranton modeling strategy, however, is like both Gary Becker's analysis of personal and social capital (Becker 1996) and Bénabou and Tirole's treatment of self-confidence and personal rules as personal capital stocks in that individuals have "self-image stocks" they wish to maintain vis-à-vis others' social behavior. In Becker's time allocation model, personal and social capital are stocks of noncommodity wealth inherited and further produced with time and market goods such that individuals maximize utility given these stocks. In Bénabou and Tirole's analysis, self-confidence and personal rules are forms of personal capital individuals create that are seen as a means of overcoming present bias. For Akerlof and Kranton, an individual's various social identities are the individual's social capital, and their corresponding self-images are the individual's personal capital. Akerlof and Kranton do not use the language of capital and investment in their paper, but their self-image function (2) operates like a production function, albeit in a strategic, game-theoretic setting in which others' choices influence individuals' own choices, whereby individuals construct their personalities or self-images (but not themselves) by using social prescriptions $\mathbf{P}$ to tell them how to match their own characteristics $\mathbf{e}_j$ and their ideal characteristics according to the social categories $\mathbf{c}_j$ assignable to them, all based on a internal technology of anxiety reduction. Akerlof and

Kranton's analysis is also a personal capital approach in that individuals engaged in anxiety or cognitive dissonance reduction act to offset depreciation in personal capital self-image stocks. However, their analysis offers no mechanism by which the individual would also invest in self-image capital. Rather, the model is homeostatic in character in employing a regulatory feedback principle that maintains a given self-image stock, in which the regulatory principle works by balancing the state of the individual's ideal social characteristics and assignable social categories c_j.

4.3 Social Identity and Social Group Multiple Selves

How, then, does the social identity theory Akerlof and Kranton adopt fit into the larger social psychology landscape of thinking about social identity? In its primary emphasis on individual cognitive processes, social identity theory, despite its name and emphasis on social groups, is in its disciplinary origins a psychological theory, not a sociological one. This becomes clearer when it is compared to the alternative approach to social identity found in sociology.[4] Though the dividing lines within the field of social psychology on social identity and self concepts between primarily psychological and primarily sociological approaches are often blurred, and though the two types of approaches are complementary in important respects, there remain significant differences between them that reflect their respective disciplinary origins and main concerns. Psychology's social identity approach focuses on the given individual and asks how individuals align themselves through self-categorization with given social categories. Sociology's social identity approach, in contrast, investigates how individuals and social structures are mutually determining. From the perspective of social psychology as a whole, these differences can be seen as a part of a general division of labor on the subject of social identity within a jointly shared social psychology framework.

Yet Akerlof and Kranton's way of introducing identity into economics selectively privileges psychology's social identity approach. This implies two important assumptions underlie their analysis. One is that the examination of identity in economics can be confined to the concept of social identity, and that the concept of personal identity can be ignored or implicitly taken as being adequately represented by the individual utility function. A second assumption is that the atomistic individual can be taken as a

---

[4]   For an overview of the social identity approach, see Hogg, Terry, and White (1995). For an overview of the sociological approach to identity, see Stets and Burke (2000).

satisfactory entry point for the explanation of social identity in economics, as reflected in Akerlof and Kranton's strategy of treating social identity as "a new type of externality" and as a modification of the standard conception of the individual. Both assumptions, we will see, appear problematic from the perspective of how social identity is understood in sociology's social identity approach. Moreover, it is worth recalling that psychology's social identity approach allows that individuals may have multiple selves associated with their multiple social group identities. In Section 4.3.1, then, I look at the sociological approach to identity for comparison with psychology's social identity approach. In the following section, I show how Akerlof and Kranton's selectively privileging psychology's concept of social identity produces an intractable multiple selves problem.

4.3.1 The Sociological Approach to Identity

The sociological approach to identity derives from George Mead's symbolic interactionism (Mead 1934), whereas current work generally follows the approach of Sheldon Stryker (Stryker 1980). Its main assumption is that there is an interactive reciprocal relation between the self and society in which each influences the other. Individuals always act in structured social settings and influence society through the effects their actions have on groups, organizations, and institutions, which are themselves interrelated; on the other hand, social structures influence individuals through shared language meanings and through social roles that determine how individuals interact. In regard to its conception of social identity, the sociological approach also explains individuals' social identities in terms of their affiliations to social groups, but social groups are instead understood in terms of their place in a social architecture (a group of employees in a business, people in types of community organizations, people organized by occupations, etc.) rather than by societywide social categories that make no such reference. Moreover, as social structure is complex, so that any given social group operates across multiple dimensions of social structure, social groups are themselves internally differentiated and are not well described by characteristics that apply to all members. Indeed, individuals can belong to the same social groups in quite different ways, whereas in psychology's social identity approach individuals are subsumed under social categories all in essentially the same way. This means that as individuals relate to the same groups differently, it is necessary to simultaneously conceptualize them both *in relation to* and *apart from* their social group identities, or in terms of their having personal identities as well social identities. Thus, the sociological approach to identity opens the door to an expanded, more comprehensive view of identity.

Internally, social groups are often seen as being structured by roles that produce cohesion for the group in a complex social structural world that makes competing demands on the group and threatens its integrity as a group (Stets and Burke 2000). A role identity is defined as "the character and the role that an individual devises for himself as an occupant of a particular social position" (McCall and Simmons 1978, 65). This combines the idea of pre-given social positions with their interpretation on the part of individuals – what the "individual devises for himself." On the one hand, then, roles and positions are almost always subject to interpretation and negotiation; on the other hand, individuals generally seek to match their own self-conceptions with the expectations others have of them in their roles. This negotiation of roles also needs to be understood in the context of the overall structure of a set of roles within a social group. In the simplest kind of setting, roles are paired with counterroles (such as parent and child), whereas in more complicated group and institutional settings (such as in business firms), roles are more highly differentiated, networked, and have a variety of cross relations and network interconnections with one another. All this serves to create a basis for saying that people are individualized by their many different relationships in the social groups of which they are members.

This naturally brings up the issue of individuals' multiple social identities. Psychology's social identity approach recognizes that individuals have multiple identities, but it does not seek to explain their possible interconnections. Therefore, not surprisingly, it does not consider how individuals might have personal identities vis-à-vis their multiple social identities. Because the systems of social category classification on which the social identity approach draws treat individuals merely as members of given populations constructed for reasons unrelated to how individuals come to have their multiple identities, there is indeed little it can say about individuals per se. In contrast, because the sociological approach explains individuals' social identities in connection with how they occupy different roles in social structures, their multiple social identities can in principle be explained in terms of how individuals act on social structure in managing their interconnected social roles – what the "individual devises for himself." Multiple identities still remains an important problem for the sociological identity approach, but at least it offers a strategy for addressing the problem through the idea that overlapping social roles create distinct circumstances for individuals – a personal identity type idea – and by suggesting that people actively negotiate their own individual pathways across their multiple roles and social identities.

In addition to this, we should add that the sociological approach also emphasizes the idea that the individual is a reflexive being. Reflexivity, we saw in connection with Bénabou and Tirole's analysis, is valuable for emphasizing individuals' distinctness from one another, because it involves individuals taking themselves as distinct from one another. Note, then, how this idea works in one sociological approach to the relationship between the intragroup settings and the intergroup settings individuals may occupy, as influentially developed by Albert Bandura. In *intra*group settings, he argues, individuals' sense of membership depends on how they develop self-conceptions and activate what has been labeled a sense of "self-efficacy" (Bandura 1977). Self-efficacy is defined as having beliefs about one's ability to "organize and execute the courses of action required to produce given attainments" (Bandura 1997, 3), or more generally as having beliefs about one's competencies and one's ability to exercise them (Mischel 1973). In *inter*group settings, in contrast, individuals are thought to develop self-worth views based on their relations to groups where they are outsiders, such as when they judge themselves favorably or unfavorably in the eyes of outsiders. Here self-efficacy and self-worth are understood reflexively and in relation to one another in a general analysis of how individuals negotiate their multidimensional roles and positions in complex social structures. Of course, there are many other strategies in sociology for explaining the interconnectedness of social roles. Nonetheless, reflexivity often plays an important role in accounting for how individuals are able to take stock of themselves in complex settings. Some of these ideas will reappear in later chapters of this book, but here we return to Akerlof and Kranton.

4.3.2 Akerlof and Kranton and the Multiple Selves Problem

How exactly then do Akerlof and Kranton address the multiple selves problem that individuals have multiple competing social identities? Essentially they avoid the problem by adopting a partial equilibrium type of social identity analysis that prevents it from even arising. As noted previously, their analysis focuses on one social identity at a time, letting "the 'situation' ... determine ... which [social identity] categories are most salient" (Akerlof and Kranton 2000, 731n.). Thus, only one social identity is at issue at any one time. The difficulty is that from their own utility-maximizing point of view this cannot be a satisfactory strategy. Suppose individuals faced with losses to a given self-image stock are able to generate offsetting gains in another self-image stock by selecting a subset of social identities and games with others they would prefer to regard as salient. They might then be able to maximize utility (and minimize cognitive dissonance) by accepting losses in some games and focusing on games in which there were greater gains. Isolating one game in the analysis of self-image, then, neither adequately explains utility maximization, nor arguably captures how many people behave when it comes to how they manage their different social identities. Akerlof and Kranton understand self-image to be multidimensional, but their account of choice behavior ignores this. Indeed, the representation of individuals' multiple self-images as a vector is a purely formal device that lacks behavioral implications. On the one hand it requires they employ a partial equilibrium approach, whereas on the other it precludes their addressing how utility-maximizing individuals might address complex social identity problems.

There is another important reason why their analysis cannot be developed to accommodate how individuals might address their multiple social identities. The self-image vector I_j is an argument in the utility function, so for individuals to be able to rank and order the games they play, they would need to be able to make choices about their own utility functions. Indeed, they would also need to be able to change how they did this, because "the 'situation'" or context might change in terms of how easy or difficult it might for individuals to reduce cognitive dissonance across different social identities. However, on the standard view that Akerlof and Kranton accept the utility function represents the individual, so there is no external vantage point from which individuals could step outside of themselves to make those choices. Essentially, individuals would need to take a reflexive stance toward themselves to be able to determine how they get utility from their actions in different games, but the individual does not exist outside of the utility function. Akerlof and Kranton offer a brief comment on identity "choice" but do not incorporate this in their formal model on the grounds that "identity" choice is "very often limited" (2000, 725–6, 737–8). This rationale, however, seems more driven by the assumption that the utility function only represents individuals in terms of how they are affected by their actions than by any evidence from social psychology.[5]

To this it might be replied that the self-image vector I_j could be given structure in terms of personal rules for ordering individuals' social identity games (along the lines of Bénabou and Tirole's personal rules), perhaps

---

[5]   I offer suggestions regarding how individuals might take a stance toward themselves by representing the individual objective function as an identity function in Davis (2007a).

by prioritizing certain types of games. But what would the basis for such prioritizing be? Because in psychology's social identity approach individuals' social identity categories are simply given, there is no account of how individuals might begin to determine their social identity priorities according to situations in which they find themselves. If individuals' social identity categories did happen to come in some ranking or order, this prioritizing would then need to be standardized across types of situations. It is difficult to believe, however, that individuals prioritize their social identities in any standard way. Circumstances and context vary too widely, and even were people to exhibit somewhat typical patterns of prioritizing, they would certainly not suit individuals in nontypical situations. In this regard, recall that in the sociological identity approach, rather than social identity functioning as an externality or external effect on individual behavior, self and society both have effects on one another. Individuals are affected by their social roles, just as in the Akerlof-Kranton analysis, but they also affect their social roles by interpreting what those roles require and how they can be reconciled when they conflict. Broadly speaking, this understanding requires a conception of the individual that includes a concept of ability, but as argued previously this concept has no place in the utility function framework.

Thus, Akerlof and Kranton fail to show that individuals do not fragment into multiple selves or how they might manage themselves in such a way as to maintain a sense of unity as single individuals. This reflects their reliance on psychology's social identity theory because the social categories and corresponding social identities this approach generates are not structured by any overall theory of how individuals' social identities are related. Rather, the construction of broad social categories applied to individuals reflects a multisided social statistical process historically driven by many, often weakly related different social forces – effectively the product of what Nancy Cartwright terms a "dappled world" (Cartwright 1999) – so that assigning social identities to individuals in such a way inevitably serves to "internalize" multiple unrelated identities within individuals. This point naturally directs us on to the social preferences approach, because its introduction or internalization of social preferences in the utility function similarly draws on many distinct accounts of what social preferences we might have. That is, just as there are many social category foundations for social identities, so there are many social theory foundations for social preferences. In contrast to the ad hoc treatment of social categories in psychology's social identity approach, perhaps there is a more systematic basis in social preference analysis regarding how self-interested preferences and social preferences relate to one another. Does treating self-interest and social concerns both as kinds of preferences then provide a way of reconstituting the individual as a single person?

4.4 The Social Preferences Approach

I begin with a review of what this approach involves. Social preferences, or other-regarding preferences, are individual preferences not motivated by self-interest but rather by material payoffs to others (Fehr and Fischbacher 2002). The possibility that individuals might have such preferences and do not always act out of self-interest was suggested by experimental research initiated by Werner Güth into how people play the ultimatum game (Güth, Schmittberger, and Schwarze 1982). Individuals' having social preferences was not thought to preclude their still having preferences regarding payoffs for themselves, and individuals are accordingly seen as having both self-regarding preferences and other-regarding social preferences in their individual utility functions. The form social preferences take and the way the utility function needs to be revised have thus been the main objects of research, and there is a very large number of competing accounts regarding what social preferences individuals have. More recent research also investigates how social preferences vary across cultures (Henrich et al. 2004; Henrich et al. 2005).

Here I provide only a small sample of four influential types of strategies for investigating social preferences. One type of social preference is altruism, or a willingness to act in the interest of others without ulterior motives. James Andreoni models utility functions as including egoistic preferences and altruistic preferences, and argues that the "warm-glow" feeling people get from giving apart from any concern for others and genuinely altruistic behavior are complements that produce "impure" altruism (Andreoni 1989a, 1989b). A second type of social preference is for fairness, or reciprocal fairness, in which an individual responds to actions perceived to be kind in a kind manner and actions perceived to be hostile in a hostile manner. In Matthew Rabin's early fairness model, an action is perceived as fair if the intention behind the action is seen as kind, and vice versa, in which the (un)kindness of the intention is determined by the equitability of the payoff distribution produced by the action (Rabin 1993). A third type of social preference is inequity aversion, in which individuals are averse to inequality in the distribution of material resources. In Ernst Fehr and Klaus Schmidt's model (1999), individuals feel altruistic toward others and want to increase their material payoffs when those payoffs fall below some benchmark, and they feel envy toward others and want to decrease their payoffs when those payoffs exceed some benchmark. A fourth type of social preference is for social welfare with a concern for both low payoffs and efficiency – a Rawlsian or "me-min-us" approach. Gary Charness and Matthew Rabin (2002) argue, against difference aversion, that experimental results show that people care more about people who fall behind than people who get ahead, and that they also may make sacrifices for those who are ahead if they believe this favors efficiency.

In all four cases, sociality is introduced into the utility function, though we should note that this is done quite differently from Akerlof and Kranton's analysis of social identity as "a new type of externality." For Akerlof and Kranton, social identification with others can generate cognitive dissonance type negative externalities that need to be minimized in order to maximize utility. Thus, social identity often produces costs for the individual and acts as drag on utility maximization. If the people with whom one identifies do not violate shared social group prescriptions, individuals would be better off. In the social preference approach, on the other hand, social interaction with others is directly utility-generating. Individuals may trade off or substitute between self-regardingness and other-regardingness, but when they favor the latter it is no less utility-maximizing than favoring the former. The social preference approach, then, might instead be seen to more resemble Becker's earlier expansion of the utility function to include social tastes such as a taste for discrimination (Becker 1971 [1957]), because individuals gain utility from satisfying that taste just as they do when their ordinary preferences are satisfied. It is true that Becker saw satisfying social tastes as serving the individual's own interest and basically regards the individual's social and private concerns as opposed to one another, whereas the social preference approach arose out of extensive experimental research investigating whether individuals sacrifice their self-interest for other-regarding concerns. Both nonetheless treat social concern as a taste or preference. In contrast, Akerlof and Kranton have self-image in the utility function, and the individual's concerns about others with whom they identify enter not as a taste but as a relationship that needs to be managed in strategic interaction to maintain self-image.

Yet whereas the social preference approach is more like Becker's approach, there is also an important difference. Becker's social tastes are basically tied to the like or dislike of kinds of people, whereas social preferences are preferences for kinds of social structures or forms of social organization, such as would minimize inequality, promote the well-being of the worst off, and so forth. Liking or disliking someone or something can be understood as an affective state of the individual, and so can a social preference. However, it is easier to argue that the affective characterization essentially captures the meaning of liking or disliking someone or something than it is to say this about a social preference. With a social preference there seems to be something additional involved that concerns understanding and cognitive appraisal. When one says one prefers some social states of affairs, one is usually able to give some explanation of what that social state of affairs involves. Otherwise, that preference is taken as uninformed. Of course, people can and do have social preferences that are uninformed, but in comparison with their ordinary preferences this is often taken as self-defeating and potentially incoherent. How can one even be said to have a preference about something about which one basically knows nothing? In contrast, it does seem acceptable to say ordinary preferences regarding things one likes or dislikes require no explanation, because they concern an individual's private tastes where the same burden does not apply. So it can be argued that the social preference approach is different from Becker's approach in that having to give an explanation for one's preference means reasons underlie and constitute a partial motivation for social preferences.

Despite this argument, social preference theorists do not treat social preferences as ostensibly different from ordinary preferences. Individuals substitute between social and ordinary preferences no differently than they do between different kinds of ordinary preferences, and there is no account of reasons constituting a motivation for social preferences. At the same time, explanation plays a clear role in experimental settings in which researchers employ specific protocols to investigate whether individuals act on social preferences. Specifically, experimental subjects must have the nature of the strategic interaction they are to be involved in explained to them to successfully participate in the experiment and make the experimental results internally valid. This role for explanation in the experiment thus means that experimental subjects rely on reasons in addition to preferences in motivating their choices. For example, in the ultimatum game, subjects might make certain allocations because they believe that such allocations are fair or just, and ought for this reason be promoted. They might personally rather prefer an allocation that is not taken to be the fair or just one, but allow their reasoned conclusion to determine their "preference." In this case, they have what may appear to simply be a preference, albeit a social one, but the basis for their choice cannot really be said to be entirely affective.

On this view, the social preferences approach ought not to be formulated as a pure preferences approach. In effect, it would have a wrong theory of motivation. However, this view is rejected by social preference theorists who see social preferences as simply a different kind of preference and therefore as not having any fundamentally different motivational basis from all other preferences. This can be seen as another dimension of their strategy for internalizing sociality because it keeps the motivation for acting socially fully internal to the individual; whereas reasons, which might motivate the same behavior, are by nature socially shared, cannot be seen as purely subjective, and thus cannot be fully internalized. Seeing social preferences as strictly preferences may also seem to be an advantage in that it appears to sustain clear boundaries between individuals, individuals each having only their own preferences (whatever their nature), thus representing individuals as distinct from one another. I argued in Chapter 1 that it is circular to argue that individuals represented as a collection of own preferences are distinct from one another, but here I put this aside to ask in what follows whether the social preference approach can even be successful in representing social preferences as essentially the same as ordinary preferences. That is, I ask whether their strategy of internalizing sociality as a preference in the atomistic individual can be successful, and if it is not, what the consequences are of this for this version of a revised *Homo economicus*.

4.5 From Sympathy to Empathy?

Let us take altruism as a paradigm case of a social preference on the grounds that the concept has some inescapably other-regarding content, and for contrast begin by looking at a non-preference-based account of altruism that emphasizes this other-regardingness to the extreme: Thomas Nagel's reason-based, agent-neutral account (Nagel 1970). Nagel extracts from the meaning of other-regardingness the idea of neutrality regarding one's own interest versus those of others, and then argues that such neutrality can only be motivated by reasons that are objective and shared rather than subjective and private. This defines for him the idea of an impersonal standpoint, which he takes to be central to the idea of altruism. Altruists, it follows, are people who do not privilege their own case over that of others. Indeed, altruists – or perhaps saints! – fully abandon their own personal positions, a view Nagel later embraced in his *The View from Nowhere* (1986). In effect, his view is one in which individuals live a life of reason and are fully absorbed by social concerns. As such, Nagel's view is the polar opposite of the social preference strategy that internalizes social concerns by explaining them entirely from a personal point of view.

Nagel might then say that the social preference approach is incoherent, at least when it comes to explaining altruism. However, we might rather ask how the personal point of view is understood to link to other-regardingness when we emphasize social preferences as being about different kinds of social arrangements. Consider again the four different types of social preference strategies distinguished in the previous section in terms of the conclusions their proponents draw about them. If impure altruism obtains, it is because "giving" situations somehow combine people's altruistic and egoistic behavior in particular ways that public policy may exploit (Andreoni). If people act reciprocally, they have an expectation that a certain pattern of interaction is in place in the world, and accordingly know how to judge those who infringe upon it (Rabin). If inequity aversion motivates people, they must see society as structured in terms of desirable and undesirable differences (Fehr and Schmidt). If people believe in efficiency and also in protecting the worst off, they have some view of how society can be better organized (Charness and Rabin). In each case, individuals are assumed to have an understanding of how social relationships are or can be structured, but their preference for one state of affairs or another is still affective and personal. How might people have such a single orientation as this that yet accommodates such a variety of different understandings of social arrangements?

Because we are building on the standard *Homo economicus* model but want it to include a social orientation, the appropriate way to proceed would seem to be, like Akerlof and Kranton, in terms of the idea of an externality, though one now seen as positive. On the standard view, sympathy is the externality defined as concern for others. Individuals might then be said to be concerned with fairness and inequity in any variety of ways these phenomena can be manifested in social life if they are simply said to feel sympathy toward others. Sympathy, that is, can function as an "all-things-considered" type of externality in the sense of constituting a universal bedrock for all specific types of social preferences. The expression "all-things-considered" comes from Daniel Hausman who uses it to give the definition of "preference" that he thinks most appropriate to economics (2005, 36–39). For him, the concept of "all-things-considered" preferences is a technical term in economics that incorporates folk psychological meaning associated with decision making based on beliefs and desires:

> An agent's preferences consist of his or her overall evaluation of the objects over which preferences are defined. This evaluation implies a ranking of these objects with respect to everything that matters to the agent: desirability, social norms, moral principles, habits – everything relevant to evaluation. (ibid., 37)

If we accordingly understand sympathy as an "all-things-considered" preference for others, or as a single orientation toward others that encompasses all the sorts of social arrangements that social preference theorists investigate, this would preclude needing to provide any sort of reason-based account of why people might be other-regarding and would thus provide a comprehensive basis for a fully affective view of social preferences.

Does sympathy in this extended sense then do the job that social preference theorists ask of it? Traditionally, the idea of sympathy (and antipathy) has had a much narrower scope, as with feelings one has for family members, close friends, and others with whom one is in regular contact – an emphasis we can find in Becker's social tastes idea. However, sympathy in the extended sense suggested appropriate to social preferences goes beyond this, and so the issue is whether the feelings involved can be translated into settings in which individuals make choices relative to reciprocity, inequity aversion, and so forth. Consider inequity aversion. If this is to be motivated by a kind of sympathy, one needs to have positive feelings toward unknown individuals who suffer inequity, as the reach of inequity extends beyond the people one can know. This essentially defines the concept of empathy understood as favorable feelings one has toward others based on imagining their situation – "putting oneself in their shoes." Note the advantage for the social preference approach, then, of treating extended sympathy as empathy. Though the idea of "putting oneself in someone else's shoes" suggests a reasoned evaluation of how one person's situation abstractly compares to another's, emphasizing the imaginative grasp of another's situation equally allows empathy to be interpreted as feeling-based. Should we additionally suppose that feelings of empathy toward others generally derive from the experience we ourselves have in like circumstances, then this extended concept of sympathy can well be argued to be affective in nature. From this it follows that social preferences are like ordinary preferences, and contra Nagel, other-regardingness can be explained from personal point of view.

However, interpreting social preferences as a form of empathy produces a clear multiple selves problem for the social preference approach. The standard view of sympathy is the idea of a feeling a person has *toward* another. Empathy goes beyond this because the idea of imagining another's feelings involves effectively taking the other's position in order to know his or her preferences. That is, as one must imagine another person's feelings as they would have them, by definition these imagined feelings are different from the feelings that underlie one's own preferences. Indeed, if we were to explain this in social identity terms as Akerlof and Kranton do, empathy would be one mechanism whereby people identify *with* others, either individually with respect to unknown representative others or by subsuming themselves under a shared social group identity, as for example when they identify with all people who suffer inequity. This would then mean that individuals are actually somehow made up of multiple selves or utility functions: the self or utility function that applies to the preferences specific to them and selves or utility functions that apply to the preferences of others with whom they empathize (or identify). Minus having this double set of preferences and utility functions, they would not be able to have social preferences regarding such things as inequity aversion, at most feeling sympathy toward those to whom they are related or know.

In reply, the social preference theorist could argue that both sets of preferences are still the individual's own preferences because individuals are the ones who have them, and thus no multiple selves or utility functions problem arises. However, this reply really only assumes away the possibility that individuals have multiple selves or utility functions by denying there is any important difference in nature and origin between ordinary preferences and social preferences, even though the latter are based on imagining others' ordinary preferences. Further, it is not clear how this response could be defended other than by insisting that individuals must always be represented by single utility functions. Another reply would be to reject the explanation of social preferences as an "all-things-considered" type of externality and in particular that an extended sympathy involves upon empathy. The problem with this response is that it leaves us with no account of how individuals understood as utility maximizers have distinctively social preferences and, given accounts such as Nagel's, invites us to consider how individuals might simply be motivated to be other-regarding for reasons rather than affectively.

The general difficulty, it seems fair to say, stems from the strategy of combining ordinary preferences that are self-regarding and social preferences that are other-regarding in one utility function. Formally, it is a simple thing to add a new argument to a utility function and employ the traditional *Homo economicus* logic to give an expanded but standard account of how people make choices. The question this strategy raises, however, is whether this formal revision of the standard model is substantively justified when the content of this new argument is considered. Broadly speaking, that is, can we internalize sociality in the form of other-regardingness and make it essentially the same type of individual motive as self-regardingness? The case for doing so is yet to be made in the social preferences approach.

4.6 Internalizing Sociality versus Socially Embedding Individuality

This chapter has examined two strategies inspired by behavioral economics for developing a more realistic conception of the individual for economics, each with a particular take on how to proceed. Each begins with the standard *Homo economicus* atomistic individual conception but transforms it by incorporating social motives in the utility function. This is at once a conservative and radical strategy – conservative in simply revising the atomistic view and radical in seeking to demonstrate that the atomistic individual is also a social being. Both also go substantially beyond the two strategies examined in the last chapter, which are in turn closer to prospect theory in seeking to anchor the atomistic individual in real-world contexts, but are much weaker in their characterization of the nature of social interaction, sociality, and its relation to the individual. Indeed, both of the strategies discussed here have a genuine appeal for many who have long complained that economics is too individualistic. They not only cleverly make sociality a part of individuality but also admirably open up new conceptual domains for the theory of individual economic behavior: social identity, reciprocity, inequity aversion, and so forth. Further, there seems to be no limit to the number and variety of social concepts that these new frameworks might ultimately accommodate, promising an increasing, long-desired rapprochement between economics and the other social sciences.

The argument advanced in this chapter against these strategies is that these revised atomistic individual conceptions nonetheless do not succeed in showing how a person is a single distinct individual, albeit with multiple selves, rather than a disunified collection of different selves. In this respect, the conclusions here as well as in the last two chapters are an implication of what was argued in Chapter 1. There it was argued that atomistic individual conceptions can only treat individuals as distinct and independent by reference to their own characteristics, but as this involves circular reasoning, we ought to expect that atomistic individual conceptions of all kinds fail to explain what the unity of being a single individual consists in – the problem of the sub-personal bound on single-individual explanations. That is, they are all ultimately multiple selves conceptions of individuals and, as such, cannot provide an account of how individuals act as single agents. The implication of this, however, is not that single-individual explanations are impossible, but rather that they need another basis than atomism offers, and thus that atomism is a dead end when it comes to understanding individuals, however much momentum it may inherit from the past in the new approaches that have contributed to recent economics.

Rejecting atomism in conceptualizing individuals means explaining individuality somehow in terms of relationships between individuals. People are individualized, as it were, by their social interaction with one another. They are distinct and independent from one another, not because of characteristics we can assign them abstractly and in isolation apart from interaction, but because social interaction as it works in the world produces this result. In effect then, rather than internalize sociality, this view calls for embedding individuality in sociality. Prospect theory's realist emphasis on context actually involves a step in this direction, especially as we saw reflected in social psychological thinking about context, but behavioral economics' attachment to utility function representations of individuals has rather given impetus to the internalizing strategy. At the same time, there are other currents in recent economics that premise interaction in their accounts of individuals. Game theory, despite its early connection to the atomistic individual conception, begins with the idea that individuals directly interact with one another – strategic interaction – rather than just indirectly through the isolating medium of markets, and thus makes interaction somehow part of the individual. The next three chapters, accordingly, look at ways of representing individuals that more or less begin from the perspective of their interaction, moving from accounts that depart the least from the standard view of individuals to those that depart significantly from it.

PART 2

INTERACTION

FIVE

The Individual in Game Theory

From Fixed Points to Experiments

5.1 Game Theory's Wild Card

The conception of the individual in noncooperative game theory is an extension of the standard utility function conception of the individual that differs in making individuals strategically interactive. Whereas on the standard view individuals' interaction through markets is indirect and their choices are independent of one another, in game theory individuals' interaction is direct and their choices depend on one another. Individuals need to know something about one another to make their choices, and this means that interaction is built into the conception of the individual in game theory. The question is: How significant is the effect of this? There are two polar answers to this question in contemporary game theory representing two different views of games, the nature of strategic interaction, and the appropriate methods for their investigation: one emphasizes single-play (and finitely repeated) noncooperative games and has been developed in an a priori logical-deductive manner; the other emphasizes indefinitely repeated play games that may be cooperative and has been developed through experimental investigation. The answer from the former approach is that interaction makes little difference to the standard individual conception; the answer from the latter approach is that interaction can make quite a difference. In this chapter, I argue that the former approach fails to show how the standard individual view can accommodate interaction, whereas the latter approach generates an open-ended approach to interaction that can produce similar open-endedness about individuals.

Adding interaction to our account of individuals consequently functions as something of a wild card in our thinking about them. It also gives us a potentially quite different way of thinking about the individual in economics compared to the views examined in Part 1. If we say that in game theory

strategic interaction frames how we think about individuals, we no longer ask how we might embody sociality in individuals but rather ask how
we embed individuals in sociality. Economists, of course, have voted with
their feet since the 1980s regarding the centrality of game-theoretic interaction to economics. This does not imply that the internalizing strategies
discussed in Part 1 will cease to play a role in economics in the future, but
it does suggest that they are likely to be increasingly captive to the alternative logic of interaction. Game theory, the first of the important departures
in recent economics from the postwar price equilibration framework, has
been seen by many of its critics as looking backward, tied to an inflexible
Homo economicus conception. The argument here is that this tie is tenuous,
and that game theory across its many forms on the whole shifts the balance
in our thinking about what individuals are.

Single-play (or one-shot) noncooperative games were the main point of
entry for game theory's reemergence and rise in economics in the 1980s
when it began to be more widely used to examine questions perceived to
be fundamental to economics. Their investigation has been associated with
intensive examination of a small set of paradigmatic games (the prisoner's
dilemma, hawk-dove, chicken, etc.) and the building of game theory around
John Nash's equilibrium concept rather than John von Neumann's earlier
minimax solution concept. The limitations of the Nash "classical" game theory framework, in particular the problem of multiple equilibria, gave rise
to the refinement program as a collection of initiatives aimed at producing
stronger solution concepts than Nash equilibrium provides (cf. Rizvi 1994;
Hargreaves Heap and Varoufakis 2004 [1995], 80–125; Ross 2005, 201–4).
Central to this project is the Harsanyi doctrine to be discussed in Section
5.2, where my focus is not the issues connected to these foundational concerns, such as the plausibility of mixed strategies, problems of multiple
equilibria, and so on, but rather how the core ideas of this program are
interrelated with assumptions about the nature of individuals, particularly
in connection with John Harsanyi's view of individuals as being of certain
types, as developed in his transformation of games of incomplete information into complete information games.

In what I treat as the other pole of game theory with respect to conceptualizing the individual, the second half of this chapter turns to a quite
different set of issues that arise in connection with games of indefinitely
repeated play. There, courtesy of the folk theorem, the utter abundance
of solution concepts makes it unclear what game theory can accomplish
when it addresses ongoing situations, a circumstance arguably reflective
of many real-world market and nonmarket situations. Repeated play also

complicates the conception of individuals in games because of their propensity to behave cooperatively, contrary to the standard *Homo economicus* view. Game theorists from early on have sought to make sense of the abundance of solution concepts in repeated play by using experiments to determine equilibrium outcomes. Interestingly, a key center was at the University of Michigan about the same time that Edwards's Behavioral Decision Research Program was in full swing, though in this case not in psychology (see Mirowski 2002, 484–8). However, recourse to experiments also raises new issues about economic explanation long overlooked in the field. Experimenters design the settings in which experimental subjects interact. Do they also construct individuals according to their construction of their forms of interaction? Many experimentalists largely take this to be a nonissue confined to the technical problem of good experimental design, but I will argue that the issue is more difficult than it may appear and this follows from taking seriously the idea that interaction is central to our understanding of the individual – and that individuality is somehow embedded in sociality.

Section 5.2 begins by developing a conception of the individual appropriate to the Harsanyi doctrine (the Nash-Harsanyi-Aumann refinement program) by transferring the logic of fixed point theorems used in equilibrium existence proofs for noncooperative games to a conception of the individual in games. It then compares this view to the standard subjective preferences conception of the individual. The discussion then distinguishes between complete and incomplete information games and summarizes Harsanyi's method for transforming the latter into the former by describing individuals or players as being of certain types. Section 5.3 evaluates his incomplete information game conception of the individual and argues that in important respects it equates to the standard subjective preferences conception of the individual, implying that game theory's ties to the standard *Homo economicus* conception of the individual limit the contribution that strategic interaction can make to rethinking the individual.

Section 5.4 turns to indefinitely repeated games, looks at Robert Axelrod's experiments at the University of Michigan and some of the history of experimental game theory that followed, and then frames the discussion of the role the experimenter plays in terms of the issue of artificiality of experiments and their external validity. I also argue that though the repeated play framework has been from the beginning something of the poor stepchild in game theory in economics, its exploration has had important implications for economics and the more standard single-play noncooperative framework. In Section 5.5, I go on to ask what conception of the individual it is that an experimentalism interactionist framework produces, and I conclude that though many researchers remain steadfast in their attachment to *Homo economicus*, they fail to rule out alternative views that may be equally plausible.

Section 5.6 concludes the chapter with a discussion of the limitations of simply emphasizing interaction as a way of explaining people as distinct single individuals. This serves as an introduction to the two remaining chapters in Part 2 that lay out a number of strategies that are relatively successful in this regard, some of which employ evolutionary and other forms of game-theoretic reasoning to solve multiple selves problems. Thus, this chapter also opens up a general discussion of how a possible paradigm shift may be under way in standard economics, from atomist to interactionist types of reasoning about the nature of individuals.

5.2 The Nash-Harsanyi-Aumann Program: Fixed-Point Identity

How should we approach the topic of the conception of the individual in the Nash-Harsanyi-Aumann refinement program? Because central to that program is Nash's demonstration of how equilibria exist in strategic games, we might elicit an individual conception appropriate to that framework by employing the same logic to demonstrate how individuals exist in games. That is, the formal or ontological basis for explaining the existence of Nash equilibria in games also provides a formal or ontological basis for explaining the existence of the individuals playing those games. Let us explain this in terms of the Brouwer-Kakutani fixed point theorem that underlies equilibrium existence proofs in both multiequation Walrasian competitive economies and n-tuple strategies in many-person noncooperative games (cf. Giocoli 2003a). A fixed point theorem is a mathematical proposition stating that a mapping f that transforms each point x in a set X to a point $f(x)$ within X has a fixed point x^* that is transformed to itself, so that $f(x^*) = x^*$. That is, a fixed point theorem demonstrates the existence of some consistent system of relationships by anchoring that system in one self-identical relationship within that system. If we transfer this understanding to individuals in games, then they could also be seen to be consistent systems of relationships (thus recalling the consistency view of rationality or individuality from Chapter 2). For each individual seen as being made up of many points x representing them in a set of such representations X, the mapping f that transforms each point x in that set X to a point $f(x)$ within X would then have a fixed point x^* that is transformed to itself, so that $f(x^*) = x^*$. These fixed points would make the existence of each individual a matter of this one self-identical relationship, much in the way that personal identity is explained in philosophy when individuals are said to exist in virtue of possessing some self-same feature despite change in many of their other features. In philosophy, this self-identical feature is often seen as holding temporally so as to explain personal identity in time, but the more general consistency idea that the fixed point analogy permits does not require temporal framing. All it requires is that, just as equilibria exist in games in virtue of one self-identical relationship, so in the parallel conception of individuals in games they also exist in virtue of one self-identical relationship.

To translate this formal conception of an individual into an economic one, let us say that for a fixed point x^* to be transformed to itself, or that $f(x^*) = x^*$, it is necessary to characterize x^* reflexively in that in all transformations of x in X, x^* always reproduces itself and only itself. Individuals are then reflexive in that, in all possible transformations of the individual, one self-identical relationship is constantly reproduced if the individual exists as a single system of relationships. In standard utility theory, individuals are reflexive in this sense in that in all transformations of the individual, the individual's self-same preferences are always reproduced. That is, the identity and the existence of the individual are determined in terms of these self-same preferences. Understanding this reflexivity epistemically, individuals can be said to always "know" their own preferences, or at least know them in the sense that they always draw on these self-same preferences when they act.

This interpretive strategy, however, encounters a problem associated with the private, subjective character of preferences. Because they are subjective in nature, they cannot be described as other than the individual's "own" preferences, and thus they presuppose the individual's existence rather than provide the basis for explaining it, as was argued in Chapter 1. Indeed, seen as intrinsically private in nature, it is hard to see what subjective preferences could possibly refer to and accordingly how they might constitute a basis for a single self-identical relationship in the individual in terms of which the individual is constantly reproduced. This points us, however, to an important difference between standard utility theory and game theory as it was initially developed in the Nash-Harsanyi-Aumann program. In that development in connection with complete information games, all individuals' preferences are known by all players, thus effectively grounding their subjectivity in the interaction of the game rather than in the idea of being their "own" preferences. This then makes it possible to treat individuals' self-same preferences re-understood in this way as the source of one self-identical relationship in terms of which the individual is constantly reproduced. In this respect, game theory might be thought to make an advance over the standard utility conception of the individual in explaining individuals from the outset in terms of strategic interaction rather than as atomistic beings. The underpinnings of this argument are examined in Section 5.2.1, and then its extension by Harsanyi and Aumann to incomplete information games and Harsanyi's representation of individuals as being of certain types is examined in the section following.

5.2.1 Complete Information Games

Game theory shares expected utility reasoning with the standard model of the individual but goes beyond the latter's focus on lotteries and choice under risk for isolated individuals to emphasize the additional complications created by the individual's interactions with others as a source of uncertainty in the world. What does this involve? Because Harsanyi (1967/1968, 1995) argues that games of incomplete information can always be transformed into games of complete information, let us begin with the requirements for the latter as more basic.[1] Players in a game need to know the rules of the game being played (or what kind of game it is), the utility payoffs for the other players, and that players play rationally (rather than, say, habitually). Robert Aumann put these requirements in terms of common knowledge:

It is not enough that each player be fully aware of the rules of the game and the utility functions of the players. Each player must also be aware of this fact, i.e., of the awareness of all the players; moreover, each player must be aware that each player is aware that each player is aware, and so on ad infinitum. In brief, the awareness of the description of the game by all players must be a part of the description itself. (Aumann 1989, 473)

This was later refined by Aumann and Adam Brandenburger to say that Nash equilibrium only requires that players have mutual knowledge of one another's rationality and common knowledge of one another's beliefs (Aumann and Brandenburger 1995).

Note, then, the fundamental departure from standard utility theory this involves. Because the standard view sidesteps the interactive aspects

---

[1] Strictly speaking, he produces games that function like or "as if" they are complete information games, because they are still games in which "players have less than full information about each other's *payoff functions*." Or, "the new game G^* will be one with *complete* information because its basic mathematical structure will be defined by the probabilistic model for the game, which will be fully known to both players" (Harsanyi 1995, 293, 295).

of economic behavior by postulating perfect competition and price-taking behavior, individuals need not be aware of what other players are aware of, nor aware that other players are aware of what they are aware of, and so on. Individuals only consult their own private preferences, given prices, and this means that individuals' private preferences are essentially unrelated to one another except by way of the mediating role of prices. In the early Nash-Harsanyi-Aumann program, in contrast, players' mutual knowledge of one another's rationality and common knowledge of one another's beliefs organizes individual preferences into a single transparent structure that all take into account in making their decisions. Moreover, because by the fixed point theorem this structure has a reflexive nature, what individuals know is a structure of preferences that is reflexive in nature. Their own individual preferences, then, are reflexively consulted from this perspective.

Individual preferences are still subjective, of course, in the sense that individuals have their own preferences and not one another's. However, this subjectivity is now couched in an intersubjective framework of interaction in games that provides an interpretative frame for each individual's consultation of their own preferences. At the same time, each individual's preferences are seen as their preferences by all others. Thus individuals' preferences are their own and not one another's, not in virtue of being private, but in virtue of being seen by them and others as their respective preferences. Accordingly, if we transfer the fixed point logic from equilibria to individuals, then the game theory conception of the individual that emerges from the early Nash-Harsanyi-Aumann program posits the existence of individuals as systems of relationships, each organized around a single self-identical relationship in terms of which the individual is constantly reproduced. Just as in standard utility theory, individuals are reflexive in the sense in that in all transformations of the individual, the individual's self-same system of preferences is always reproduced, so here also in the fixed point framework, the identity and the existence of the individual is determined in terms of these self-same preferences. In the interactive context of game theory, however, these self-same preferences take on different meaning, effectively thereby transforming the standard preference-subjective account of the individual into what can be termed a game-objective account – thus embedding individuality in sociality.

5.2.2 Incomplete Information Games

Harsanyi's arguments regarding how games of incomplete information function as if they were games of complete information simultaneously solved two problems. One was that, whereas most games are presumably games of incomplete information, the Nash equilibrium framework required complete information. The other problem involved the rationale for mixed strategies (players playing a number of pure strategies with different probabilities). Nash equilibria always exist in finite games when mixed strategies are allowed but are absent in a large number of games in pure strategies. At the same time, mixed strategies lack plausibility, both because they do not seem to be common in real-world decision making and because it can be shown that "a player will not lose if he abandons the randomization and uses instead any arbitrary one of the pure strategy components of the randomization" (Aumann 1985, 44). In Harsanyi's (1973) formulation of incomplete games, however, a player employs pure strategies that appear as mixed strategies in the form of other players' best guesses or conjectures as to which pure strategy a player is playing. This device made it possible to suppose that the Nash framework had wide application, because it allowed one to say that players play pure strategies, but that games could nonetheless still be analyzed as if they played mixed strategies.

Harsanyi used his analysis to show that players might regard one another as being of certain types. There are two conditions under which his formulation holds: there must be common knowledge of players' conjectures, and players must have common priors regarding the set of states of the world – labeled the "Harsanyi doctrine" by Aumann (1976). The common knowledge of players' conjectures condition follows from the common knowledge assumption. The common priors condition means that individuals or players share the same probability distributions over all possible states of the world. Whereas individuals may differ in their preferences, "probabilities reflect information, so that prior to information being received, probabilities should be the same" (Rizvi 1994, 18; cf. Aumann 1987, 13–14). Once information is received, probabilities can then differ such that, in principle, informational differences would be important to explaining the outcomes of games. However, Aumann's (1976) extension of the Harsanyi doctrine eliminates informational differences by arguing that if individuals begin with common priors, and if their beliefs concerning any given event are common knowledge, then their posterior probabilities concerning that event must be the same because rational individuals would revise their beliefs through Bayesian updating when faced with informational differences.[2] Common knowledge thus trumps asymmetric information, so that, as Aumann famously put it, "players cannot agree to disagree."

---

[2]   See Hargreaves Heap and Varoufakis (2004 [1995], 28–9 for a brief summary of Aumann's argument.

This is the context in which to view Harsanyi's focus on types of individuals. In his later work, he says that whereas a complete information game (or C-game) is always analyzed on the assumption that "the centers of activity" are players or individuals – a player-centered representation – incomplete information games (or I-games) should be formulated as being with types of players or types of individuals as the "centers of activity" – a type-centered representation (Harsanyi 1995, 295). At the same time, Harsanyi takes the player-centered representation and type-centered representation in I-games as being ultimately equivalent, and in important expositions of his thinking on the subject (e.g., ibid., 298–9), he relies on the player-centered language to provide what he regards as the more intuitive understanding of his argument. How is this justified?

The means by which Harsanyi treats these two forms of representation as equivalent is his reinterpretation of games of incomplete information in accordance with the probabilistic model (that is, by adding a lottery to the game) in which facts about players not known to all players are replaced by probability assessments regarding players' characteristics that are known to all players. Players are then represented as types because they may be represented in terms of certain sets of characteristics. Broadly speaking, they may be represented in terms of certain characteristics and as being of certain types, because "causal factors" or "social forces" in the world determine what characteristics different individuals are likely to possess (ibid., 297).[3] In particular games, then, before any moves are made, players estimate the probabilities that other players have certain characteristics and act on the assumption that every other player will estimate these probabilities much in the same way (thus the need for the common priors and updating assumptions). Harsanyi also assumes that players know which type they themselves represent – "know their own identities" (ibid., 296) – and rely on this information and perspective to assess the probability that other players are of certain types. This makes each player's assessment that another player is of a certain type a conditional probability assessment, one conditional on knowing one's own type. All players make such assessments, and consequently any given player (player 1) will act "so as to protect his interests not only against his unknown *actual* opponent ... but ... against all *M* types of player 2 because, for all he knows, *any* of them could now be his opponent in the game" (ibid., 299; Harsanyi's emphasis). Thus, each player's expected payoff depends, not just on the strategy of the actual unknown opponent, but

---

[3] Drawing on game theory applications to the Cold War, Harsanyi's example distinguishes American and Russian types whose causal factors pertain to their locations in the United States and the Soviet Union.

also on the strategies of any one of M potential opponents.[4] Then, regarding types of players as "the real 'players'" and their payoff functions as the "real payoff functions, one can easily define the *Nash equilibrium...* of this [constructed] C-game G^*" (ibid., 300; Harsanyi's emphasis).

5.3 Knowing Your Own Identity

The argument above is that complete information games replace the preference-subjective conception of the individual with a game-objective one, and that this constitutes an advance in thinking about the individual whereby private individual preferences are replaced by intersubjectively recognized individual preferences. Intersubjectively recognized individual preferences, that is, do not suffer from the circularity in the private preferences concept because they are framed in terms of a single transparent structure that all players take into account in consulting their own individual preferences in deciding how to play. Unfortunately, this intersubjective preferences view does not carry over to the Harsanyi-Aumann incomplete information game account of individuals as being of certain types, and indeed this framework restores the problematic private preferences concept of the standard utility account in a new way.

The key point is that, in games of incomplete information, players know their own types with certainty but only know that other players are one of M possible types with some probability. More accurately, players are not concerned to know their own types, which are probabilistic assessments other players make of them, since they directly know who they are in terms of their own preferences because they "know their own identities" (ibid., 296). Indeed, individuals must know their own identities in order to form their conditional probability assessments of other players' types. This means, then, that players have special access to themselves, or that their "own" preferences are privately known to them. If preferences are fully private, however, they cannot be said to be framed by the intersubjective structure of the game as they are in transparent complete information games. We are back, consequently, in the world of standard subjective utility theory in which individuals are defined in terms of their "own" preferences. However, as this notion is circular and empty and presupposes individuals rather than explains them, it cannot provide an adequate conception of the individual as a distinct being. Thus, in a more realistic world of incomplete information, game theory fails to put forward an alternative conception of individuals

---

[4] These are labeled semiconditional payoff functions.

as interactive that successfully departs from the inadequate standard utility conception of individuals as isolated independent beings.

Of course the Harsanyi-Aumann analysis has been used extensively to explain outcomes in games of incomplete information between different players of given types, as for example in the industrial organization application of the incomplete information game model to the strategic interaction between a monopoly supplier of an energy source and a monopoly producer of electricity described by Drew Fudenberg and Jean Tirole (Fudenberg and Tirole 1989). Indeed, applied incomplete information game modeling in economics only plays lip service to the concept of player preferences, and that concept really has no functional role in an analysis in which the main idea is that players are simply of different types, know their own types, and are able to probabilistically determine other players' types. Obviously the focus is on the nature of interaction between players under certain assumptions about their types, which need not be examined to carry out the analysis. Note what even this methodological position implies.

The assumption that the types of individuals or players can be taken as given rules out the possibility that strategic interaction endogenizes or changes the nature of the players. Yet it is entirely reasonable to consider that individuals might change their types, and indeed change in other ways as well, as a result of their strategic interaction with others. This same issue arose in the Akerlof-Kranton analysis in connection with whether individuals might re-rank their social group social identifications in order to maximize utility. There also it was strategic interaction (but over social group identities) that was involved and the same conclusion implicitly arrived at regarding its limited effect on what individuals are. In fairness to both Fudenberg and Tirole and Akerlof and Kranton, the consequences of allowing that interaction might somehow endogenize the individual are arguably severe, because this would also endogenize payoffs and thereby undermine the idea that strategic interaction can be understood in terms of a set structure of payoffs. Yet also note that evolutionary game theory explicitly investigates the evolution of types of individuals (or agents) and thus offers a framework in which the goal is to explain how interaction endogenizes players along payoff pathways. In Chapter 7, I will return to evolutionary game theory (along with a number of related views) in connection with a discussion of how "dynamic" conceptions of the individual make their response to change the basis of their status as distinct beings. In the balance of this chapter, I focus on how experimental investigation of repeated-play games gives strategic interaction an open-endedness that can significantly open up the conception of the individual in game theory.

5.4 Repeated Play Games and Experiment

Finitely repeated games have many of the properties of single-play games in that players can use backward induction to play in the first round of a many-round game what they would play in the final round of the game. For example, the unique equilibrium strategy for a prisoner's dilemma game played repeatedly for a finite number of rounds is to defect at every stage. Thus, the logic of repeated play, if expected to end, collapses onto the logic of single-play games. In contrast, in games of indefinitely repeated play, in which players do not foresee an end to play, this reasoning breaks down and, as encapsulated in the folk theorem, there is an infinite number of equilibrium strategies. Unfortunately, the folk theorem alone does not explain why standard reasoning breaks down. The impression this leaves is that thinking about strategic interaction inhabits two completely different worlds, neither of which can be explained in terms of the other. Moreover, both seem to reflect ordinary experience, because many real-world strategic interactions have a single-play or a finitely repeated character and many have an indefinitely repeated-play character.

Perhaps the main difference between the two types of strategic interaction concerns their differences regarding the nature of the individual. Research into indefinitely repeated-play games has from the beginning brought into question the *Homo economicus* conception. Contrary to that view, experimental evidence has long shown that individuals in indefinitely repeated games often cooperate rather than simply pursue their own payoffs. However, if we regularly see this kind of behavior in these types of games, might it not also have a role in single- and finitely repeated-play games when we observe how they are played in the real world? Indeed, recent experimental research shows that individuals do not always behave as predicted even in these types of games (cf. Roth 1995). Nonetheless, many game theorists still believe that the difficulties associated with explaining single-play and finitely repeated games point to the need to "refine" our understanding of their equilibrium properties. That is, they reject the idea that indefinitely repeated play might teach us something new about single play, assume that the standard conception of the individual applied to strategic interaction is essentially correct, and suppose that the way forward for game theory is to further extend foundational principles consistent with the Nash equilibrium concept.

This section examines these assumptions by specifically emphasizing the role experimental investigation has played in the development of thinking about indefinitely repeated-play games. In contrast to how interaction is locked in to the *Homo economicus* conception in standard single-play game explanations, the multiplicity of solutions to repeated-play games combined with the variety of ways in which they can be experimentally investigated creates a wide range of ways to understand the relationship between interaction and the nature of individuals. At the same time, clearly an experiment's design influences the character of the interaction between the experimental subjects. My argument, then, is that because the design process can result in both *Homo economicus* and non-*Homo economicus* sorts of explanations of behavior, experimental research in game theory effectively endogenizes the individual conception – contrary to the standard view discussed previously. Further, just how the individual conception is endogenized to the form of interaction the experiment creates depends on the specific way in which the interaction between experimental subjects is designed. The question this will leave us with is: What does this do to help us understand the role that interaction plays in determining what individuals are?

5.4.1 Indefinitely Repeated Games

Indefinitely repeated games have a bit of an odd status in game theory. From the early recognition of the folk theorem (e.g., Luce and Raiffa 1957) to its subsequent formalization (Rubinstein 1979), the views of their importance have ranged from not very important to very important. On the former score, they are something of the poor stepchild to the much larger research program of classical game theory. On the latter score, it has been argued that they could be a model for all strategic behavior. For example, it can be argued that people sometimes cooperate in prisoner's dilemma games, because they "fail to recognise the discrete nature of these one-shot versions of the games ... [and] behave as if they were engaged in repeated interaction" (Hargreaves Heap and Varoufakis 2004 [1995], 191). From this it is a short step to arguing, not that players fail to recognize the character of one-shot games, but that they are simply disposed to think in terms of repeated interaction, even when they know a particular interaction is not going to be repeated or will occur only so many times. One issue that this division in opinion about indefinitely repeated play brings up is the degree of fit between game theory and the real world. Might we assess how games are played empirically? This is a complicated issue in the history of game theory, particularly when we consider efforts to impose fit between game theory and the world for such reasons as military advantage (cf. Poundstone 1992; Schelling 1960) and widespread disregard for the whole question of fit associated with much of game theory's formal development and interpretation as a field of mathematics. However, the issue of fit is essentially where serious investigation of repeated-play games begins because their experimental investigation has been the main way of dealing with the multiplicity of solutions the folk theorem permits.

Particularly influential in initiating the investigation of repeated-play games were Robert Axelrod's early experiments at the University of Michigan (Axelrod 1980a, 1980b, 1981, 1984).[5] Influenced by evidence that reciprocity might play a role in strategic decision making and interested in the idea that cooperation may evolve in certain social contexts, Axelrod ran two repeated-game experimental tournaments in which different computer programs played a round-robin sequence of prisoner's dilemma games against one another – a Computer Prisoner's Dilemma Tournament. The programs were submitted by people expert in game theory, and those submitting to the second round knew the results of the first round. Though the games were repeated a finite number of times (200 each), they were played by computer programs simulated to play indefinitely repeated games. The victorious program in the first tournament was Anatol Rapoport's TIT FOR TAT program, which had the strategy of starting with cooperation and then doing whatever the opponent does thereafter. In the second tournament, Rapoport's TIT FOR TAT strategy was victorious again. Axelrod's method of investigation was interesting in that, not only did he invite experts in game theory to participate as experimental subjects as authors of the competing programs, but he essentially encouraged them to design programs to defeat TIT FOR TAT by informing potential participants for the second tournament that it had won the first. Thus, Axelrod was in some respects less engaged in testing the fit between interaction understood as a repeated game and people's ordinary behavior in the real world than in testing the intuitions of experts involved in the formal development of game theory regarding the nature of strategic choice.[6]

Contrary to most game theorists' predisposition to see strategic interaction of all kinds as noncooperative, then, Axelrod's targeting game theorists in his tournaments gave many good reason to associate repeated-play games with cooperation and coordination (and also in creating an interest in reciprocity in particular). This arguably renewed interest in earlier anecdotal evidence supporting the conclusion that people often cooperate in

---

5   Axelrod's PhD is in political science. The experimental game theory research program at Michigan, in which he and a number of others were and are still involved, was begun by Anatol Rapoport in the 1960s (see Mirowski 2002, 484–7).

6   For a formal extension of TIT FOR TAT as a Nash equilibrium strategy when games are repeated indefinitely, see Hargreaves Heap and Varoufakis 2004 [1995], 191–6.

prisoner's dilemma games (such as from postwar RAND researchers Merrill Flood and Melvin Drescher). More significant, I suggest, is the emergence of the issue of experimental design as a new focus for how to understand play in all types of games. Axelrod's account of how he set up his tournaments made design issues explicit. For those with more traditional expectations about behavior in games, the implication was that perhaps Axelrod's results might not be reproduced were his experiments designed differently.[7] Thus, they also found themselves reasoning in terms of experimental design. At about this same time, willingness to think about experiments in terms of how they were constructed was being stimulated by growing interest in Vernon Smith's papers on the "rules" for experimental design (Smith 1976, 1982). Smith, from the 1960s on, had worked to generate interest in what experimental research might bring to the understanding of forms of competition, particularly monopolistic competition (Smith 1992), and by the 1980s was beginning to be taken seriously. Moreover, as his views and early conclusions about the motivations behind behavior were relatively traditional, many economists may have reasoned that experimental research would be a new way of confirming standard assumptions, thus reinforcing interest in design issues.

In any case, however we judge economists' response to the relatively sudden emergence of experimental practice in economics, anyone taking experimentation seriously as a method of investigation soon came to appreciate the need to consider the role the experimental investigator played in designing the experiment. This conclusion, I argue, was reinforced by the subsequent range of experimental results regarding the nature of individual behavior. Whereas some experiments verified traditional views, others produced results contrary to standard theory even in the single-play framework, most famously early on in the case of the ultimatum game (Güth, Schmittberger, and Schwarze 1982). Experimentalists on both sides of the issue might have dismissed the results of their opponents, but they shared the view that all came down to proper experimental design. The conclusion that was less commonly drawn but nevertheless follows is that what individuals are, as manifested in their behavior, depends on how experiments are constructed. Thus, it no longer made sense to treat the individual conception as fixed and given. What individuals are depends on how their interaction is designed. Is there anything more than this that the rise of experimentalism allows us to say about individuals and interaction?

---

[7]   This same motivation, we saw in Chapter 2, operated for David Grether and Charles Plott (1979) in connection with evidence that individuals exhibit preference reversals.

5.4.2 Experimentalism and Mechanism Design

Let us consider some of the issues surrounding experimental design. Consider again Shaun Hargreaves Heap and Yanis Varoufakis' point that players in one-shot games may mistake them for ongoing forms of interaction. Seeing games as ongoing could mean that individuals see games, not as a succession of one-off exchanges each of which is relatively self-contained in terms of the structure of the game, but as one enduring relationship that exhibits variability over the long run around some expected or customary behavior. Suppose experimental investigators, however, see the experimental game in terms of single-play and finitely repeated games. If the experimental design then involves a set of protocols for experimental subjects that lead them to see the game as a succession of one-off exchanges, the experimental subjects could behave as they believe they are expected to behave even if they understand interaction differently. This raises the issue of game theory's fit with the world and the artificiality of the laboratory situation, that is, the issue of external validity (cf. Guala 2005; Santos 2010).

By comparison with the real world, the laboratory is an "artificial" environment in that it "is not a socially neutral context, but is itself an institution with its own formal or informal, explicit or tacit rules" that constitute it as "a special kind of society" (Siakantaris 2000, 274–5; also Starmer 1999; Guala 2002; Bardsley 2005). These "rules" allow experimental investigators to make inferences about behavior in this "special kind of society" based on the observations they make, which when made properly are regarded as internally valid. In contrast, external validity concerns inferences made about the real world on the basis of conclusions drawn from the "special kind of society" constituted in the laboratory:

The result of an experiment E is internally valid if the experimenter attributes the production of an effect Y to the factor (or set of factors) X, and X really is a cause of Y in E. Furthermore, it is *externally* valid if X causes Y not only in E, but also in a set of other circumstances of interest F, G, H, ... (Guala 2005, 142)

Internal validity, that is, concerns whether the experimenter has made the correct inferences from the experiment itself, whereas external validity – or "parallelism" (Smith 1982) – is a matter of whether experimental results can be generalized to the world. Obviously, it is possible to have the former without the latter should a well done experiment still not tell us much about the world. Indeed, according to a small survey done by Arthur Schram (2005, 235n.), most experiments are meant to test theory, and thus are primarily concerned with internal rather than external validity. Charles Plott, moreover, claims that the "experiment *should* be judged by the lessons it teaches about theory and not by its similarity with what nature might happened to have created" (Plott 1991, 906; emphasis added). Surely this runs the risk, however, of insulating theory and experimentation from the world. What can we say, then, about experiments and external validity?

Achieving external validity, in fact, faces significant barriers associated precisely with the artificial character of the laboratory environment and the attendant difficulties involved in representing the real world in the lab. George Loewenstein (1999) argues that external validity can be high where experiments are meant to investigate highly structured markets (such as double oral auctions) whose features can be reasonably replicated in the lab, but for most experiments it is more likely to be low because laboratory environments have many characteristics that are rarely found in the world, such as stationary replication of some kind of choice. Loewenstein also faults experimenters' efforts to remove contextual cues to produce controlled context-free experiments. Much cognitive psychology research, he argues, demonstrates that people rely on contextual cues to trigger complex inferences, and thus experimental environments stripped of such clues are unrealistic. Can the experimental investigator really be thought to be generally successful in removing contextual clues? In the case of the investigator who models an experimental game in terms of single or finitely repeated play, though experimental subjects may think in terms of ongoing interaction, it is fair to say that the experiment's protocols function as contextual clues signaling how the game ought to be played. Nicolas Bardsley emphasizes a key reason for thinking this in connection with the difference between experiments in the natural sciences and the social sciences (cf. Bardsley 2005). In the latter, we have conscious subjects who are aware that, among other things, they are participating in experiments. This awareness of course could have no effect on how they behave, but it seems more likely that it does.

Suppose, then, that we employ the standard view of individuals and treat experimental subjects as having interdependent utility functions as in social preferences experiments. Then can we say that "the [experimental] subject cares about the utility of other subjects, but not the utility of the experimenter" (Sobel 2005, 401)? If experimental subjects understood in this way do care about the utility of the experimenter, external validity then becomes altogether problematic. Suppose we think in terms of social identification. In the cognitive psychology literature, social identification can be primed by an anchor or by the way in which a question is asked (Ariely, Loewenstein, and Prelec 2003, chap. 13; 2006, chap. 14). Thus, while the experimenter has designed a game that the experimental subjects play, the experimental subjects are arguably also engaged in playing a metagame with the experimenter in which the experimental game is embedded. In terms of contextual cues, experimental subjects would interpret the experiment's protocols as implying that the experimenter wants them to play a particular kind of game; and as they get utility interdependently, they would then play the game appropriately, irrespective of whether in real-world situations they would behave differently.[8] Such cues could be associated with the authority that the experimental subjects perceive to be invested in the experimenter, or they might be associated with social customs regarding the rules that apply when one voluntarily accepts compensation for participation in some activity. Graham Loomes puts this particularly well:

> They know you're running an experiment, and so they know you're looking for something. Despite your protestations, they may believe there is *a* right answer which will be rewarded. Or they may want to please you, or create a favourable impression of themselves. Or they may simply feel pressure to do *something*, and so they look for cues, and seize upon whatever the experimental design (consciously or unconsciously) suggests to them. (Loomes 1991, 598)

The experimental investigator framing an experiment in terms of single and repeated play, then, may well succeed in demonstrating that individuals are motivated as expected. Indeed in the artificial "special kind of society" created in the laboratory game, this may well be an internally valid conclusion. However, the game and the "society" really at issue is not the game-within-the-game that the investigator has designed. Rather, it is the metagame in which the investigator is included. From this perspective, there is no external reference point from which one might ask about external validity of laboratory results, and indeed the idea of external validity in presupposing a separation between the laboratory and the world essentially loses its meaning.

If we must thus give up the idea of an "external" world, it does not follow that we must give up idea of the real world, which is in fact what experimental investigators and their experimental subjects occupy. Thus, mechanism design theory (the subject of the 2007 Nobel Prize in economics) forthrightly follows out the logic of the metagame to prescribe institutional reforms or experiments for the world itself. The economist or experimental investigator models people or experimental subjects strategically using the

---

[8]   This desire on the part of experimental subjects to act as they believe experimental investigators wish them to act has long been known as the "Hawthorne" effect, after a series of experiments performed on workers at a Western Electric consumer products factory in Hawthorne, Illinois, from 1924 to 1932 (cf. Cot 2009).

standard individual conception, and Nash efficient outcomes are employed as the basis for the policy or experiment protocols. If we generalize Loomes' evaluation of experimental subjects to people generally, we might indeed conclude that people will be expected to generally respond to this "experimental" situation as the standard individual conception and Nash strategic play predict. On the other hand, the similar but slightly different take on social experimentation taken by the libertarian paternalists examined in Chapter 3 suggests a somewhat different possibility. The two views do share a commitment to realizing *Homo economicus,* but the libertarian paternalists begin with *Homo sapiens,* who does not always behave as *Homo economicus.* Thus, it is not always clear when and whether institutional reform will produce *Homo economicus* behavior. That is, even when people or experimental subjects are disposed to behave as they believe is expected of them, they may not. This, however, affirms the experimental character of the metagame involved. Investigators or policy makers are able to influence but not fully control outcomes. Let us turn back, then, to what these perspectives on interaction teach us about individuals.

5.5 Ambiguity and Construction

I have suggested that indefinitely repeated games were originally something of the poor stepchild in game theory, because they were not very amenable to the formal analysis used to develop game theory in connection with single-play and finitely repeated games. The argument in the previous section, however, is that this spurred their empirical investigation, and this in turn has given new impetus to game theory understood as experimental investigation. Indeed, experimental game theory has arguably displaced classical game theory as the leading form of game-theoretic investigation because so many of the predications of the latter have not stood up well to empirical scrutiny, and because of the potential research opportunities available to the former. Yet this story only leads to another concerning what experimental game theory can accomplish. Though most experimental game theorists maintain a fairly conventional view of the relationship between the experimental investigator and the experimental subjects, some of those who have worried about the issue of external validity point us toward a rather unconventional view of experiments as settings in which experimental investigators construct rather than observe behavior. I make no attempt to arbitrate between the different views on this subject or say how seriously the unconventional view might impair the experimental project. The question that rather concerns me in this section is the status of the individual conception as a result of experimental investigations of strategic behavior. My conclusions come on two levels.

First, game theory, despite its original attachment to the standard individual view, has opened up active consideration of what individuals are when they interact with one another, largely as a result of the impact of experimental investigation of indefinitely repeated play and the spillover effects of this on thinking about single play. The multiplicity of solutions to repeated-play games, together with the variety of ways in which they can be experimentally investigated, opens up an exceptionally large canvas on which a wide range of ways to understand interaction and its impact on individuals can be portrayed. Thus, whereas at the outset the standard individual view was the general case and nonconforming behavior was seen as anomalous, it has since become more of a special case, and nonstandard behavior is rather now seen as common. Of course the standard view is still widely defended in economics, but having lost its earlier foundation in a priori reasoning, it now needs to be actively defended vis-à-vis rival views on the basis of evidence. So altogether, game theory has had an important impact on thinking in economics about what individuals are.

Continuing with this point, if interaction does make a difference to what individuals are in the sense that they do not appear to be just atomistic beings that also happen to come into direct contact with one another, how does their strategic interaction specifically reset the boundaries on being what an individual is? If we say that individuals are not atomistic beings, because interaction somehow breaks down their atomism, how far does this breaking down go? Because game theory seeks to explain how it is that individuals interact, its account of interaction needs to be compatible with saying people still retain the status of being individuals, however this might need to be re-understood. Clearly, however, the issue of the boundaries that apply to being a single individual has not arisen in much of game theory in a very serious way, at least as it has developed to date, and the best it accordingly seems we can say is that the conception of the individual in game theory is ambiguous. Individuals still count, but we do not know in what degree or how. Thus, the richness of the larger canvas for portraying individuals in interaction is also its weakness. There are too many possibilities for saying what individuals are, and there are few indications regarding where one should turn to begin to sort this all out.

My second conclusion concerns the metagame and the experimental investigator as a constructor of the identity of experimental subjects or individuals. Again, I do not take a position on how significant this capacity to construct or influence identity may be; it is enough to say there is little reason not to believe that it is a real capacity, whether exercised in the laboratory or in real-world policy design settings. This follows from the difference between social and natural science, noted by Bardsley, which simply records that individuals have awareness of the circumstances in which they act. Note what this awareness can involve. The idea that experimental subjects may act as they believe the experimental investigator expects them to act implies that they make judgments about both their circumstances and the role they believe they ought to play in those circumstances. That is, they do not just have a disposition to react to protocol signals (as the entities investigated in natural science), but in some degree determine a course of action for themselves that they believe they ought to adopt according to their understanding of those signals. One way to put this is to say that they play the experimental game by playing a role they conceive for themselves and into which they insert themselves. This view of the matter accordingly enlarges our account of the experiment to include two capacities rather than one. The investigator exercises a capacity to construct or influence identities, and the experimental subjects exercise a reflexive capacity to adopt or reject the identity desired.

Reflexivity is also assumed in the Nash-Harsanyi-Aumann analysis in terms of the doctrine that players "know their own identities" (Harsanyi 1995, 296), but in a much more modest way.[9] For Harsanyi, knowing your own identity is essentially the same thing as knowing what your own preferences are in the standard model, and it really comes to nothing more than an information requirement for decision making in the traditional belief-desire framework. However, in metagames between investigators and experimental subjects, the former are able to influence and the latter able to adopt *multiple* possible identities, not just one exogenously given identity (even if investigators or policy makers often seek to make it the *Homo economicus* identity). This is a further respect, then, in which the individual conception becomes endogenous to how people interact with one another. More interesting, I believe, is one additional comparison. Whereas reflexivity is tied to decision making information requirements for Harsanyi as in the standard preference model, in metagames in experimental settings it is rather tied to the nature of the relationship between the investigator and the experimental subjects. The individual's identity, therefore, is somehow a relational identity. Thus, whereas my first conclusion is that the individual conception in game theory is ambiguous because the boundaries on being

---

[9] As we saw, it also plays an important role in Bénabou and Tirole's account of self-reputation, though not in Akerlof and Kranton's view.

a single individual in interaction are left unclear, in the context here we find the outline of an idea about how those boundaries might be determined. That is, rather than the broad forces of interaction – a vaguely interactionist conception of the individual – it is the way in which specific relations between individuals cause them to interact with one another that sets the boundaries on what being a single individual involves. This view – what I call a relational conception of the individual – is the subject pursued in connection with two additional game theory views discussed in the chapter to follow.

5.6 Problems and Boundaries

This chapter first argued that, though seeing individuals in games as strategically interactive represents a step beyond standard utility function thinking, nonetheless the main path of development in game theory in the Nash-Harsanyi-Aumann equilibrium refinement program formulated in terms of incomplete information games ultimately fails to detach itself from the subjectivist limitations of the standard approach. Basically, the standard view supposes that individuals can be exogenously identified apart from their interaction with others, and thus to preserve this core idea the Nash-Harsanyi-Aumann program must ultimately reserve some element of subjectivity to individuals. However, as subjectivity presupposes individuality rather than explains it, it does not really capture how interaction affects what individuals are, and the Nash-Harsanyi-Aumann program consequently ends up simply offering an account of individuals as arbitrarily determined packages of strategies.

The chapter then moved to a second domain within game theory, indefinitely repeated games, and argued that their experimental investigation raises deep questions about what game theory as a whole is all about. At the same time, it is still unclear what experimental game theory actually tells us about the nature of individuals other than that interaction is important to our conception of them. I focused on indefinitely repeated games because alternative hypotheses about individuals are readily suggested by them, whereas the openness of the experimental setup allows for a range of types of behavior. Yet experimental investigation of play in games itself opens up a host of new issues in connection with the issue of design and external validity that on the one hand add new complications to our thinking about individuals, but on the other hand also suggest ways of thinking about what individuals are in relational terms. The following chapter thus begins with two game-theoretic accounts of individuals that are explicitly relational conceptions laid out in two disparate domains in connection with teams and neuroeconomics.

This chapter began by contrasting the internalizing sociality in individuality orientation of the views discussed in Part 1 with an alternative embedding individuality within sociality orientation of the views that are the subject of Part 2. Note, then, that the kind of problem with single-individual explanations encountered in Part 1 is also quite different from the kind of problem with them that we have just seen in this chapter. In Part 1, the problem was that the conceptions of individuals developed by different researchers cannot rule out that individuals fragment into multiple selves, and fail to address the sub-personal bound on what being an individual involves or how individuals with multiple selves are single unified beings. Here the problem was the opposite in that a vaguely interactionist view of individuals makes the supra-personal bound on single-individual explanations the main problem. How is it that people who interact are still single individuals and do not simply disappear into masses of interacting people. Whereas in Part 1 the problem arises because individuals' multiple social dimensions are unsuccessfully incorporated within individuals, the problem we face when we rather embed individuals in the social world is that they lose their individuality altogether. Looking at Parts 1 and 2 together, then, what we see are how two bounds operate on single-individual explanations in economics: one concerning the individual's fragmentation and one concerning the individual's entire disappearance. Any satisfactory account of single individuals, I argue, needs to adequately explain both to say how single individuals have multiple selves and interact with one another.

SIX

Multiple Selves in Interaction

Teams and Neuroscience

Ùɓúntú [ubuntu]: a Zulu term meaning, "a person is a person through other persons," often used by Nelson Mandela; also the name of a community-developed open source computer operating system.

6.1 Beginning with Multiple Selves

This chapter turns to two recent game-theory-based views that reject the atomistic individual conception and explain how people seen to have multiple selves can be thought to be single individuals. Interaction is central to understanding individuals as it was in the last chapter, but the interaction explained in this chapter operates simultaneously on two levels rather than on just one: interpersonally between individuals as before but now also intrapersonally between their respective multiple selves. I first discuss Michael Bacharach's view in which individuals have multiple selves because they identify with different social groups, but in which these multiple selves also identify with the single individual understood as a team. Bacharach employs the same psychology social identity framework as Akerlof and Kranton, but he replaces their utility function representation of individuals with his multiple selves team representation of individuals. Second, I discuss Don Ross's neuroeconomics individual conception in which people's different neural selves are relatively independent agents that play intrapersonal games with one another that produce single unified individuals who then play interpersonal games with one another. Like Bénabou and Tirole, Ross explains the intrapersonal interaction between an individual's multiple selves game-theoretically, but in contrast to their intrapersonal noncooperative game analysis he explains these intrapersonal games as coordination games.

Whereas Bacharach and Ross both seek to explain how having multiple selves underlies being a single individual, they have quite different views regarding what people's multiple selves are. Bacharach sees individuals' multiple selves as their supra-personal social identities. Thus, to show that people are single individuals, he needs to show that they do not dissolve into the many different social groups with which they identify. Ross sees individuals' multiple selves as their sub-personal neural selves. Thus, to show that people are single individuals, he needs to show that they do not fragment into their many competing sub-personal selves. Bacharach and Ross are thus concerned with the two different boundaries that single-individual explanations must jointly address. These are the boundaries, as was said in Chapter 1, that Nathaniel Wilcox uses in applying the concept of agency to single individuals (Wilcox 2008, 527). For him, Bacharach's supra-personal orientation makes the "*fusions* of agency" the problem that needs to be solved to explain single individuals, whereas Ross's sub-personal orientation makes the "*fission* of agency" the problem that needs to be solved to explain single individuals. That is, for Bacharach the problem is how there are individuals and not just social groups, whereas for Ross the problem is how there are individuals and not just neural activity.

The previous chapter focused on the simple idea that strategic interaction influences what individuals are. The two views discussed in this chapter go further and employ one kind of relational conception of the individual – one in which people are single individuals in virtue of how their interaction with others makes them more than collections of multiple selves. Other relational conceptions (though not developed in recent mainstream thinking about the individual) individualize people interpersonally without explaining them as collections of multiple selves. At the end of the previous chapter, we saw the outline of such an idea in connection with how experimental design places players in certain relationships that can constitute them vis-à-vis one another as single individuals. It can also be argued that the relationship between experimental investigators and experimental subjects individualizes them in those respective capacities. Previously, I also explained how shared intentions ("we" intentions) operate in this way by individualizing the person who expresses them (Davis 2003, chap. 7). A relational conception of individuals also seems to be essentially the goal in the "relational autonomy" research program pursued by recent feminist philosophers; the object is to show how individuals can be simultaneously autonomous and related to others, thus neither atomistic nor fully socialized beings (cf. Mackenzie and Stoljar 2000). What all types of relational conceptions have in common is that they use a more fine-grained view of interaction to explain individuality in terms of specific types of interactive relationships.

Section 6.2 begins with Bacharach's theories of teams and team reasoning that use social identity theory and were developed to address classic problems in game theory. Section 6.3 turns to neuroeconomics and Ross's account of individuals' neural selves and the social dynamics of their interaction. Section 6.4 follows a lead suggested by Ross in looking at how neuroscience develops representations of individuals. Here I rely on the cultural anthropologist Michael Dumit. Section 6.5 summarizes the chapter and takes stock of what a relational approach to thinking about individuals accomplishes and leaves undone.[1]

6.2 Bacharach's Individual as a Team

6.2.1 Teams and Frames

Bacharach's team conception theory of the individual stems from his theory of teams and team reasoning (Bacharach 2006).[2] The latter was motivated by the discrepancy he perceived existed between what ordinary experience suggests people often do in games, such as the prisoner's dilemma, and what rationality prescribes they ought to do. The source of the difference, he believed, is an ambiguity in the syntax of standard game theory. On the standard view, individuals in games are thought to ask themselves: "what should *I* do?" However, Bacharach suggests that people ought rather be taken to be asking themselves, particularly when they are working together with others: "what should *we* do?" When taken in this latter way, individuals could be said to choose according to what they believe best promotes the group or team's objective, which would then entail that they act so as to perform the role appropriate as a member of that team or group. Bacharach's main contribution to thinking about games such as the prisoner's dilemma was to argue that individuals could alter their view of the kind of strategic interaction they were involved in according to the different possible cognitive frames they used to think about the world, and he thus developed a "variable frame theory" for rational play in games in which the frame adopted for a decision problem determines what counts as rational play (also cf. Janssen 2001; Casajus 2001).

---

[1] For related discussions of the subjects addressed in this chapter, see Davis 2008b and 2009d.

[2] Gold and Sugden edited and published Bacharach's last work after his death. For their theory of teams, see Hollis (1998), Sugden (2000), and Gold and Sugden (2006, 2007).

In order to explain how someone acts, we have to take account of the representation or model of her situation that she is using as she thinks what to do. The model varies with the cognitive frame in which she does her thinking. Her frame stands to her thoughts as a set of axes does to a graph; it circumscribes the thoughts that are logically possible for her (not ever, but at that time) (Bacharach 2006, 69).

Robert Sugden had earlier explained framing in terms of focal points following Thomas Schelling's emphasis on the role of salience in coordination games, and his theory of focal points similarly ties decision making to the way the game is understood (Sugden 1995; cf. Schelling 1960). This all recalls what Tversky and Kahneman (1981, 1986) termed standard theory's extensionality or description invariance assumption (the idea that the description of a choice situation should not influence choice), which if abandoned makes it possible to bring a variety of insights from psychology regarding framing to bear on rationality in economics.

For Bacharach, if we suppose that the cognitive frames people adopt determine how they see themselves as agents, we can distinguish between choice reasoning that is instrumentally rational for individuals acting independently from choice reasoning that is instrumentally rational for them in the teams or groups to which they belong. In the latter case, when individuals think in terms of teams, Bacharach says that their agency undergoes a transformation in that people cease to think as independent individuals and come to think of themselves as team members. It may then be rational for them to cooperate rather than defect in prisoner's dilemma games because this is rational from the perspective of their being members of the team. Of course, the idea of agency transformation raises many questions regarding how teams are formed and how individuals come to identify with them. Bacharach's view, like Akerlof and Kranton, draws on social psychology's social identity theory, and like them he explicitly makes use of self-categorization theory (Turner et al. 1987) whereby individuals develop different self-concepts for themselves associated with their identification with different social groups. This makes group identification a psychological phenomenon rather than the result of rational choice, though Bacharach allows that individuals nonetheless need to recognize that they have a common interest in being members of a team. Indeed, it is this common interest that gets represented by a group utility or payoff function that individuals then seek to maximize by fulfilling their roles as members of the team (Bacharach 2006, 87–90).

If individuals are understood to be members of teams or groups, however, in what sense are they still single individuals and do not simply dissolve across their many team and group memberships? In self-categorization theory, individuals are seen to be single beings in virtue of being the "intersection" of all their group identities. In brief remarks he makes on the subject of personal identity, however, Bacharach goes further and replaces the idea of the individual as an intersection of a set of group identities with the idea of the individual as a team. His basic idea is that just as a person's multiple selves all identify with different social groups as team members of those groups, so they can equally be understood to all identify with the single person as team members of that person.

My suggestion assimilates personhood to group identity more directly and more fully. Since a person is temporally extended, we can represent her as a sequence of adjacent, linked segments – "time-slices", "dated subpersons", or what have you. Each of these parts has the essential characteristics of an agent and, in particular, is the locus of the person's thinking about what to do, now and later. (Bacharach 2006, 89)

That each of a person's temporal time-slices is the "locus of the person's thinking" means that each takes on the single person's point of view, according to whatever their respective responsibilities as team members would be. Thus, a person made up of many selves is still a single individual because each of that person's multiple selves acts in the name of the person as a whole. What is different in Bacharach's view from Akerlof and Kranton's, then, is how this identification works in two directions rather than one. On the one hand it explains social group identification; on the other it explains personal identification. Ontologically speaking, just as groups exist based on the evidence that people identify with them, so individuals as teams exist based on the idea that this same capacity can be exercised by individuals' multiple selves with respect to the person as a whole. Bacharach planned to write an entire chapter on the person as a team to further explain his view in which he intended to liken intrapersonal team reasoning to interpersonal team reasoning, but this chapter was not completed (cf. Bacharach 2006, 94n.). Natalie Gold and Sugden, however, discuss his proposal at some length based on their knowledge of this unfinished writing, and this helps further illustrate his idea of the individual as a team (2006, 191–6; also cf. 2007).

As they explain it, Bacharach was especially motivated to address the problematic absence of an enduring agent in dynamic choice theory. On the standard view, any agent at time t is treated as an independent rational decision maker, so that the "person" over time is no more than "a collection of transient agents, who may happen to have certain common preferences and beliefs" (Gold and Sugden 2006, 191). For Bacharach this did not make sense because it meant that people would unfailingly exhibit present bias. It was as if their different transient selves were always playing an intrapersonal prisoner's dilemma game. Thus, suppose we assumed that each of these transient selves asked themselves the question: What should *we* do? As Gold and Sugden then demonstrate, this would open the door to an explanation of how people overcome present bias without any need to reinterpret the nature of the game or change its payoffs (ibid., 194–6). Bacharach's sees the present-bias problem like Bénabou and Tirole, but uses an agency transformation of the individual's transient selves to produce a solution to the intrapersonal prisoner's dilemma. In this respect, his thinking resembles collective intentionality theory, such as developed by Margaret Gilbert in terms of plural subjects (Gilbert 1989). At the same time, Bacharach had little to say about the nature of intentions or plural subjects, leaving his view largely one about the role of different cognitive frames in decision making.[3]

6.2.2 The Individual as a Team as a Relational Individual Conception

Consider, then, how Bacharach's team view of the individual operates as a relational individual conception. Individuals have many temporal selves, because they belong to many different social groups over time (and also at any one point in time). These temporal selves identify themselves as both team members of these social groups and as team members of the person. For Bacharach, this double identification simultaneously "entifies" both the groups and the person (Bacharach 2006, 70–3). His team view of the individual is thus a relational conception of the individual, because it ties being a single unified individual to having relationships to others (in social groups in his case) by the same logic. Moreover, Bacharach's reasoning runs from social (group) identification to personal identification. It is only because an individual's temporal selves are able to see themselves as members of social groups – that is where the team idea comes from – that they are able to see themselves as belonging to a single individual. This thus gives us one example of a relational individual conception. We will see that Ross's

---

[3] Gilbert (1989, 2008) is primarily concerned with how plural subjects come about and undertake shared activities, and her paradigm example is two people going for a walk. Similarly Bacharach writes:

My current … idea is something like this: Something in the situation prompts the parties to see that they have action possibilities which have possible outcomes of common interest.… Each of us sees we could write a paper together, or have a pleasant walk round the garden together, or bring down the appalling government together. (Gold and Sugden 2006, 165)

Gold and Sugden distinguish Sugden's own theory of teams as follows: "Sugden (2003) presents a 'logic of team reasoning' without making any claims for its validity" (Gold and Sugden 2006, 167).

relational conception works somewhat differently in terms of how interaction between individuals' neural selves produces single individuals. For
now, however, I will note how Bacharach's relational view goes beyond the
simple game theory idea that interaction matters to our conception of the
individual. Interaction matters, but it matters because it involves a particular kind of interactive relationship, namely the team relationship, in which
the form of interaction and what the individual is each imply the other. For
Bacharach, that is, these are internally rather than externally related to one
another, and interaction makes a difference to our understanding of individuals when it reaches into what they are.

If Bacharach's team conception of individuals shows how we might understand individuals with multiple selves to be single unified individuals, does
it also succeed in showing them to be distinct and independent individuals? That is, does it address Wilcox's "fusions of agency" problem? When
one is a team member, one's status as an independent individual dissolves
as one's agency is fused with that of all other team members. Bacharach's
answer is that just as an individual's temporal selves can identify with social
groups, so they can also identify with the single person. In fact, social psychologists argue people exhibit both capacities. People identify with social
groups, and people employ self-concepts with which they also identify
(cf. e.g., Stevens 1996). So Bacharach's assumption that an individual's temporal selves identify with an enduring self is not without support in standard
psychological thinking. At the same time, the idea that the person is a team
is rather thin as a mechanism or account of what holds the person together
as distinct and independent from others. We might agree that it allows us
to suppose people solve intrapersonal prisoner's dilemma problems and
overcome present bias, but as the individual-as-a-team idea is really just
an analogue of the social-team idea, they might just do this because this
is what team members do in the groups with which they socially identify.
Social identification, that is, frames personal identification.

Let us look at this from the perspective of Bacharach's concern with
dynamic choice and add in the fact that social groups have dynamics as
well. They change their memberships, and often this implies that they
change what kinds of groups they are. But then, if the social groups with
which we identify change over time, so on Bacharach's argument the person our temporal selves identify with should change over time also, and
we are each as likely to be different teams over time rather than just one
team. More strongly, if the person as a team is constantly changing, then
it becomes unclear why we should refer to the person as *a* team through
time at all. It is difficult to see how this is consistent with the idea of people

being distinct and independent individuals. Note, then, that the difficulty Bacharach faces in addressing the fusions of agency problem stems from the very nature of his relational conception of the individual. Its advantage in going beyond making interaction per se central to the individual conception is how it explains interaction in a special way via the team idea. However, that idea by itself is not enough to tell us why personal identification does not ultimately collapse on social identification – or how personal identity is something over and above social identity. Thus, focusing on special forms of interaction – ones that are effectively internally related to what the individual is – does not seem to be enough to explain individuals.

6.3 Ross's Neuroeconomics-Based Relational View

Let us turn, then, to the second relational individual conception discussed in this chapter: Ross's neuroeconomics-based view, whose subject is the neurons and different neural systems that make up the human brain. Ross treats these different neural systems as relatively independent neural agents and thus as a person's multiple selves. As such, they are sub-personal multiple selves rather than supra-personal ones, and he accordingly investigates what a person is from the perspective of neuroscience rather than from the perspective of social psychology. Ross shares Bacharach's game-theoretic form of analysis of interaction; but whereas Bacharach uses social identity theory to solve intrapersonal prisoner's dilemma games, Ross explains people's multiple neural selves as being engaged in intrapersonal coordination games. The difference between their views seems to be a difference between a natural science sort of investigation and a social science one. However, Ross's view includes an important role for social forces – evolutionary social forces – that influence how people's sub-personal neural selves play coordination games with one another. This creates links between his view and cultural anthropology accounts of neuroscience and individual identity that I will explore in Section 6.4 as an important dimension of his relational individual conception.

6.3.1 The Individual in Neuroscience and Neuroeconomics

Neuroscientists come at the individual from a relatively unique perspective. Their goal is to investigate the nature and functioning of the brain, but this sort of investigation does not line up nicely with the idea that people are single unified individuals. Though neuroscientists indeed put single individuals in scanners for neural-imaging purposes, they treat them there as collections of relatively independent neural structures whose coordination can be theorized in different ways and on different levels according to the goals of research and therapy and according to the different kinds of phenomena being investigated. Neuroscience, that is, begins with the disaggregated rather than the whole individual and works with a multiplicity of theories regarding the different ways in which individuals can (but may not) function as single unified persons. This is not the view, however, that we find in neuroeconomics research whose origins are in behavioral economics. As argued by Colin Camerer and others, neuroeconomics is largely a development of behavioral economics that aims to secure additional new evidence from neuroscientific research to support and refine many of the conclusions reached by psychologists and behavioral economists about the behavior of individual economic agents (e.g., Camerer, Loewenstein, and Prelec 2005; Camerer 2006, 2008). If we take Kahneman and Tversky's prospect theory (1979) as providing the basic model on which most developments in the behavioral economics literature have been based, then essentially neuroeconomic research in this tradition assumes that individuals can be adequately represented by an individual value function analogous to the traditional individual economic agent utility function. A neuroeconomics derived from behavioral economics thus assumes from the outset that the different regions of the brain work in such a way as to produce the behavior of the single unified individual economic agent.

This, however, begs the question of whether people function as single individuals. We could reason that different structures in the brain effectively act as relatively independent neural agents, and that individuals' interaction with one another is segmented according to which of these neural selves and brain structures is involved. For example, when two people become angry with one another, the parts of their brains that produce anger response take over in each, and the persons that they each are as a whole answer to these sub-personal neural agents. People, then, would not interact as single individuals; their different neural selves would interact, as it were, "behind their backs." Thus, whereas you may place one body in the scanner at a time, this does not imply that the behavior investigated is that of one unified agent. This thus introduces Ross's perspective. As he aptly puts it, on the standard economics view neuroeconomics is simply "behavioural economics in the scanner" (Ross 2008, 374). To this he opposes a neuroeconomics he terms "neurocellular economics," which uses the modeling techniques and mathematics of standard economics – optimization and equilibrium analysis – to represent the functioning of different parts of the brain without making any assumptions about how neurocellular processes are related to the individual as a whole. For Ross, whether in neuroeconomics or other areas of investigation, an agent ought to be defined in minimalist fashion as an optimizer in a narrowly defined reward space (ibid., 378–9). More fully, an agent is "any system that observes certain consistency conditions in behavior, such that it can be interpreted *as if* it is maximizing the value of a function that maps a system of preferences over commodity bundles onto the real numbers" (Ross 2005, 245). There is nothing in this definition of an agent, however, that requires economic agents be identified as single individuals – or as Ross puts it, as "whole *people*" (Ross 2008, 378). Indeed, the objective functions that agents optimize could be ascribed to all types of agents, including sub-personal agents – "*that* neuron, or *that* neurotransmitter system, or *that* quasi-modular circuit" (ibid., 379). Ross thus rejects the idea that any sort of whole person "anthropomorphism" is the necessary starting point for neuroeconomics or indeed any other sort of investigation that concerns economic agency.

Ross's neurocellular economics understanding of neuroeconomics follows in the line of thinking initiated by psychiatrist George Ainslie that starts with individuals' multiple selves (Ainslie 2001).[4] Individuals are collections of optimizing sub-personal neural agents who interact in coordination games internal to the individual (Ross 2005, 2006, 2007; cf. Davis 2007c). Why begin with sub-personal neural agents? Ross takes the idea of an agent to be primitive and basic, and then argues that neuroscience gives us good reason to see individual neurons and other neural structures as agents on the grounds that they can be regarded as functioning in an optimizing way. Specifically, neuroscience tells us that neurons and neural structures exhibit the property of servosystematicity, or the control of entropy through negative feedback mechanisms (Ross 2005, 246–8). That is, they possess mechanisms that enable them to maintain themselves as relatively independent entities. In rational choice terms, a servosystematic mechanism is one that avoids operating as a money pump. Neurons and neural structures are agents, then, that optimize in the sense of effectively acting in their own respective neural interests, as indeed any of the human body's organs include in their activities ones designed to perpetuate the organ. The issue for Ross, consequently, is whether single individuals should play any role in a neurocellular economics. Indeed, it is not immediately clear from his starting point that we even need to individuate whole persons, because if an

---

[4] The multiple selves view is sometimes associated with Paul Glimcher's neuroeconomics research, but Ainslie's view is criticized in Glimcher, Kable, and Louie (2007). Ross et al. (2008) defends Ainslie.

individual's sub-personal neural agents play coordination games with one another, it stands to reason that they could also play coordination games with other individuals' sub-personal neural agents, thus eliminating any need to talk about the person per se. His analysis would then be no different than a generalized game-theoretic view of the world in which different neural agents play different games with one another, and there are no whole individual agents (as Bénabou and Tirole's view turns out to be). However, this is not Ross' view. He argues that this sort of representation of the world is too "flat" to capture the various macro structures, social and otherwise, that he believes we see in it. Thus, his game-theoretic world is one in which collections of neural agents successfully play coordination games with other collections of neural agents that lead to interpersonal games between whole individuals. Let us see, then, how that argument works.

6.3.2 Sculpting Individuals

The key claim Ross makes is that individuals' sub-personal neural agents find it in their interest to prioritize coordination games with other sub-personal agents internal to the same individual. The basis for this claim is evolutionary: because evolution has confined sets of sub-personal neural agents to the same individual human bodies, it turns out to be symbiotically in their interest to cooperate with one another in order that the body they jointly inhabit survives. Further, as the whole individual's survival also depends on interaction with other whole individuals (who are similarly the result of internal coordination games), Ross, like Bacharach, makes the whole individual the product of both interpersonal and intrapersonal interaction.[5] An important difference between their views lies in how they each bring these two sides of the individual together. We saw that Bacharach uses the double-sided nature of social identification to bring these two dimensions of the individual together, but that this is problematic because changing social identities then implies a changing individual. In contrast, Ross brings them together as an outcome of evolutionary processes.

Specifically, Ross argues that evolved systems of social dynamics influence the development and evolution of intrapersonal and interpersonal forms of interaction in such a way as to continuously "sculpt" and "re-sculpt"

---

[5]   Their arguments, however, proceed in opposite directions. Bacharach begins in the social world with supra-personal multiple selves, and then uses the team idea to constitute the whole individual internally; whereas Ross constitutes the whole individual internally out of the coordinated play of the person's sub-personal selves, and then explains external interaction on this basis.

individuals' neural selves into whole persons. Human language is central among these evolved dynamical systems. We know that humans are different from other animals in terms of their special capacities for language. A particularly important aspect of this is the reflexive capacity people have developed to describe themselves or produce narratives about themselves. The exercise of this capacity, Ross believes, provides the framework within which an individual's sub-personal selves operate to solve internal coordination games. Essentially, they find it in their interest to coordinate under the banner of the individual's current self-representation. Why should evolutionary forces select for the human language capacity to produce individual self-representations? Because in a complex world of many types of social interaction people need

to *make* themselves predictable. They do this *so* they can play and resolve coordination games with others. (To be predictable to others, they must be predictable to themselves, and vice versa.) Then all of this is compounded by the fact that nature doesn't exactly partition games the way analysts do in game theory texts. A person can't keep the various games she simultaneously plays with different people in encapsulated silos, so a move in a game G_i with the stranger will *also* represent moves in other games $G_{k,...,n}$ with more familiar partners – because these partners are watching, and will draw information relevant to $G_{k,...,n}$ from what she does in G_i. (ibid., 293)

The interdependent nature of games between individuals, then, constrains the games internal to individuals to be consistent with self-narratives that are recognizable as those of whole persons. For Ross, this is essentially an evolutionary story: "social dynamics *are* logically and ontogenetically prior to individual selves, because selves are sculpted into being by social processes" (ibid., 257).

Note, however, that there is an ambiguity in Ross's argument. It is one thing to say that individuals have a capacity to reflexively produce self-narratives or discursive representations of themselves, and it is another thing to say that these representations are specifically whole individual representations of themselves: *self*-reports rather than simply representations of different aspects of themselves. If neuroscience tells us that individuals are collections of relatively independent neural structures, might not individuals' representations of themselves be alternately of this neural system, then of that neural system, and so forth, just as the angry person momentarily stands in for the whole individual? Nothing in Ross' analysis of interaction between an individual's sub-personal selves quite tells us how they collectively graduate to producing whole individual self-reports. Where, then, does the self-narrative that specifically produces the individual's self-concept come from? If Ross does not answer this question directly, he nonetheless offers a framework for doing so that is worked out in terms of Daniel Dennett's idea of an intentional stance (Dennett 1987).

Dennett's intentional stance idea, or intentional stance functionalism, explains the behavior of all entities, human and nonhuman alike, using a concept of intentionality. An intention in the most basic sense is an orientation toward something, and its representation is always in the form of language as in such expressions as "believes," "thinks," "wants," and so forth. Thus, when we represent a nonhuman entity intentionally, we say, for example, that a thermostat "perceives" a change in temperature, or a computer "remembers" certain files. Dennett's goal in authorizing such expressions is not to undermine the traditional understanding of intentionality as associated with human intentions, but rather to free it of its association with so-called internal states of the human mind, and in effect "externalize" its meaning by applying it to relations between things in the world. This arguably increases the power of attributions of intentions to all sorts of entities in the world, because rather than looking "deeper and deeper" into some sort of mysterious concept of mind to understand those intentions, we are compelled to draw on features of the environment and the world to explain the nature of those intentions – an explanatory process understood as "triangulation" by Ross (2005, 49–50, 61). Thus the intentional stance, as simply a principle of orientation requiring expression in a distinct kind of language, can be taken by all sorts of entities towards all sorts of things.

A collection of sub-personal neural selves, accordingly, could conceivably take an intentional stance toward the individual as a whole they collectively inhabit, and this stance could be said to be that of the individual's self-concept. We can reinforce this conclusion by emphasizing the syntactic and semantic properties of language. We can thus use language syntactically in a reflexive manner to make the individual using language itself an object of linguistic expression, whereas semantically these individuals can be named the single persons who interact in games. Ross can thus say that in human language the interaction between collections of sub-personal selves reflexively produces individual self-concepts that we associate with whole persons. Consider further what the nature of self-narratives typically involves.[6]

---

[6]   The literature in psychology on the self-concept is extensive and I only lightly summarize it in Chapter 8, in which the idea of a self-concept as a self-narrative is discussed more extensively. Epstein (1973) ignited recent interest in the idea. See surveys of the literature in Markus and Wurf (1987) and Banaji and Prentice (1994). The literature on self-concepts that take the form of self-narratives is associated with a subfield of psychology called

Narratives generally are discursive language structures that take the form of a "story" from a particular perspective, and as such must have consistency and integrity as a single account of how events transpire for a subject or number of subjects. That is, a story must hold together, and in the case of self-narratives must do so for the subject at the center of that narrative. Consequently, if a person's self-concept is seen in extended form as self-narrative, the whole person is individuated as a single being as long as that person's story retains some sort of integrity. Of course saying that a story must "hold together" can seem very subjective, but Ross provides a criterion for this. His view is that the predictive role we see in the social dynamics of language increasingly sculpts the person and her story by narrowing the possibility space the individual's life occupies as the individual ages, so that the continually reduced space in which the individual's self-narrative takes place always defines the self, even if the "story" never comes down to one simple final message (Ross 2007; cf. Dennett 1991). This convergence argument arguably allows a kind of dynamic reidentification of the individual as a single being, because the narrative of the person at earlier points in time is always contained in the narrative of the person at later points in time. Ross's further argument is thus that if we look at how self-narratives actually work, we can conclude that the social dynamics of language work to make interaction between people predictable as single individuals.

Let us then draw together the different sides of Ross's relational view of the individual. We saw that he begins with a neuroscience account of how people's sub-personal neural selves play internal coordination games, and then further develops this view via Dennett's intentional stance thinking as an account of how people's intrapersonal and interpersonal interaction have become embedded in a social dynamics of human language. I have characterized his account as a neuroeconomics-based one, because his multiple selves are sub-personal neural selves, but we can also emphasize the latter side of it and say that Ross explains individuality as the product of the institution of human language: people function as single individuals because language has evolved to structure their internal and external interaction in such a way as to bring this about. Seeing his view in this way particularly makes sense when we treat language as an "external scaffolding" for human cognition as Andy Clark does (1998) – an interpretation Ross favors. Clark

narrative psychology (Sarbin 1986; Polkinghorne 1988; Bruner 1992, 2002; Herman, Jahn, and Ryan 2005). Self-narratives are taken as the basis for personal identity by a number of philosophers (MacIntryre 1981; Ricoeur 1988, 1992; Taylor 1989; Dennett 1991; Schechtman 1996; Ross 2007). For a critical view of self-narratives as a basis for personal identity, see Strawson (2004).

argues that in the long history of human cognitive development, human beings have continually offloaded to constructed and natural structures in the world those cognitive functions they are not especially good at while retaining and specializing in those functions at which human beings excel.[7] Ross's frequent example is that because human brains "aren't very good at arithmetical calculation ... [people] solve the problem by writing the sequence of outputs on a piece of paper, using a special-purpose visual-display format," and so forth (Ross 2005, 260–1). From this perspective, we would say that human self-narratives take the form they do because our accumulated social-cultural practices constitute an external scaffolding for the nature of storytelling. Then our view of the individual would essentially be an evolutionary institutional one applied to modern neuroscience.

In Section 6.4, I follow up on this lead and look more closely at how some of the technological and scientific practices contemporary neuroscience employs in neural imaging provide specific forms of scaffolding for neuro-scientists' representations of individuals. I will use this discussion to further develop Ross's relational individual conception when we place emphasis on the role social institutions play, but I will also use it to open up a new set of issues regarding the ways in which individuals get represented in social narratives in general. I take as my main source in this regard Dumit's cultural anthropological account of how neuroscience characterizes individuals.[8]

6.4 Picturing Personhood

Picturing Personhood is the title of Dumit's book on brain scans and individuals' biomedical identities (2004). Dumit is a cultural anthropologist, and though he writes from the perspective of science and technology studies about neuroscience in general rather than about neuroeconomics per se, the issues he addresses are no less relevant to neuroeconomics and its

---

[7] Clark's (anti-Cartesian) external scaffolds idea treats cognition as distributed across the environment people occupy. It was developed following the thinking of psychologist Lev Vygotsky and sees human mental processing, whether involving cognitive or motor tasks, as relying on found and created features of the external world (Clark 1998, 45–7). Relatedly, Wilcox, who we saw is concerned with the fusions and fission of agency, also argues that we should see human cognition as being distributed across individuals and external cognitive artifacts in social systems of information processing "which implement *external* information representations and algorithms," and reduce "*the importance of individual brains* to economically important information-processing tasks" (Wilcox 2008, 524; his emphasis). For an excellent set of papers examining the nature of human cognition in relation to agency, see Ross et al. (2007).

[8] However, also see the complementary discussions of Radden (1996) and Lloyd (2007).

representation of the individual. Indeed, much of his discussion focuses on laboratory experimentation, a central focus of neuroeconomics. A key difference from neuroeconomics, however, is that Dumit focuses on how the laboratory is socially organized by disparate groups of scientists (physicists, chemists, nuclear chemists, biologists, computer scientists, electrical engineers, statisticians, psychologists, etc.) who play different roles in making experiments possible, most of whom are only marginally interested in the experimental outcomes themselves, and who are primarily concerned with the technical-scientific development and employment of their own areas of expertise. This scientific production process, moreover, is also explained by Dumit in terms of the organization of neuroscience as a whole around research institutes, universities, medical centers, government agencies, and proprietary entities, all of which are represented as being in competition for resources in a climate in which scientific and often popularly understood social goals for the use of science are intermixed and contend.

Ross, we saw, argues that individuals are collections of sub-personal agents constructed as single individuals through a "sculpting" process operating within a set of language practices. Dumit brings whole communities of individual scientists in complex social-scientific settings into this sculpting process and the business of determining when and how neuroscience counts people as single individuals. His focus is the biomedical identity of single individuals. Of course, neuroscience has many concerns besides this one, but it has been an important one on account of the historical development of neuroscience as one means of addressing certain forms of mental illness that prevent people from behaving as is expected of single individuals (for example, schizophrenia and addictions of various kinds). If, behaviorally speaking, people are sometimes "not themselves," then an ambition of neuroscience is to determine why and how they might be treated so as to be able to "be themselves." As we will see, whether particular individuals are able to "be themselves" is determined in neuroscience by comparing them to the average behavior of individuals in carefully constructed control groups of individuals who are represented as able to "be themselves" according to conventional views of behavior. Neuroscience for Dumit, then, also employs a relational conception of individuals, though one that explains individuals by the standard of a class of individuals in the social groups of which they are said to be members. This is not Bacharach's social group team view. Rather, people are individuals by comparison with the representative group member taken to be a single individual in regard to the behavior at issue. Individuals still acquire their status as individuals in relation to other individuals, but only relative to the representative individual of the social group in which they are included. Moreover, whereas Bacharach's social groups are basically given, for Dumit they are constructed according to the way in which research is organized in the neuroscience community.

Though he does not refer to Clark, Dumit's framework can be understood in terms of Clark's idea of external scaffolds, because neuroscience across its many constituent disciplines makes heavy use of a wide array of advanced technologies (all the apparatus of brain scans with all the supporting science, techniques, procedures, testing methods, equipment, systems of organizing labs, etc., that scans require) that allows it to accomplish computational and information-processing tasks that far exceed and yet also simultaneously enhance scientists' natural abilities. This emphasis on the importance of the institutions of science also recalls Wilcox's fusions of agency issue. For Dumit, it is not the fragmentation of individuals into neural multiple selves – the fission of agency question that Ross emphasizes – that is at issue in the way that the neuroscience community constructs individuality. The issue is rather subsuming individuality under the idea of representative-ness understood in terms of the social-statistical scientific construction of classes of average behavior. That is, if people are identified as individuals only relative to the classes to which they belong, their distinctness as indi-viduals can only be of a typical kind. Then, because neuroscience constructs many classes of average behavior, the conception of the individual that emerges is that of a collection of average behaviors. However, this hardly captures what the idea of being a single individual involves. Individuality is broken up and disappears into a social classification process. If Ross, then, is worried about how people fragment into multiple selves, Dumit is wor-ried about how people disappear in the scientific narrative. In effect, they are lost in the social.

Note also, then, that Dumit's examination of how neural imaging and scanner technology produce a conception of the average individual recalls how experimental game theory employs a laboratory technology that pro-duces a conception of the experimental subject. In the previous chapter, my conclusion was that once one designs a particular type of laboratory environment, one has also created a set of rules for research in that lab that have implications for the interpretation of experimental subjects. Let us see, then, how for Dumit neuroscience accomplishes this with scan-ning. Neuroscience seeks to model single individuals as "normal human" individuals. However, it needs to use advanced statistical and technological means to transform that latter concept into something measurable. Here in outline are the steps involved in doing so according to Dumit.

First, one must isolate a sample of the "relevant" human population for scanning in order to produce a "normal" image to be compared to the individual images of particular people in research and therapy.[9] Second, a set of controls is imposed on this sample group of individuals for such things as smoking, a history of past depression, and so forth, as well as for the state of these subjects prior to scanning (what each subject eats or drinks beforehand, their state of rest, instructions regarding how to behave while being scanned, etc.). Third, after this sample of individuals is scanned, the individual brainset data produced for each subject is normalized for differences in brain size, physical functioning, and so on, in order that each individual's brain locations can be correlated with those of all other individuals in the sample, or in order that all the individual brainsets are comparable.[10] Fourth, these normalized individual brainsets are then combined to produce one collective group individual brainset that establishes what being a "normal human" involves, at least as represented by this particular population sample. Finally, needed throughout the whole process are sophisticated statistical and computational techniques for data processing, the tuning and calibration of the scanner technology selected, and considerable chemistry and physics associated with the registering and capturing of satisfactory brain images.

Given all this, whether the particular individuals later examined in research and for medical purposes can be called single individuals – understood as independent "normal human" individuals – is a matter of whether they fall into a scientifically constructed class of similar objects all characterized as "normal single individuals." Of course, we cannot forget that there are many avenues of investigation in neuroscience, and so there are many ways in which the reference idea of the collective individual brainset can be produced. Therefore, "normal human individual" really refers to a heterogeneous class of such representations of individuals, as reflects the many-sided multidisciplinary character of neuroscience. Indeed, neuroscience can only be loosely called a single investigative community because the aims and goals of individual researchers and medical practitioners are

---

[9] There are many interesting problems associated with the representativeness of these samples, particularly as concern the age, gender, and social circumstances of the individuals sampled in creating them, but they go beyond the purposes of the discussion here.

[10] There are different types of normalization procedures – the original standard being the "Talairach brain" – but they all essentially adjust nonaverage individual characteristics toward the average. I also put aside here that various researchers intentionally "inflate" or "flatten" the scans they produce to enhance their usefulness in exhibiting phenomena of special interest (cf. Alač 2004).

highly diverse. There is one thing, however, that is common to all neuroscientific representations of the single individual that bears final comment.

As the representation of an instance of a class, "normal human individual" in all cases is a third-person representation of what an individual is. I characterize third-person representations as ones that use the language of "he," "she," "it," and "they" to refer to others (as objects) distinct from the party (the subject) formulating the relevant representation – here, neuroscientists representing those who are the object of research and therapy. By contrast, a "first-person" representation is one that uses the language of "I" and "me." Ross, we saw, puts special weight on "first-person" representations that are also reflexive; in a self-narrative, someone (the subject) refers to herself (the object) using the language of "I" and "me." This is all important, because part of what being a human individual seems to involve is having this reflexive capacity of self-representation, because if people's representations of themselves are only third-person representations, again, they are arguably lost in the social. Yet there is nothing in the concept of "normal human individual" that gets at this. Neuroscience, also all human and social science, only creates third-person conceptions of average individuals. Indeed, third-person representations of individuals are pervasive throughout human society and certainly not the sole province of science. I return to this issue in the concluding section as it is central to the chapter to follow.[11]

6.5 Taking Stock

The previous chapter argued that game theory embeds thinking about individuals in strategic interaction, but it concluded that this simple "interactionist" idea alone does not take us very far, as classical game theory still largely retains the standard individual conception, and the status of the individual in experimental game theory is ambiguous. The current chapter consequently adopted a new point of entry compared to the last and also previous chapters – the idea of a relational conception of the individual – and used Bacharach and Ross's views to develop this conception. Their general strategy of explaining the individual both intrapersonally and interpersonally clearly distinguishes their approaches from most reasoning

[11] Korsgaard makes a similar distinction to the one I use here, differentiating between "a third-person point of view" and a first-person "description under which you value yourself, a description under which you find your life to be worth living" (1996, 100, 101; cf. Davis 2009b). My distinction here is more neutral in that it does not make her normative emphasis on a "life worth living" part of this distinction.

in economics about individuals, but their more important departure from past thinking is to genuinely make what individuals are endogenous to their interaction with others rather than treat them exogenously as atomistic beings whose choices are also interdependent. Thus, why people seen to have multiple selves are nonetheless single individuals for Bacharach and Ross depends on just how people interact with others. For Bacharach, it is their belonging to social groups that provides the basis for regarding people as single individuals, specifically as a team. Compare this conception to Akerlof and Kranton's. They also see people as belonging to social groups, and employ the same psychology social identity theory as Bacharach, but individuals are still defined by exogenous utility functions. For Ross, people are single individuals despite being made up of collections of relatively independent sub-personal neural agents, because of the way that social dynamics, especially of language, "sculpts" them as such in their interaction with others. Compare this with Bénabou and Tirole's approach. They also seek to explain individuals as the result of intrapersonal games, but how these games are played is essentially independent of how people play games with one another.

We saw also in this chapter that Bacharach and Ross were concerned with different types of multiple selves problems. Bacharach treats an individual's multiple selves as supra-personal social identities, and Ross treats them as sub-personal neural selves. Thus, Bacharach's problem in explaining the single individual is to address Wilcox's fusions of agency issue, and to show that individuals do not disappear into the various social groups with which they identify (the same issue that Dumit's analysis addresses). Ross, in contrast, is concerned with Wilcox's fission of agency issue, and that people do not fragment into competing internal interests. Together, these two issues and these two different accounts of single individuals help to jointly set out the two boundaries on adequate single-individual explanations. Adequate explanations of what single individuals are, that is, need to explain both how they hold together as unified beings in the face of both ways in which they may fail to do so. This framework for single-individual explanations was used at the end of the previous chapter to make a distinction between the difficulties that the revised atomistic individual conceptions discussed in Part 1 encounter and the difficulties that characterize individual conceptions emphasizing interaction, the subject of Part 2. This chapter introducing the relational individual conception relocates these boundaries within the analysis of interaction in virtue of the different ways in which Bacharach and Ross understand individuals relationally. I assume in the balance of this book that the main conclusions of this chapter are central to our thinking about what individuals are: that people have multiple selves, that single individuals must somehow be understood relationally in terms of interaction between people, and that single-individual explanations stand or fall depending on their ability to account for the boundaries on them described here.[12]

At the end of the previous section, third-person individual representations were distinguished from first-person individual representations, especially reflexive self-representations. The need for this distinction arose out of an evaluation of Dumit's account of how neuroscience constructs conceptions of individuals through the application of a variety of social-statistical scientific methods. What these third-person characterizations do, as reflects the scientist's third-person perspective, is produce average behavior representations of individuals who are all seen to be members of sets of similar individuals. This is indeed one understanding of individuality, and I will argue in Chapter 9 that it is an important component of our understanding of individuals – that much of the "material" we believe makes them up, as well as in their own view, comes from others" appraisals and characterizations of them. However, I claim that this understanding of individuality is also only a part of what we generally include in that idea, and that what also needs to be included in our conception of individuals is some capacity to produce first-person self-representations. The point is that without making this part – an important part – of what individuals are, we cannot rule out that their individuality is simply socially constructed, and indeed constructed as a heterogeneous collection of average behaviors as reflects the fact that there are multiple sorts of third parties in the world (from science, media, government, etc.) engaged in some form of social statistical classification of kinds of individuals. In effect, individuals also have to be subjects whose self-construction of themselves as individuals somehow combines with how they are constructed by others.

This latter idea is missing from the relational conceptions discussed in this chapter. The closest we come to it is Ross's use of Dennett's intentional stance idea. That idea embeds subjectivity in the world as intentionality,

---

[12] There are other strategies for developing relational conceptions of individuals that are not game-theory-based, and thus not discussed here. For example, some have emphasized commitment as a capacity that individuals exercise in interaction with others (Sen 1977; Hollis 1998; Minkler 2008). Commitment may individuate the person who makes it if those to whom it is made see it as tying that person's temporal selves together under one conception of the person (Davis 2007b). The other approach I have noted concerns collective intentions (Tuomela and Miller 1988; Gilbert 1989, 2008; Searle 1990; Davis 2002; de Boer 2008). Collective intentions, it can be argued, create obligations for those who express them, and this serves to individuate persons over and above their temporal selves (cf. Davis 2003, 145–7).

but it does not explain how it comes about or why it should be thought to exist. The way the social dynamics of language works for Ross produces individual self-concepts as objects of self-narratives, but why it should produce this result is not clear. Bacharach assumes individuals function as team subjects – "what should *we* do?" – but he does not develop subjectivity as intentionality nor explain why we should suppose people have this capacity. The following chapter, then, looks at a set of views I characterize as developing an evolutionary-relational conception of the individual. The addition of evolutionary thinking appropriates and employs the concept of a self-organizing entity to attribute to the individual the idea of being a self-sustaining subject. The concept was introduced in this chapter by Ross in his treatment of agents as servosystematic, or as agents able to control entropy through exercise of negative feedback mechanisms that are part of their nature. In the following chapter, I look at the development of this idea in discussions in psychology and economics that make evolutionary reasoning about individuals their point of entry, and that involve a different point of departure for introducing psychological thinking into recent economics than offered by the Behavioral Decision Research program and behavioral economics.

SEVEN

Evolution and the Individual

Identity Through Change

You imagine you are a secondhand car whose odometer has been reset to zero by exile, that craftiest of dealers. With all old parts, you are recast as a brand-new human engine. Within you is all the clanking, hissing, and racket of past rides. But you muffle it all and press on.

(Hakakian 2004, 14–15)

7.1 Self-organization

The question examined in this chapter is how individuals are to be looked upon when we understand them as self-organizing systems. This perspective is associated with a view of the economic world as an evolutionary system of change rather than as a static structure of unchanging relationships. This change in perspective places new emphasis on an issue central to understanding what individuals are: how they are to be reidentified in systems of change that affect themselves as well as the world they occupy. We have already encountered this issue in connection with the analysis of present bias in behavioral economics, because there people fail to act rationally because they do not behave as the selfsame individuals through time. In that case, the reidentification issue is narrower, because the world itself is not treated in an evolutionary way but is seen as a stable backdrop – indeed, one in which policy makers believe they can determine what rationality requires, and thereby make it possible for people to act "as if" they are single individuals through time. Clearly, things are significantly more complicated in an evolutionary world in which both individuals and the world are constantly changing. This chapter then argues that an alternative line of thinking in recent economics beginning in the 1950s with Simon – who rejected Edwards' Behavioral Decision Research view of what psychology brings to economics – takes this more comprehensive view of change in economic life and produces an individual conception, which

I term an evolutionary-relational conception, that makes a key contribution to our thinking about individuals in the form of the idea that they are self-organizing systems.

How individuals can change and paradoxically still be reidentified as the selfsame individuals, all in a world that is also changing, is not a question that has been central to evolutionary economics. Rather, the focus there has been on how thinking in evolutionary terms changes our understanding of entire social economic systems. This more aggregative perspective may reserve a role for individuals in general, but often has little to offer regarding what happens to specific individuals in evolutionary processes. For example, most of evolutionary game theory sets aside the question of particular individuals' persistence to focus on the persistence of types of individuals, as inspired by the classic hawks and doves game (cf. Maynard Smith 1982); and Joseph Schumpeter's use of the idea of creative destruction describes turnover in the population of individual entrepreneurs as a consequence of their actions as a type of agent in capitalist economies (Schumpeter 1942). However, this perspective seems incomplete, because if types of individuals endure in evolutionary processes, then individuals of those types must also endure, at least to some degree. Thus, I suggest that a more complete evolutionary economics also needs to explain the nature of individuals in evolutionary systems, which requires addressing the basis on which they may be said to endure, if this can indeed be argued.

There are different strategies for going about trying to explain the paradoxical idea of how individuals might both change and endure. One is to first establish the basis on which they can be regarded as distinct and independent beings, and then seek to determine when they can be reidentified on that basis through a process of change. Establishing how individuals are distinct and independent – a concern that has occupied much of the discussion in the previous chapters – gives us a baseline idea of an individual against which we might then allow various changes in that individual's makeup that are nonetheless consistent with what makes the individual distinct and independent. The difficulty with this strategy is that what makes an individual distinct and independent may also change, as we saw with Bacharach's view. In his relational conception, individuality was explained in terms of how individuals are related to other individuals in social groups. If we look at the world in a more evolutionary way, then we should expect people's relationships to others to change, as our social group memberships constantly change. Then the strategy of first getting straight distinctness and independence and then mixing in change is a risky one because the basis for distinctness and independence is constantly changing. Evolutionary theorists, however, seem to employ a second strategy for conceptualizing individuals, at least as I interpret them: they reverse the strategy above and explain what makes individuals distinct beings in terms of what makes them enduring beings; they do so by showing how changing interaction with others reinforces rather than undermines individuality. I characterize conceptions of individuals that have this sort of basis evolutionary-relational kinds of views.

This chapter tracks the development of an evolutionary conception of the individual across a number of important contributors. It begins in the immediate postwar period with Simon's environmental or ecological rationality conception of individuals that emphasizes the idea that individuals function homeostatically, and moves on to other individual conceptions in recent economics that retain and develop this assumption, particularly by emphasizing learning and adaptation in complex environments. Central to the evolutionary-relational individual conception as it emerges across these views is a conception of the individual as a self-organizing system – a concept developed for other purposes in the rather different context of postwar physics, natural science, mathematics, and especially cybernetics.[1] My view is that this concept makes a key contribution to understanding individuals as agents in dynamic and evolutionary systems. This chapter attempts to set out how the figures to be discussed here jointly contributed to this type of individual conception. It involves, we will see, the idea of the individual as a reflexive being, one that has first-person representations of itself, the idea introduced at the end of the previous chapter.

To begin, two caveats are in order. First, in contrast to previous chapters, the first three (of the four) theorists whose views are examined here generally do not make the nature of the individual their focus, and thus I have reconstructed their individual conceptions from their treatments of economic agents in evolutionary processes. However, the fourth of the individuals examined, Brian Arthur, is explicitly concerned with individuals or agents – indeed as an early contributor to agent-based modeling in

---

[1] Ashby (1947) originated the modern usage of the term "self-organizing." Hayek (1945) described the market as a self-organizing system. See Wiener (1961) for early development of the idea in cybernetics. For an influential sociological application, see Niklas Luhmann (1984). Mirowski's (2002), which has done the most to foreground this idea in economics, argues that von Neumann's theory of automata as self-organizing systems is one of the most fundamental developments in postwar thinking, underlying not just the adoption of computational processing representations of a multitude of natural and social phenomena in a range of key current technologies but also much of contemporary economics.

economics – so treating his view last in this sequence hopefully helps justify my reconstruction of the others' individual conceptions. Second, though all the views discussed here are seen by their proponents as being evolutionary ones, the meaning of "evolutionary" is very broad, means different things to different people, and only loosely follows along the lines of Darwinian theory. Indeed, evolutionary theorizing in economics has always been rather uneven in its allegiance to Darwinian theory, as perhaps befits the problems of applying biological science to the social sciences to develop an account of cultural evolution (cf. Hodgson and Knudsen 2006, 2008; Vromen 2004, 2009).

Section 7.2 discusses Simon's early rejection of utility functions and his strategy of explaining individuals in terms of aspiration levels and the environments they occupy. Simon influenced the "fast and frugal heuristics" approach of Gerd Gigerenzer, Reinhard Selten, and other cognitive psychologists; seen together they provide the basis for an understanding of rationality as ecological rationality. Section 7.3 turns to market experimentalist Vernon Smith, influenced by Simon especially later in his career, who argues that individuals develop rational behavior in competitive markets, an outcome he sees as combining constructivist and ecological forms of rationality. Smith's account does not quite explain how individuals adjust to competitive markets, nor is he especially explicit about the nature of individuals. However, evolutionary game theorist Ken Binmore, discussed next in Section 7.4, does make an argument on this score that shares a number of Smith's philosophical commitments. Binmore does not characterize rationality as ecological rationality, but his evolutionary naturalist approach shares a number of its assumptions about rationality and evolutionary processes. I focus on Binmore because he places important emphasis on learning, and this allows me to explain how the idea that individuals are reflexive beings is key to an evolutionary individual conception. Binmore does not actually give an account of how individuals learn, and so Section 7.4 circles back to Simon's early thinking about complex systems to treat agent-based modeling as a means for explaining how individuals learn and coevolve with their forms of interaction. Brian Arthur's complex adaptive systems thinking about individuals' cognitive capacities in evolutionary settings is then used in Section 7.5 to expand the evolutionary individual conception developed stage by stage across the previous sections. Finally, Section 7.6 closes the chapter with brief comments on the importance of the concept of human capacities in this framework and asks whether we ought to also consider whether they evolve.

7.2 Ecological Rationality: Simon's Intervention

Simon, we saw in Chapter 2, was an important source of thinking in postwar psychology about individuals in connection with his early critique of rationality theory and influence on the development of the field of Behavioral Decision Research (BDR). Simon and Ward Edwards both had a role in the emergence of this field, but their work gave rise to two different research programs, with Edwards' impact chiefly on the line of thinking that pursued revising the standard utility function approach, and Simon having his impact on those inclined to abandon it. Simon was from early on interested in information processing and the cognitive capacities of decision makers relative to the context of decision making, and this led him to argue that complex environments required "only very simple perceptual and *choice mechanisms to satisfy* [the decision-maker's] several needs," and that "no 'utility function' needs to be postulated" (Simon 1956, 137–8; his emphasis). His approach thus needs to be distinguished from that of Edwards, though it is easy to miss this if one associates Simon's ideas strictly with the idea of bounded rationality, contrasts this with "unbounded" rationality, and then reduces the difference between the two to simply whether the information and processing capacities of the decision maker are limited. Gigerenzer is clear about what is wrong with this interpretation: "In his 1956 article entitled 'Rational Choice and the Structure of the Environment,' Herbert Simon pointed out that there are two sides to bounded rationality: the decision-maker's 'cognitive limitations' and the 'structure of environments'" (Gigerenzer 2001, 39). Simon's argument, then, was that the decision maker's "cognitive limitations" need to be understood relative to the "structure of environments" the decision maker occupies, because those environments determine the kinds of decisions that must be made. Further, because the decision maker's environments are complex and changeable, it makes no sense to represent the individual as optimizing a fixed utility function. Decision makers, as it were, are "in" the world, and their boundedness needs to be understood relative to that world, not relative to some abstract standard of rationality.

Simon's thinking about rationality and the individual accordingly gives rise to a type of evolutionary thinking that emphasizes decision makers' continual adjustment and adaptation. He does not operate with a broad macro view of evolutionary processes, but instead examines the decision maker's adjustment to particular decision contexts. Thus, in his 1955 paper in which he focuses on "the properties of the choosing organism" and explains what came to be known as satisficing, he distinguishes the "behavioral alternatives" (or alternative kinds of choices) decision makers perceive they have and their aspiration levels for achieving satisfactory outcomes, and he argues that because both may adjust, a dynamic account of decision making is necessary (Simon 1955, 100, 112). Selten later reformulated and labeled this approach aspiration adaptation theory (Selten 1998), and also characterized it more broadly as learning (direction) theory (Selten and Stoecker 1986). Also building on Simon, Gigerenzer went on to argue that decision makers employ what he terms an adaptive toolbox made up of a variety of domain-specific or "fast and frugal heuristics" that do better in changing and varied environments than do general-purpose algorithms (Gigerenzer et al. 1999). He characterizes this as involving an ecological rationality: "A heuristic is ecologically rational to the degree that it is adapted to the structure of an environment" (ibid., 13).

Simon, then, initiated a line of thinking quite different from the one associated with Edwards, as reflected in his satisficing critique of rationality as utility function optimization. However, might Simon's dismissal of utility function analysis still allow us to understand rationality on its alternative Samuelsonian basis as consistency in choice? Not if we take adaptation seriously. As Gigerenzer explains it,

Consistency in choice and judgment is not a general norm to follow, but rather a tool for achieving certain proximal goals. For a given goal, consistent behavior can be an advantage, a disadvantage, or unimportant. (Gigerenzer 2001, 41)

Being ecologically rational, then, does not require consistency in choice or indeed even rule out preference reversals. Consistency in choice may be adaptive or it may not be adaptive, depending on immediate and past circumstances. Simon's dual emphasis on decision makers' "cognitive limitations" and the "structure of environments" they occupy portrays decision makers as adaptable and responsive to their circumstances, which themselves change and evolve, and neither the utility maximization view nor the consistency in choice view of rationality captures this understanding.

Simon's thinking, we saw in Chapter 2, was particularly influential for the construction of preferences line of thinking in BDR, which argues that preferences are elicited rather than revealed according to the ways individuals interact with the world. Nonetheless, the construction of preferences line of thinking in BDR is generally less evolutionary in its approach and more focused on the mechanisms by which preferences are constructed (though see Payne, Bettman, and Johnson 1993). This difference becomes significant when we ask about the underlying conception of the individual, because as we saw, the preference construction approach really does not support any clear view of the individual. Having undermined the traditional view in economics that identifies individuals with their given preferences without producing an alternative account, the preference construction approach essentially creates a vacuum on the subject. What then should we say in this regard of Simon, whose emphasis on the decision maker's continual adjustment and adaption seems to imply that the decision maker is an enduring agent, though also one who evolves according to the changing circumstances of choice?

Simon had a long and fertile career in which his thinking ranged across a wide variety of subjects. Yet I suggest that an answer to this question can be located in his early thinking – going back to his first work (Simon 1947) – when he determined many of his foundational beliefs regarding the nature of decision making. His 1955 paper on "the properties of the choosing organism" (Simon 1955, 100), in contrast to its 1956 companion paper on the properties of the environments organisms occupy, is particularly interesting in this respect, because there we see Simon take in some respects a traditionally economic rather than psychological approach to the decision maker, and do so in a way that has definite implications for thinking about what individuals are. My argument, in fact, is that the route he took here saved him from the BDR preference construction "no individual" result and introduced a key idea for understanding individuals dynamically or as enduring beings that are reidentifiable across change in an evolutionary conception of the individual.

Much of the 1955 paper is devoted to the problem of "simplifying" the decision maker's payoff space on the assumption that choice situations of any complexity need to be recast so as to allow effective choice. Here accordingly, Simon explains outcomes as being satisfactory for decision makers when they allow them to achieve certain levels of aspiration. Then, after setting out a representation of a feasible or viable payoff space in this way, Simon turns to economics' traditional concern with the existence and uniqueness of equilibrium solutions to decision problems. He asserts that in human decision making, alternatives are generally examined sequentially, and that when a satisfactory outcome is reached and an aspiration level is achieved, the decision-making process terminates at that stage of the sequence. However, he sees that the problem in explaining choice in this way is that the individual's aspiration levels can be affected by the sequencing of alternatives. Then the decision pathway may be unclear, and we cannot rule out the possibility that the decision maker never reaches satisfactory outcomes. Simon's response is to attribute a capacity to the decision maker to sort through choice alternatives to determine the order in which they should be addressed. His claim is that the decision maker's aspiration levels rise or fall as the alternatives faced are respectively easy or difficult to discover, and this allows the decision maker to follow a decision pathway that produces a determinate outcome (ibid., 111). This in turn leads to another possible indeterminacy addressed in similar fashion. The size of the set of "behavioral alternatives" (or alternative choices) decision makers perceive they have is also affected by the sequence of alternatives. Simon's response in this case is to say that the size of the set is enlarged or narrowed if the alternatives are respectively easy or difficult to discover, and thus again decision makers can be said to have a capacity to move to determinate outcomes in environments to which they must adapt (ibid., 112).

It is not my goal, however, to say whether Simon has successfully explained satisficing as a determinate choice process. More important for the discussion here is what Simon's view implies about the nature of decision makers when he says that we have capacities for dynamic adjustment to an environment. That the adjustment mechanisms Simon describes are properly termed capacities follows from his view that they are powers that can be exercised in varying degrees by different decision makers. Thus, to understand how different decision makers behave, he tells us that we need to take into account the degree to which each adjustment capacity is exercised by the decision maker. In particular, Simon makes the interesting claim that the latter capacity – determining the set of alternative choices the decision maker has – is likely to be especially evident the "more *persistent* the organism," presumably because a capacity to continually broaden the alternatives set is associated with decision makers being able to sustain more extended decision pathways, so much so that it may even be possible to speak, as he does, of an "optimal degree of persistence in behavior" (ibid.; his emphasis). Thus, whereas the first capacity concerns whether the decision maker is able to settle at an aspiration level, the second concerns whether the decision maker is able to do so repeatedly over a sequence of decision contexts. As such, it provides the basic idea that decision makers are enduringly individual in virtue of their capacity to adjust to change.

Simon does not follow up on this view in his 1955 paper, but turns to a different issue, namely that organisms may exhibit an entire hierarchy of adjustment mechanisms. Thus, let us simply state what is new about Simon's view of decision makers, and so about individuals, and also ask what it implies about them in identity terms. First, he says that if we are to suppose that decision making has a reasonable degree of determinacy in changing environments, we need to attribute dynamic adjustment mechanisms or capacities to decision makers. Second, he says that having these capacities can be tied to the persistence or durability of the decision maker itself. The logic of this thinking might be stated as follows. Were decision makers constantly changed as they adjust to their circumstances, we would have no reason to suppose that they have any integrity or independence as coherent decision makers. This cannot be the case, however, because we suppose they do carry out coherent patterns of decision making in changing environments; and so there must be something about them, which we may understand in terms of some set of mechanisms or capacities they possess that provides them some measure of control over the effects of the environment on them. Then, when we individuate them as decision makers, we understand them as persisting as coherent decision makers in virtue of the way these capacities allow them to adjust to their environments in this adaptive fashion. In Simon's later language, in fact, this adaptation is associated with the idea of homeostasis and the view that a decision maker's capacity to respond to its environment is broadly a matter of acting on or controlling feedback from the environment (Simon 1962, 467). On this view, decision makers – and individuals – are relatively distinct and independent beings precisely in virtue of being able to respond to change. That is, in identity terms it is how we understand their reidentification through an account of adaptation and adjustment that explains their individuation.

Much more needs to be said to fill out these ideas, particularly in connection with an issue Simon turns to later, namely, just how a decision maker's capacities might operate in complex systems (Simon 1962). However, we can still review his basic view. Specifically, Simon's idea of a decision maker's individuality deriving from its stabilizing mechanisms or inherent capacities is an idea of feedback principles that reinforce some set of identifying characteristics it possesses. In effect, rather than suppose adjustment and adaptation undermine individuation, Simon rather supposes they produce it. Interaction with the environment is then determined by how the decision maker's feedback control system directs a path of adjustment and adaptation to that environment. This basic idea came out of Simon's satisficing thinking about adaptive decision making, but there were likely other sources as well. Thus, it seems fair to say that one was his early acquaintance with the mathematical idea of a self-reproducing system, encountered when he "was dragooned as discussant of [John] von Neumann's 1950 address to the Econometrics Society ... entitled 'The Theory of Automata'" (Mirowski 2002, 459). Simon demurred from von Neumann's computer-brain views, but the latter's concept of automata as self-reproducing systems, as well as much of the new postwar thinking about cybernetic systems, broadly fit Simon's own thinking about adaptation. Beyond this, Simon was likely also well aware of the general development of thinking at the time about other types of self-organizing systems. Thinking about self-organizing systems had received considerable impetus during World War II in the development of self-adjusting or servo-mechanistic weapons systems – such as in aircraft gun sight adjustment systems for high-speed aerial combat (Klein 1998). After the war, the engineering of self-stabilizing systems also expanded exponentially in the technology of rocket and missile guidance systems.[2] So in fact, Simon's thinking was really more central to what was going on at the time than it might seem – especially compared to most postwar economists who saw things in deductive axiomatic terms.

I close this section with one last point about what feedback mechanisms involve that we encountered in the previous chapter and that points forward to the balance of this one. Ross, recall, also employs the feedback idea and uses it specifically in a reflexive way when he argues that collections of neural selves generate whole individual self-narratives. I take this point to be central to understanding feedback mechanisms in intentional agents in that when they succeed in adapting to their environments by using environmental feedback, they do so by reflexively revising their past strategies that effectively act as summary accounts of themselves. In effect, the latter are "working self-concepts" that are continually redeveloped to anchor and reanchor how decision makers respond to successive choice situations. Adaptation and feedback, then, as Simon intuited in his attention to the persistence of the decision maker, imply some sort reflexivity, and this presupposes some sort of self-concept. This latter idea, the following sections argue, underlies evolutionary individual conceptions that develop Simon's view in terms of the claim that individuals have a capacity to learn. Because learning in any substantive sense implies that individuals can say when they learn, "*I* didn't know that; now *I* do," it provides the grounds for saying that evolutionary conceptions treat individuals as reidentifiably distinct and independent. Next up, then, is market experimentalist Vernon Smith's view of individuals as able to adapt and learn in a particular type of institutional setting: the market.

7.3 Ecological Rationality: Smith's Extension

Smith's market experimentalism is based on his conception of a microeconomic system as being made up of an environment and an institution (Smith

---

[2] See Klein (1999) for the extension of the logic of control engineering technologies to economic stabilization policies.

1982). He has used this framework to show how rationality is manifested in individuals in their market interaction with one another, rather than as isolated individuals. The idea that individuals are rational per se is a product of what he terms constructivist rationality. The idea that individuals are rational in markets is the result of Smith pairing constructivist rationality with an ecological rationality, together with his critique of the notion that the former should be thought the sole dimension of rationality appropriate to economics. Combining the two forms of rationality to explain markets and experiments in this way is a late career project of Smith's, outlined in his Nobel lecture (2002), and then stated more fully in his *Rationality in Economics: Constructivist and Ecological Forms* (2008), which it seems fair to say involved an effort on his part to provide a broader interpretive framework for his life's research. We might say that through his connection to Gigerenzer, who is particularly responsible for developing the idea of ecological rationality emphasizing Simon's thinking, Smith rediscovered Simon, or at least discovered what he found relevant in Simon's thinking to his own work when he adopted ecological rationality as a key part of the organizing frame for his market experimentalism.[3] I use this connection to reconstruct the contribution I believe Smith thereby makes to an evolutionary conception of the individual, one that goes beyond Simon's pure feedback idea; though I do not argue that Smith sees himself as explicitly contributing to this particular understanding. Indeed, Smith is considerably more concerned with the market as an institution, and so his understanding of the individual as I describe it should rather be seen as a by-product of this primary concern.

Constructivist rationality, then, is rationality in the traditional sense: conscious, deliberative, and deductive – in a word, Cartesian. However Smith argues, constructivist rationality cannot fully explain much of human decision making or the emergence and nature of human institutions. The philosophy that it can, which he calls constructivism,

uses reason deliberatively to create rules of action, and to design human socioeconomic institutions that yield outcomes deemed preferable.... Although constructivism is one of the crowning achievements of the human intellect, it is important to be sensitive to the fact that human institutions and most decision making are not guided only or primarily by constructivism. Emergent arrangements, even if

---

[3] Smith co-contributed to Gigerenzer and Selten (2001) in McCabe and Smith (2001), and Gigerenzer made six contributions to Plott and Smith's *Handbook of Experimental Economic Results, Volume 1* (2008). In 2008, Smith also agreed to become co-director of Gigerenzer's Adaptive Behavior and Cognition (ABC) research group at the Max Planck Institute for Human Development in Berlin.

initially constructivist in form, must have fitness properties that take account of opportunity costs and environmental challenges invisible to our modeling efforts. (Smith 2008, 31–2)

"Emergent arrangements" moreover have their "fitness properties," Smith believes, as did Simon, because they have an important characteristic of natural systems – the capacity to be self-regulating. In Simon's words quoted as an epigraph by Smith,

We have become accustomed to the idea that a natural system like the human body or an ecosystem regulates itself. To explain the regulation, we look for feedback loops rather than a central planning and directing body. But somehow our intuitions about self-regulation do not carry over to the artificial systems of human society. (Simon 1981/1996, 33; quoted in Smith 2008, vi)

Smith shares this complaint. The long history of constructivist thinking about rationality and social order, he argues, has blinded us to the self-regulating properties of socioeconomic institutions. As these properties are important to explaining how social systems operate, we ought to develop an understanding of their specific form of rationality, an ecological rationality, in which the "behavior of an individual, a market, an institution, or other social system ... is adapted to the structure of its environment" (Smith 2008, 36). This idea goes back to Simon's early influential critique of standard rationality theory. It also links up with Smith's conviction that Hayek employed a concept of ecological rationality (ibid., e.g., 9–10). Smith's later adoption of the idea enables him to argue that constructivist and ecological rationality operate in tandem in social systems. I argue that this has significant implications for how we explain individual decision making.

Psychologists, Smith goes on, have appreciated the limitations of constructivist rationality since the 1970s. At the same time, in general their experimental practice typically tests individual decision making in nonmarket contexts, operates in laboratory settings that are highly artificial institutionally speaking, and thus minimizes or ignores institutionally motivated reward behavior in which monetary stakes are involved. They accordingly judge institutional behavior, in markets in particular, from the perspective of experiments on individuals and infer from their experimental results that "[m]arkets cannot be rational if agents are not fully rational in the sense in which we have modeled it as theorists" (ibid., 157). However, Smith argues, "this is an inference based on how the theorist, not the subject, models decision problems, and it ignores the demonstrated capacity of subjects to find equilibrium outcomes by repeat interactions in market experiments with no cognitive awareness of this capacity" (ibid.). That is, markets and the decision making in them may be ecologically rational if not rational in the constructivist sense, because the institutional setting provides clues absent from experimental decision-making contexts that emphasize individuals per se. Better then not to focus exclusively on whether experimental subjects reason in the traditional manner, and rather focus on how their decision-making may be reasonable by the standard of the successful functioning of socioeconomic institutions, in particular for Smith in markets. Indeed, the evidence from many market-based experiments dating back many years, he believes, is that competitive equilibria (CE) do not require that agents have complete or "perfect" information about the equations defining competitive equilibria or common knowledge about the strategies of other agents, both components of a traditional constructivist approach to decision making. The "idea that agents need complete information," Smith thus concludes, seems to be

derived from introspective error: As theorists, we need complete information to calculate the CE. But this is not a theory of how information or its absence causes agent behavior to yield, or fail to yield, a CE. It is simply an unmotivated statement declaring, without evidence, that every agent is a constructivist in exactly the same way as we are as theorists. And the claim that it is "as if" agents had complete information helps not a whit to understand the wellsprings of behavior. (Smith 2008, 62)

If individuals are not complete information agents, how are we to conceive of them? For Smith, the answer lies in understanding what kind of decision making it is that agents actually engage in according to the environments they occupy.

Consider what is involved in saying that individuals somehow go through a process of decision making that enables them to ultimately find their way to CE. Because we do not understand how they do this, and because they do not appear to rely on the kinds of information resources theorists attribute to them in Cartesian constructivist terms, from an ecological rationality perspective we might accordingly just say that they have some capacity that enables them to engage in decision making that allows them to endure as decision-making agents through to achieving CE. Smith points to just such a view, I argue, when he draws special attention to the work of Roy Radner and his co-researchers, who model success in going through decision-making processes as a simple matter of survival (ibid., 169–73.). The issue of survival gets at the fundamental requirements of life, satisfaction of which we may say comes down to having certain capacities whose exercise may help achieve it. Radner and his co-researchers in fact emphasize that decision making guided by survival concerns (they consider firms) in a world of uncertainty and incomplete markets readily produces behavior at odds with what utility and profit maximization (and constructivist rationality) predict (cf., Radner 1997; Dutta and Radner 1999). For example, when firms have diverse technologies and behaviors but nonetheless offer the same rate of return to investors, firms that have better technologies earn rents they use to maintain survival, such that in the long run the population of firms includes only "survivalist" firms. Their technology practices in effect summarize their special capacity for survival, and they are thus ecologically rational in their exercise of this special capacity. For Smith, this argument gets at the heart of what is missing from constructivist rationality: a capacity the decision maker has to adapt to environments that are likely changing, and that thus render constructivist maximizing rationality ineffective.

To emphasize adaptation and having a survival motive, however, is not to say that individual behavior is blindly driven by forces independent of socioeconomic institutions. Rather on Smith's view, the nature of these institutions, particularly market institutions, determines what particular individual decision making is in fact adaptive and ecologically rational. That is, Smith, as Simon, employs a feedback principle in his conception of individuals in that what individuals are depends on the capacities they exercise in interacting with specific socioeconomic institutional environments. Further, Smith's idea that individuals go through a process that preserves their status as decision-making agents, a process likened to survival, implies that their autonomy as individuals derives directly from their dynamic interaction with others in the space of institutions – thus implying a dynamic principle of autonomy as associated previously with Simon's early thinking. In outline, the specifics of his view with respect to market institutions in particular are essentially as follows.

Market institutions define the language of trade and state the rules providing algorithms that carry agent messages into outcomes. Based on these rules, the social brains of subject agents provide algorithms that process incoming market-trading information, and respond with messages that over time converge to equilibrium outcomes best for the individual and the group. What we observe is the outcome of an interaction between the institutional and mental algorithms. (Smith 2008, 317)

Institutional arrangements and individual behaviors – indeed individual autonomy – are thus seen as emergent upon this dynamic of interaction. We may rationally reconstruct in traditional constructivist fashion what is ecologically rational for individuals and institutions, but the essentially "trial-and error" nature of this evolutionary process and the "home- and socially-grown" character of "the rules of action, traditions, and moral principles" it involves ultimately preclude their analysis in fully constructivist terms (ibid., 322). Individuals are separate and distinct beings, then, not by assumption but as a result of the way they adapt and adjust over time in interaction with others in concrete social institutional settings – for Smith, especially market settings.

Of course, there is much in this Smithian sketch of an evolutionary conception of the individual that is left unexplained. On the one hand, the socioeconomic institutions he examines, namely, markets, are still described in quite abstract terms – the language of bids and offers, the order in which agents move, the rules under which messages become contracts, and so forth (Smith 1989) – so that is hard to see how they could be associated with any particular conception of the individual. Indeed, in contrast to the relational conceptions of the individual discussed in the previous chapter, there is no fine-grained account of how interaction with others might explain individuals' relative autonomy. On the other hand, whereas Smith follows Simon in explaining individuals as adaptive in terms of a dynamic feedback principle, there is little more in his analysis that explains how this principle actually stabilizes individuals as individuals – the larger idea that they might be self-organizing as autonomous beings. In the following section, then, I look at what I regard as another evolutionary conception of individuals – Ken Binmore's – that is more specific about the capacities individuals have that enable them to adapt to changing circumstances, and that moreover shares a number of the same underlying theoretical commitments of Simon and Smith.

7.4 Binmore: Playing the "Game of Life"

Much as Smith criticizes constructivist rationality as Cartesian, Binmore rejects what he characterizes as rationalist approaches to philosophy (especially moral philosophy) from Plato through Descartes and Kant (Binmore 2005b, 37–45). Binmore is a mathematician and developer of evolutionary game theory, and his early formal models of evolutionary games apply to types of individuals rather than single individuals. However, his more recent work on game theory, justice, and the social contract addresses the nature of single individuals (Binmore 2005a, 2006). There, he seeks to explain the emergence of social norms without appealing to abstract ethical principles and does so by making a number of anthropological claims about human beings, primitive society, and the origins of social interaction. In particular, he argues that cooperative norms such as fairness as reciprocity or reciprocal altruism (sharing in response to sharing) have natural origins in the evolution of close-knit kin groups in early human societies, and that this principle has taken on a variety of different forms in modern societies when extended to nonkin according to these societies' various cultural histories. He argues that social interaction can be broadly represented as a "game of life" modeled as an indefinitely repeated game that can accordingly be understood in terms of game theory's folk theorem (thus aptly named). The multiplicity of solutions the folk theorem permits in the game of life then creates a role for culture in which an evolutionary ancestral logic nonetheless still acts as an equilibrium selection device. Fairness as reciprocity remains the main historical solution in human interaction, because it produces a stable equilibrium in the sense of one that brings the pursuit of advantage in evolutionary competition to a halt. In Nash terms, it is a state of affairs in which none can do better given what all others are doing.

One of Binmore's goals is to reinterpret John Rawls' justice as fairness view (Rawls 1971) along Humean lines rather than Rawls' Kantian ones. But Binmore, like Smith, is also motivated by a critical view of the recent challenge to the standard *Homo economicus* conception of the individual from behavioral economics. Behavioral economics, we saw, seeks to revise the traditional utility function representation of *Homo economicus* in order to introduce greater realism into economics. That realism is seen to result from experimental research in cognitive psychology thought to produce better explanations of individual motivation than provided by the standard rationality view. One important strand in this literature, we have seen, involves the introduction of social preferences into the utility function. As discussed in Chapter 4, experimental research employing these expanded utility functions is then tested in ultimatum games, public goods games, trust games, and so forth. One of the main findings is that individuals are motivated by other-regarding sentiments more often than seems consistent with the standard *Homo economicus* representation of the individual as essentially a selfish being. The inference drawn from this is that the *Homo economicus* conception is an incorrect representation of the individual (cf. Henrich et al., 2004, 2005; Henrich 2006).

However, both Smith and Binmore regard the selfishness characterization of *Homo economicus* as a red herring, because, in their view, that conception already allows individuals to have both other-regarding and self-regarding motives and only requires that they make consistent choices (Smith 2008; Binmore 2005b). Smith sees the problem with the social preferences critique as deriving from its testing individual decision making in nonmarket contexts that minimize or ignore reward-motivated behavior. He argues that because market experiments show competitive equilibria widely obtain, the idea that individuals are generally motivated by other-regarding motives cannot be supported. Binmore has a related view of what is wrong with the social preferences literature that derives from his own criticism of its empirical practice, and that tells us something about his conception of individuals. Games played in the laboratory, he tells us, need to be understood from the perspective of games played in real life. That is, experimental subjects make the choices they do in the laboratory, because they are the choices they would make in real life in similar situations. Thus, it is no surprise to him that people cooperate in single-play games in the laboratory, because in real life there are many social norms that involve cooperation that people regularly apply in single-interaction situations. However, this does not imply individuals are inspired by the motive to cooperate, because we cannot rule out that these social norms are not best explained as reciprocal altruism with its basis in self-regarding behavior. Rather, to determine whether people are inspired to cooperate or are closer in nature to the traditional *Homo economicus* conception, we need to see whether we can say for experimental subjects that "the relevant real-life game is an *indefinitely repeated* game, for which the folk theorem tells us that cooperation can be sustained as a Nash equilibrium by strategies that punish anyone who defects" (Binmore 2006, 85). This, Smith and market experimentalists would argue, requires that experiments are clearly explained to experimental subjects, those subjects are adequately incentivized, and they have time for trial-and-error learning (ibid., 82). Behavioralists, Binmore charges, construct their experiments in such a way that reciprocally altruist social norms drawn from the games of real life kick in, but not in such a way as to determine whether their underlying basis lies in Nash behavior.[4]

My goal here, however, is not to arbitrate this dispute or even determine the character of cooperative behavior in human life – something that both sides agree exists but disagree about philosophically and anthropologically in terms of its interpretation and extent. Rather, the goal is to get at the conception of the individual implicit in Binmore's reasoning. The point immediately in contention concerns adequate incentives for experimental subjects in trial-and-error learning. The important thing about an emphasis on trial-and-error learning is that it essentially makes a process of adjustment and change part of the individual conception. Of course, what learning is and what role it plays in the constitution of the individual are difficult questions.

---

[4] Also see Binmore and Avner Shaked's (2009) recent criticism of behavioral economics' experimental practice.

Binmore, however, simplifies these questions by explaining learning strictly in terms of evolutionary forces – as a matter of ultimate causation – and not in terms of psychological behaviors – or as a matter of proximate causation (Binmore 2005b, 6).[5] This allows him to make a straightforward argument about the evolutionary fitness of fairness as reciprocity in that he can say that our ability to learn is essentially hard-wired into our natures, so that we respond to learning opportunities in a highly determinate and predictable manner. Let us see, then, what this all means in terms of his thinking about the nature of the individual.

A main point of Binmore's attack on the social preferences literature lies in his rejection of utility function reasoning and its goal of generating more realistic utility functions. A genuinely realistic view of individual behavior, he argues, needs to emphasize how people adapt to new circumstances, not how they act on given sets of preferences.

We know that in most games, subjects' behavior changes over time as they adapt to a new game. In such games, we therefore cannot use a utility function fitted to the behavior of inexperienced subjects in order to predict their future behavior even in the same game. (ibid., 86)

People's behavior changes as they learn how to adapt to new games, so learning both produces new knowledge and also changes the individual. This means that if we want to understand the real game of life rather than artificial laboratory games, what we need to do is to operate with a conception of individuals that makes change central to what they are. For Binmore, this begins with explaining learning as a human capacity:

My own view is that we waste our time trying to work out what utility function inexperienced subjects are maximizing, because it is not useful to model them as maximizing anything at all. Economics is not the answer to everything, because we do not automatically behave rationally when confronted with novel problems. Insofar as we ever behave rationally, it is largely because we have the capacity to learn. (ibid., 87)

Rationality is better understood as involving exercising a "capacity to learn." What does it mean to say people have a capacity of this kind? What does specifically referring to a capacity add to the story? There seem to be two main implications, the first of which requires that we further develop the idea of what learning is, and the second of which requires we emphasize Binmore's idea of empathetic identification.

---

[5] Mayr (1961) is the source of this important distinction. For its further development, see Vromen (2009).

First, learning of course can be taken to simply involve information collection, as in standard economics. On that view, because individuals' preferences are given, learning does not have any impact on what the individual is. However, Binmore has a stronger meaning of learning in mind in which people adjust to what is learned. Taking learning to be a capacity involves, not only being able to acquire information, but also being able to change one's preferences in response to the information one acquires. We could of course suppose this all happens entirely unconsciously. However, I argue that to say learning is occurring requires that people are able to take stock of the effects that learning has on them. Learning is generally agreed to be something more than just reacting differently to changing circumstances. It involves recognizing that circumstances have changed, and this recognition is from the perspective of the learner. When learning occurs, someone has to be able to say, "*I* didn't know that; now *I* do." What this "*I*" refers to is obviously quite open, but following Ross's line of thinking it can still be characterized as a "working self-concept," that is, an anchor to learning that is continually being repositioned. Thus, when we say learning is a capacity, we also need to say that part of this capacity is people being able to recognize and represent themselves with open-ended self-concepts.

This takes the evolutionary understanding of individuals elicited thus far from Simon and Smith a clear step further. Simon treats being able to successfully respond to one's environment as pointing toward "persistence in behavior" (1955, 122). Smith sees people as having a "demonstrated capacity" to respond and adapt in their interaction with others (2008, 157). However, when we think of this capacity in Binmore's terms as specifically involving learning, we are able to locate all this in the conception of an agent continually able to exercise this capacity to adapt and adjust in a reflexive way. This then gives us the fundamentals of an evolutionary individual conception. I linked this conception at the beginning of this chapter to the idea that individuals might be thought of as self-organizing systems. The argument here develops that idea from the principle that an individual's behavioral response to the environment reinforces rather than undermines individuality to the conclusion that the individual has some sort of enduring identity in continually being a learner. There is still considerable ambiguity about what this latter conclusion implies. Binmore adds further content to it, however, in his discussion of empathetic identification.

Second, then, Binmore also assumes that people have a second key capacity: a capacity to identify empathetically with one another. His general argument is that pursuit of evolutionary advantage comes to a halt when individuals find themselves in circumstances that none believe they can improve upon. A social norm then emerges in which individuals reciprocally cooperate. How do individuals actually discover what social norms apply in specific circumstances? In Nash terms, what one learns is not just what one ought to do oneself to reciprocally cooperate, but also what others expect one to do in that regard. Then one also comes to see oneself in terms of the conception others have of oneself, meaning that one's self-concept is not just a product of one's own learning, but a product of one's "own" learning as influenced by others. Binmore explains this all in terms of empathetic preferences, which are hypothetical preferences we have when we imagine what we would prefer were we to identify with someone else (ibid., 113–116). Consider what is involved. Empathizing with another person involves somehow putting oneself in their place and imagining seeing things as they would. That includes seeing oneself as they would. Thus, the capacity to empathetically identify with others in social interaction means that one's self-concept is an object for oneself in some degree detached from one's own perception of it. On this view, then, not only do individuals operate with self-concepts that are essentially dynamic, but these self-concepts are also reflexively constructed in individuals' interaction with others in the process that determines social norms. This larger self-concept idea accordingly combines the two natural capacities Binmore attributes to people (learning and empathy) and makes his self-organizing conception of the individual not only an evolutionary but also a relational one.

I close this section, then, by returning to Binmore's grounding of his argument in terms of ultimate and not proximate causation. This means that the two important capacities he believes we have are the result of early human evolution, not cultural factors that map the subsequent history of human development. Thus, modern social norms only express our fundamental nature. This clearly limits what one can say about the processes by which this later cultural evolution occurs. By restricting his analysis to an account of early human evolution as an ultimate cause of behavior, Binmore rules out explaining behavior by such proximate causes as just how individuals learn from others or what psychological learning mechanisms might apply in particular cultural settings. Jack Vromen (2009), however, seems right to argue that cultural evolutionary processes significantly break down the distinction between early human and cultural evolution, and that proximate causes of behavior in the form of how individuals socially learn from one another, while certainly also present in early evolution, surely become fundamental in the latter. Douglass North is even more critical. He sees Binmore's position in this regard as a fundamental barrier to advancing an understanding of how people interact and evolve in the world we live in. The world we live in, he says, is non-ergodic, meaning that what happens today inescapably changes what we can do tomorrow, so that "we are continually evolving in new and novel ways" (North 2006, 102). To understand our behavior in this world, he argues, we need to pay close attention to the institutions, norms, habits, and rules we regularly rely on to negotiate our constantly changing forms of interaction with others.

How, we ought to then ask, might we use Binmore's important emphasis on learning and empathy as a basis for understanding individuals as self-organizing beings in an evolving cultural world? To address this question, the next section turns to another path of development in recent evolutionary thinking and its implications for thinking about the individual that explicitly emphasizes learning mechanisms as psychological – one also influenced by Simon – so as to be able to say more about the proximate causes of evolutionary processes: complex adaptive systems theory. This discussion adds an account of how both individuals and their forms of interaction coevolve by way of individuals learning across different dispersed sites of interaction. A full evolutionary individual conception, then, explains, not just how individuals evolve as relatively autonomous beings through their interaction with others, but how they evolve as their many forms of interaction evolve as well. To develop this idea, the next section returns briefly to Simon and his early thinking about complex systems as the framework in which he explained the evolution of interaction between individuals. The discussion then goes on to Arthur's complex adaptive systems view as a further development of this understanding, and as one that provides an expanded statement of the evolutionary-relational individual conception in which individuals and their forms of interaction coevolve.

7.5 Individuals in Complex Adaptive Systems

Simon's early thinking about evolutionary processes and "behavior in adaptive systems in terms of the concepts of feedback and homeostasis" was closely connected to his investigation of complex systems, which he defined broadly as systems "made up of a large number of parts that interact in a nonsimple way" (Simon 1962, 467, 468). His view of complex systems was that they are hierarchically composed out of weakly interrelated subsystems, each of which is in turn composed out of additional weakly interrelated subsystems, with those perhaps composed of additional interrelated subsystems, and so on until "we reach some lowest level of elementary subsystem" (ibid., 468). What counts as "elementary" in this modular world, he allowed, may be arbitrary, and depends on the purposes of our analysis. The key point was rather that complex systems are decomposable into subsystems, and this meant that "we can distinguish between the interactions *among* subsystems ... and the interactions *within* subsystems" (ibid., 473; his emphasis). More precisely, Simon focused on what he called "*nearly decomposable* systems, in which the interactions among the subsystems are weak, but not negligible" (ibid., 474; cf. Simon and Ando 1961). For example, in social systems near decomposability exists in connection with well-defined formal organizations within which interaction is stronger than between organizations. At the same time, "near" decomposability is not complete decomposability, so that interaction within a given subsystem still bears the effects of that subsystem's interaction with other subsystems. Consider, then, the implications this has for how individuals learn as they move across weakly interrelated subsystems, seen specifically as sites of interaction, such as when they move across firms, neighborhoods, social settings, and so forth.

As individuals move across different subsystems or different sites of interaction, they transfer and redevelop learning strategies developed in one site to others they enter. This is one way of explaining Simon's principle of weak interaction between subsystems. Different sites retain their relative independence in the way they encapsulate social interaction within them, but these interactive practices are influenced by those in other sites via individuals' circulation across sites. In the institutionally dense world North emphasizes, individuals can then be seen to be moving continuously across many different sites of interaction – games of life – each with their own respective forms of play and guiding social norms, rather than just continually playing one single indefinitely repeated game of life. They engage, then, in what might be called a continually dispersed interaction with one another, in which the way they play in one game in one social location is relevant but not definitive in determining the way they play another game in another social location. Binmore's evolutionary individual conception, we saw, explains individuals' learning evolution in modern social systems as depending on their ability to apply an ancestral fairness norm to new, culturally evolved forms of interaction. When we now open the door to proximate causation in the way here, and see people moving across many interrelated games of life, individuals' learning evolution gets nested in whole complex systems of interaction. Then explaining how individuals evolve as relatively autonomous beings through learning in interaction with others requires that we add in the effects of this systemic evolution, both in the changing character of subsystems and in the whole they make up, so as to explain how individuals' learning and multiple forms of interaction coevolve.

A complexity theory-evolutionary account of agent behavior, generally referred to as agent-based modeling, involves an account of the dynamic coevolution of individuals and their forms of interaction that emphasizes the proximate causes of individual behavior in the form of belief and expectation formation in interactive settings.[6] Agent-based modeling starts from the view that agents or individuals are heterogeneous. They engage in dispersed interaction neither reconciled nor organized by any global authority (such as the traditional Walrasian auctioneer), there are a variety of cross-cutting channels and paths of influence between the different sites of their interaction, the system of interaction as a whole – called a complex adaptive system – displays perpetual novelty and out-of-equilibrium dynamics, and this all requires individuals' continual adaptation (cf. Arthur, Durlauf, and Lane 1997). The idea of dispersed interaction can be likened to there being different games of life or social economic subsystems that involve different social norms and strategies of behavior for individuals. The idea of continual adaptation implies that individuals need to continually learn, in Binmore's terms, the social norms appropriate to games at any one site, and also how to revise how they play those games as they move across sites. Arthur's specific contribution here was to develop a psychological or cognitive view of individuals operating in markets, which serves as one kind of model for this kind of playing. "Agents 'learn' which hypotheses work, and from time to time they may discard poorly performing hypotheses and generate new 'ideas' to put in their place" (Arthur 1994, 407; cf. Arthur 1995). There are various ways in which this might be explained. Arthur notes three possibilities: individuals might draw from a bank of strategies at their disposal, they can be thought to employ "genetic algorithms" (Holland 1975) that enable them to progressively search for better strategies, and they might borrow or appropriate models from others (Arthur 1994, 408). The basic point, however, is that individuals are not just learners but have a variety of possible learning methods, and these methods evolve as their forms of interaction change. Indeed, we can see individuals as complex adaptive

---

[6] The literature on agent-based modeling is immense and rapidly expanding. One source lies in von Neumann's conception of agents as automata or self-reproducing machines combined with mathematician Stanislaw Ulam's idea that this might be represented in a cellular or grid format. Mathematician John Conway's simplified "game of life" significantly influenced the development of agent-based modeling across many sciences (cf. Garner 1970). An important early application to economics is Schelling's residential segregation checkerboard model (Schelling 1969, 1971). Much of the early development of complexity reasoning with respect to economics came out of the Santa Fe Institute where economists and physicists debated the methods of economics (cf. Arthur, Durlauf, and Lane 1997). Also see Holland (1995), Axelrod (1997), Tesfatsion (2006), and Rosser (2009).

systems themselves. Individuals are made up of different interactive learning methods or subsystems whose (weak) interaction affects each learning method, which, put together, explain the adaptive evolutionary development of the individual.

Consider, then, how these points allow us to extend Binmore's evolutionary individual conception. On his view, first, individuals have the capacity to learn, implying that we can ascribe self-concepts to them, and second, they have the capacity to empathize with others in the sense of seeing things from their point of view, implying that their self-concepts are developed in interaction with other individuals. In a complex adaptive systems framework with multiple interrelated sites of dispersed interaction, individuals also then need, first, self-concepts that are seen explicitly as revisable, meaning that this need to revise their self-concepts is part of individuals' understanding of them; and second, individuals need self-concepts that develop, not just in interaction with other specific individuals, but also with changes in the forms of social interaction. The first point deepens the meaning of learning, because individuals not only model strategies in different ways according to the kind of interaction they encounter but also learn to model their self-concepts in different ways. In effect, they develop a richer understanding of the logic of having a self-concept in which this includes an awareness of how it changes in a history of interaction with others. The second point arguably deepens the basis for empathy, because, in contrast to Binmore's idea that cultural evolution simply extends sympathy from kin to nonkin – an essentially affective basis for empathy – here empathy now requires also that individuals' have fairly well-developed beliefs and understanding about how they see themselves interacting with others. Essentially, they need to develop "theories" about the character and nature of their interaction with others, and this goes hand in hand with the development of their "theories" about their working self-concepts.

It should be emphasized that an important step in the development of agent-based modeling methods in the social sciences that underlies this larger view of learning and interaction is the incorporation of memory capacities in agents. It may seem odd that memory – clearly an important dimension of our ordinary understanding of individuals – has made no significant appearance in the discussion thus far. This is due, it should be clear, to the framing of thinking about individuals in most of the views discussed previously in largely static terms and in terms of given preferences. In any event, whereas there are many ways that the extent, character, and depreciation of memory can be modeled in connection with different types of interaction, it seems that some form of memory needs to be assumed to give realistic accounts of interactive behavior. Indeed, memory is especially important to the meaning of an evolutionary conception of individuals as beings able to adapt to changing circumstances and revise their behavior, because without memory it is hard to imagine how they would judge that circumstances have changed. Extending this to the idea that individuals have self-concepts, then, includes individuals' past selves in what they remember. In effect, the prospective or forward-looking side of individuals needs to be complemented with a retrospective or backward-looking one as well. If we combine these two dimensions of individuals' self-concepts, we have a fuller idea of the temporal structure of an individual's self-narrative. People project their self-concepts in interaction with others across multiple sites of interaction, taking into account their memory of themselves in past interaction.

The agent-based modeling approach to individuals' adaptation to changing circumstances thus enlarges the evolutionary individual conception developed in the previous sections of this chapter by further developing the way in which reflexivity operates in agents characterized as subjective or intentional. Essentially, the argument is that more complex accounts of social interaction as dispersed and evolving require a stronger explanation of how individuals account for how their own identities undergo change. This begins to tell us how to deal with the paradoxical idea that an individual persists and changes at the same time. Individuals' particular self-concepts indeed change, but in this larger view they also can be argued to have a capacity to understand the change in those self-concepts, depending on how we explain learning, empathy, and memory. It is this capacity to understand their self-concepts that provides people an identity through change; it might thus be called a capacity to manage one's personal identity.

7.6 From an Evolutionary-Complexity Individual Conception to a Social Conception

The ecological-adaptive perspective of the evolutionary individual conception is clearly quite removed from the traditional maximizing representation of the individual. The latter makes the constitution of the individual exogenous to social economic processes, and does not succeed in showing how individuals function as relatively distinct and autonomous beings. The former makes the constitution of the individual endogenous to social economic processes, but precludes their disappearing or fragmenting as individuals by arguing that interaction reinforces rather than undermines individuality. Thus, it addresses the supra-personal bound on single-individual explanations, mapping out an account of how people are individual and social at the same time. Though the self-organizing idea that underlies this reconstruction of the individual comes from outside economics and social science at the beginning of the postwar period, it takes on a form particularly appropriate to them when it gets explained in terms of the idea of the capacities of agents and individuals. The idea of a capacity, clearly, is not an important part of preference-based thinking about individuals understood as beings only having the single reactive capacity to respond to changes in price and income signals. The conclusion that follows from this is that the standard framework is not adequate to a dynamic analysis of economies and individuals, and that, as recommended by those discussed in this chapter, the utility function representation of individuals ought therefore be abandoned.

The way forward on this alternative basis, however, is hardly simple, and there are many aspects of the general explanation put forward here that can be disputed. Endogenizing individuality to social economic processes – the problem of negotiating the supra-personal bound on single-individual explanations – threatens to so vastly complicate the individual conception as to cause us to lose our grip on it altogether. In terms of what this chapter has argued, a serious problem arises in connection with the reasonable possibility that individuals' capacities might coevolve together with their forms of interaction. If this were the case, why should we suppose that the ones distinguished thus far – learning, empathy, memory, and (perhaps) personal identity – continue to function in such a way as to allow us to characterize individuals as *self*-organizing? Surely much more needs to be said on this score if we are to understand individuals to be relatively autonomous and enduring in connection with the capacities they possess. Thus, the chapter that follows makes the first of three further steps in the chapters of Part 3 of this book that jointly seek to build up this general idea of individuals as self-organizing by investigating what is involved in treating individuals as collections of capacities – or capabilities.

PART 3

SOCIALLY EMBEDDED INDIVIDUALS

EIGHT

Evolution and Capabilities

Human Heterogeneity

Human beings are thoroughly diverse.

(Sen 1992, 1)

[M]ost of what is relevant and interesting in economic life has to do with the inter-action and coordination of ensembles of heterogeneous economic actors ...

(Colander et al. 2009, 9)

8.1 From Capacities to Capabilities

The evolutionary, or evolutionary-relational, individual conception developed in the previous chapter explains how individuals and their forms of interaction coevolve according to a line of thinking that draws on Simon's feedback idea, finds development in the context of markets in Smith, is explained in terms of human capacities by Binmore, and is applied across multiple interrelated sites of interaction by Arthur. I argued that this explanation relies on the view that human beings self-organize themselves through the exercise of certain basic capacities. However, it seems fair to say that people's capacities are not given and unchanging, but they develop or coevolve together with their forms of interaction. How would this then affect this evolutionary understanding of individuals? I investigate this issue in this chapter, and to do so replace the concept of capacities with that of capabilities. I use the capabilities concept because representing individu-als in terms of whole arrays of capabilities gives a thicker account of them in terms of what they are and what they can do, and because the capa-bilities concept has been developed more extensively in recent economics in connection with thinking about the nature of individuals, particularly by Amartya Sen in his effort to redevelop the foundations of norma-tive evaluation in economics. Accordingly, whereas the previous chapter explained individuals' makeup in terms of their having certain basic human capacities, this chapter explains their makeup in terms of their being able to develop whole sets of capabilities. Individuals are collections of capabilities. I label this the capabilities conception of the individual (cf. Davis 2009c) and evaluate it here as a further development of the evolutionary-relational individual conception.[1]

This chapter and the two following examine the idea of individuals as socially embedded. Relational conceptions of individuals are also social conceptions, but they tend to emphasize direct interaction almost exclusively as the way to get beyond asocial atomism. The more indirect social effects that institutions and social structures, conventions and customs, and social practices have on individuals need to be included beyond interaction if we are to account for a full range of social influences on individuals. That these effects have not been generally integrated into individual conceptions in economics, it seems fair to say, is due to the fact that they make explaining how people can be social and individual at the same time even more difficult than accommodating interaction. This, however, points us toward one potential advantage of using the capabilities concept. On the one hand, it is difficult to not think of people's capabilities as social in character, because their exercise depends in so many ways on how society is organized; on the other hand, we can surely also say that people individually possess capabilities. In contrast, capacities are often seen as natural endowments, as in Binmore's argument. Thus, a capabilities conception of the individual in principle offers, not only a way of "thickening" our understanding of people's capacities in the evolutionary-relational argument of the previous chapter, but also a way of producing an expanded understanding of how social life affects individuality.

Characterizing individuals as collections of capabilities, however, also opens the door to the possibility that individuals are sets of multiple selves and are not single unified beings. In Part 1 on the different strategies for revising the utility function approach to explaining individuals, one way in which this problem arose was in connection with individuals having multiple social identities. However having social identities also has to be regarded as one important type of capability, and so because people have multiple social identities associated with the multiple ways they interact with

---

[1] The capabilities concept also has been applied to firms and organizations as the idea of dynamic or organizational capabilities (cf. Nelson and Winter 1982; Winter 1990) and is now used to analyze strategy in business organizations particularly in connection with resource-based theories of firms: "A *dynamic capability* is the capacity of an organization to purposefully create, extend, or modify its resource base" (Helfat et al. 2007).

others, this problem is particularly immediate to a capabilities approach to explaining individuals (Davis 2007b, 2009c). A possible solution to it, outlined in the previous chapter, lies in the emphasis the evolutionary conception places on individuals as self-organizing. There, it was argued that people develop working self-concepts in their changing interaction with others, which reinforce rather than undermine individuality. If people are now seen as collections of capabilities, do they develop their capabilities in such a way that they can be said to function as self-organizing beings? Or is personal capability development just as likely to undermine individuality, in that people are pulled in different directions by the many social identities they accumulate?

I address these questions by first examining the foundations of Sen's thinking about individual capability development and then comparing what this implies about individuals as self-organizing to what social psychologists have had to say about people having self-concepts, especially when they are understood as working self-concepts. Then I look at how the philosopher Pierre Livet has used Sen's capability approach to explain how capability development relates to personal identity, in which that idea is understood very much in the ways social psychologists understand the working self-concept idea. Finally, I return to a topic introduced in Chapter 6, the idea of a self-narrative, to look more closely at how people might construct personal identities for themselves in the form of autobiographies. The conclusion of the chapter is that a capabilities conception of the individual does provide an account of people as unified individuals, but their success in exercising the special capability on which this depends – a capability to construct their own personal identities as self-narratives – is contingent on the ways in which societies promote the well-being of people as individuals.

In Section 8.2, I discuss Sen's thinking about capability development in terms of the distinction he makes between elementary and complex capabilities in order to say how individuals might be seen to evolve as collections of capabilities. Section 8.3 turns to the idea of a working self-concept and reviews the state of thinking about it in social psychology. Section 8.4 discusses how, from Livet's perspective, people maintain something akin to personal identities despite sometimes reversing their capability development pathways. Section 8.5 looks at two philosophers' accounts of how individuals' self-narratives function autobiographically: Marya Schechtman's and Daniel Dennett's. Section 8.6 draws together the chapter's conclusions and introduces the topic of the following chapter.

8.2 Sen on Capabilities and Capability Development

Sen's first main distinction is between capabilities and functionings. "*Functionings* represent parts of the state of a person – in particular the various things that he or she manages to do or be in leading a life" (Sen 1993, 31). Indeed, practically anything we can say about people in connection with distinctively human activities and states of being counts as a functioning. Functionings can range from things that are socially significant, such as being in good health or being employed, to things that are comparatively inconsequential, such as having a particular hobby or remembering childhood experiences. Functionings also comprehend activities believed both socially desirable and undesirable, such as doing someone a favor or committing a crime. So thinking in terms of capabilities takes us considerably beyond learning and empathy, which might now be said to comprehend categories of capabilities with many variants. This broadly follows Aristotle in the method of anthropologically characterizing human life through a technique of cataloguing (Aristotle's parallel concept is *ergon*, or the function or task of something), though Aristotle was more parsimonious in terms of what he included and is often understood to have thought that there exists a unique objective list of central human functionings – an idea Sen rejects with his larger canvas (ibid., 46–9; Nussbaum 1988, 152; Crespo 2008). Capabilities, then, are defined relative to functionings. "The *capability* of a person reflects the alternative combinations of functionings the person can achieve, and from which he or she can choose one collection" (Sen 1993, 31). More fully:

The "capability set" would consist of the alternative functioning vectors that she can choose from. While the combination of a person's functionings reflects her actual *achievements*, the capability set represents the *freedom* to achieve: the alternative functioning combinations from which this person can choose. (Sen 1999a, 75)

A second important distinction Sen makes cuts across functionings and capabilities. Functionings and capabilities can be either elementary or complex. Sen explains this in terms of functionings, but the distinction carries over to capabilities.

Some functionings are very elementary, such as being adequately nourished, being in good health, etc., and these may be strongly valued by all for obvious reasons. Others may be more complex, but still widely valued, such as achieving self-respect or being socially integrated. Individuals may ... differ a good deal from each other in the weights they attach to these different functionings – valuable though they may all be. (Sen 1993, 31)

Whereas there are many possible ways in which one might attempt to distinguish elementary and complex human activities and thus functionings, notice that Sen avoids entering into this debate by simply stating that they can be differentiated according to how people value them. Elementary functionings – and capabilities – are valued by everyone, whereas some complex functionings – and capabilities – are valued by some people and others are valued by other people. It seems fair to say, then, that elementary functionings and capabilities are strongly associated with human survival, because in most circumstances in life people value survival. In contrast, because complex functionings and capabilities are valued differently by different people, they do not seem to be associated with pure human survival. They concern all the different skills and activities that people may choose to develop to live their lives in ways they value that go beyond the questions of survival, whether they help in sustaining a particular type of livelihood or simply constitute things people wish to be able to do.[2]

This second distinction provides the basis for Sen's view of individual capability development. It also tells us something about his conception of individuals. In the first instance, then, people develop their elementary capabilities to be able to sustain themselves as individuals. As elementary capabilities are valued by all, in this respect people are fairly similar. In the second instance, people go on to also develop complex capabilities. It is true that people are also similar in that they all seek to develop complex capabilities, but to say just this misses an important point. Because people differ in what they value, they elect different complex capabilities, and in this respect they are quite different. Note, then, that from the perspective of individual capability development overall, should people be so fortunate that their concern with achieving elementary capabilities diminishes over their lifetimes, the share of complex capabilities in their makeups would tend to rise. Then they would not only increasingly be made up of

---

[2] Sen also frames the distinction between elementary and complex functionings in terms of the economic development process as a whole:

In the context of some types of social analysis, for example, in dealing with extreme poverty in developing economies, we may be able to go a fairly long distance with a relatively small number of centrally important functionings and the corresponding basic capabilities (e.g., the ability to be well nourished and well sheltered, the capability of escaping avoidable morbidity and premature mortality, and so for). In other contexts, including more general problems of economic development, the list may have to be much longer and much more diverse. (Sen 1993, 31)

Of course, "survival" has many social dimensions, and its requirements vary across societies, so that where the line falls between having elementary and complex capabilities is subject to debate.

heterogeneous collections of capabilities but would also become increasingly different from one another. We can explain this as a matter of their capability sets becoming increasingly incommensurable. Whereas sets of elementary capabilities tend to be relatively commensurable, sets of complex capabilities possess a high degree of incommensurability. Sen's view of capability development – based on the view that people value things differently – thus makes a principle of human heterogeneity. Indeed, when we get beyond elementary capabilities: "Human beings are thoroughly diverse" (Sen 1992, 1).[3]

I take this view to have an important implication for how we understand the representation of individuals as developing collections of capabilities. Recall from Chapter 6 Dumit's treatment of what I called third-person representations of individuals in connection with how neuroscience constructs the "normal human" individual representation. The requirement for such a representation is that people can all be taken to be essentially alike in some respect. Sen's view of capability development, however, creates a barrier to such representations. Whereas any particular complex capability a person develops could be represented as being of a type that a "normal human" could develop, this would not apply to the person understood as a whole as a heterogeneous collection of complex capabilities. This in effect leaves an important element of indeterminacy in the representation of whole individuals. Sen in fact often exploits this in his remarks on individual identity. Responding to the claim that our identities are there to be "discovered" or that we are somehow compelled to adopt certain social identities that others assign to us, his view is that people are able to reason about and choose what identities they wish to have (Sen 1999b, 2006). Basically, he claims that individuals are able to make first-person reflexive representations of themselves to counter others' third-person representations of them.[4]

This indeed is consistent with the link Sen has long emphasized between being able to reason and choose and his concept of agency freedom – a dimension of freedom he believes absent from standard economics. Agency freedom refers to "what the person is free to do and achieve in pursuit of

---

[3] Comparability between different things depends on there being a "covering value" (Chang 1997). Incommensurability exists when different things can be compared via some "covering value" but there is significant ambiguity in the application of that value (Broome 1978). On Sen's view, it becomes increasingly difficult to compare individuals as they develop complex capabilities.

[4] Robert Urquhart captures especially well what first-person representations involve when he says that our choices are fundamentally qualitative and incommensurable, and always "from a particular perspective – *from* [a] *here*" that others cannot occupy (2005, 74).

whatever goals or values *he or she regards* as important" (Sen 1985a 203; emphasis added). Taken by itself, this seems a remarkably open-ended interpretation of personal freedom, and one might well be tempted to think it too strong. Yet when agency freedom is seen as underlying complex capability development, and as being under an individual's own direction in some important degree, this seems a reasonable way of capturing the highly elective character of choices between activities that possess high degrees of incommensurability. More recently Sen has written: "Rationality is ... the discipline of subjecting one's choices – of actions as well as of objectives, values and priorities – to reasoned scrutiny" (Sen 2002, 4). Some might find "reasoned scrutiny" opaque, but a fair reply is that when dealing with incommensurables we do not have much else to go on. Note, then, three additional ways that Sen makes human heterogeneity central to his thinking about capabilities.

First, his long-standing argument for the capability approach – that it does a better job than the utilitarian approach with respect to explaining social choice – makes a strong suit of human heterogeneity. On the one hand, the capabilities approach is about the plurality of human values and the multitude of things that people value: "The capability perspective is inescapably pluralist" (Sen 1999a, 76). On the other hand, he criticizes utilitarianism for its one-dimensional character.

Is this plurality an embarrassment for advocacy of the capability perspective for evaluative purposes? Quite the contrary. To insist that there should be only one homogeneous magnitude that we value is to reduce drastically the range of our evaluative reasoning. It is not, for example, to the credit of classical utilitarianism that it values only pleasure.... To insist on the mechanical comfort of having just one homogeneous "good thing" would be to deny our humanity as reasoning creatures.... Heterogeneity of factors that influence individual advantage is a pervasive feature of actual evaluation. (ibid., 77)

We might indeed say that for Sen the whole problem with standard choice reasoning is its failure to recognize human heterogeneity and the limits this failure places on the informational base or evaluative space available to us in determining the nature of human well-being.[5]

---

[5] This is also a problem with respect to making interpersonal comparisons: "Concentrating exclusively on mental characteristics (such as pleasure, happiness or desires) can be particularly restrictive when making *interpersonal* comparisons of well-being and deprivation" (ibid., 62). If we regard the standard prohibition on interpersonal (utility) comparisons as one of the chief barriers to advancing economic policy beyond Pareto judgments, then for Sen this barrier can be traced to failing to recognize human heterogeneity.

Second, Sen's aversion to the idea that for policy evaluation purposes we ought to come up with a unique objective list of capabilities can also be understood in this connection. His stated objection to the idea is that pure theory cannot anticipate what capabilities will be relevant for all societies for all time to come, because we cannot know what individuals will understand about the world and value in the future – not to mention that attempting to theoretically legislate such a list would involve a denial of democracy (Sen 2005). However, put in terms of complex capabilities, because people are fundamentally different, we cannot say what capabilities they are likely to value, at least once we go beyond their relatively shared desire for elementary capabilities. That is, the idea of a list of key capabilities is fundamentally misconceived when it comes to understanding human life.

Third, Sen's grounding his thinking in human heterogeneity is further reflected in his oft-stated emphasis on the nature of rationality as being chiefly about what people have reason to value rather than being simply about their making choices, given what they value.

The idea of rational choice must be founded, in one way or another, on the basic requirement that choices be based on reason. But the interpretation of how reason is to be used can vary so radically between different formulations of rationality that there is frequently little in common between the different uses of the idea of rational choice. There are differences over the *domain* of reason: for example, whether it should apply only to the selection of alternatives *given* one's preferences over the alternatives, or also be used in the determination of the preferences themselves. (Sen 2007, 17)

Thus, we can reason about the ends of action as well as about the means to those ends. The distinction here is clear, even if Sen's reference to preferences suggests he is solely concerned with their determination. Yet when we take personal capability development to be the primary concern of people especially seen as making choices over which complex capabilities they seek to develop, their preferences are better thought to be like working plans than tastes. As such they are not determinate ways in which people respond to the world but rather general strategies for action in a changing world. Much, of course, is left unexplained in all this regarding how individuals might in fact play this sort of role in their capability development, that is, how they might be in some sense self-organizing. To investigate this, the section following thus returns to the self-concept idea introduced earlier and examines what social psychologists have concluded about what self-concepts are, especially when understood as dynamic or working self-concepts.

8.3 Social Psychology's Working Self-concept

The working or dynamic self-concept idea is one particular focus in social psychology's large research program on the self – a program that compares in size and breadth to the research program on rationality in economics. Much of this research is devoted to exploring competing theories regarding the weights different kinds of self-motivation have in social settings, such as self-knowledge, self-enhancement, and self-improvement (cf. Banaji and Prentice 1994). However, my goal here is to simply elicit what psychologists generally agree research has shown is involved in simply having a self-concept (cf. Markus and Wurf 1987). I draw on this literature to see what more we can say about the conception of individuals seen as developing capabilities. Four main conclusions seem to give a reasonably complete picture of what psychologists believe a working self-concept is.

First, people's self-concepts are dynamic in that they are continually being revised. This implies they have a dual character as a structure constantly being constituted and a process whereby that structure is revised. Second, self-concepts include multiple types of self-representations, which moreover vary in their accessibility to the person. There is much debate about how this variety should be understood, and distinctions have been made between actual and ideal self-representations, positive and negative ones, and in terms of temporal orientation. At a more general level, a particularly important distinction is between core and periphery types of self-representations. The former – the individual's more "salient" identities or ones said to be "chronically accessible" (Higgins, King, and Mavin 1982) – are distinguished as being better elaborated and as having stronger effects on individuals' information processing and behavior. The latter peripheral self-representations change more frequently and may be more easily cued by an individual's experiences. At the same time, particular core and periphery self-representations can sometimes change places, displacing the former and elevating the latter. Third, the set of self-representations that make up a person's self-concept is active in the sense that it exercises influence over the individual's functioning. Without going into the different theories of how this occurs, it can be said that the working self-concept exercises something akin to a regulatory role. It may or may not direct behavior, such as in goal setting, but it seems fair to say it can constrain it. In this regard, it at least functions homeostatically, and thus does indeed play a self-organizing role, albeit on the changing terrain of an individual's multiple and varying self-representations. Fourth, this active functioning applies to both intrapersonal and interpersonal processes. That is, internally speaking, individuals' multiple self-representations undergo some sort of coordination (though what this involves is controversial); externally speaking, individuals' interaction with others is affected by the overall state of their working self-concepts.

This picture of a loose system of dynamic self-organization, then, can cast new light on Sen's understanding of complex capability development. For him, people's different values direct them along the pathways they follow out of all the possible types of functionings they might develop. What the social psychology literature on the working self-concept adds to this is that the individual's pathway in developing new capabilities takes place against a backdrop of multiple self-representations that play a role in influencing a person's choices and behavior. How this occurs naturally depends on how an individual's self-representations are organized. Thus, an individual's more enduring core self-representations are likely to reflect past development of an individual's capabilities, and accordingly have an important influence on future capability development. However, because an individual's core and peripheral self-representations can change, we must also suppose that past pathways may be altered and even reversed. At the same time, an individual's more peripheral self-representations could play an important role in redirecting an individual's capability development with respect to new complex capabilities, particularly when we emphasize their inherent incommensurability. All of this does not imply, however, that the values people have that are Sen's focus are not involved in determining their choices. However, if we are to take the conclusions of social psychology regarding the nature of individual self-concepts seriously, these values should also be seen as likely reflecting the changing constellation of self-representations with which individuals operate.

Note that this view does not make a case for a new atomism. Thus, just as individuals' interaction with others is affected by the state of their working self-concepts, that social interaction feeds back upon the system of self-representations an individual has at any one time and contributes to its change. The dynamics of an individual's self-concept are both intrapersonal and interpersonal. How people develop complex capabilities is both due to how their systems of self-representations have happened to develop and how those systems are influenced by their interaction with others. This picture still sustains the idea that individuals are self-organizing, though it makes the individual only relatively autonomous. Sen's critical response to the claim that we are somehow compelled to adopt certain social identities gives us one way to interpret the character of this relative autonomy. When others assign social identities to us, they cast us as being of certain types, and thus employ various third-person representations of us. We are only relatively autonomous because at least some of the specific contents that we are called on to arbitrate come from others, not ourselves. Even if we go so far as to suppose that all the specific contents we manage are socially constructed, the idea of having an active working self-concept implies that individuals possess some sort of autonomy.

I make no effort here to deal with the question of whether or in what degree individuals in this capabilities conception might behave consciously, deliberately, or rationally, as that question is independent of the one that has motivated the discussion in this chapter, namely, Wilcox's "fusions of agency" concern. Thus, I asked at the outset whether individuals seen as collections of capabilities can be regarded as relatively independent. The answer, in terms of the idea that individuals' capability development involves having self-organizing working self-concepts, is that they should indeed be regarded as relatively independent. We do not need to know whether they behave consciously, deliberately, or rationally to say this. This clearly then involves a departure from the emphasis Sen places on the need to engage in "reasoned scrutiny" regarding one's "objectives, values and priorities." It does not imply, however, that we cannot speak of behavior as deliberate and rational in some sense. There is nothing per se incompatible between what psychologists have learned about working self-concepts and placing an emphasis on deliberation. Indeed, the social psychology literature on the self-concept certainly countenances people giving reasons for what they do. However, we might also investigate how their reasons might be related to the way that they organize their many self-representations and working self-concepts.

8.4 Working Self-concepts as Personal Identities: Livet

Let us use this understanding of the individual, then, to take a closer look at the process of capability development. One framework for doing so has been provided by Livet, who draws on Sen's capability approach to explain how people's capability development pathways create personal identities for them (2004; 2006; cf. Davis 2009b). Livet's starting point is that the idea of an unchanging personal identity is incompatible with thinking that people freely develop their capabilities. Because he believes people do freely develop their capabilities, individuals' personal identities must somehow be understood in terms of their capability development. This may seem inconsistent with the idea of even having a personal identity, but it is consistent with understanding personal identity dynamically as a working self-concept, particularly when we say self-concepts operate in some sort of self-organizing way. What this section then seeks to do is use Livet's analysis of capability development to give a capability interpretation of the working self-concept idea as a way of understanding individuals having personal identities. I argue that when we treat individuals as collections of capabilities, having a working self-concept is equivalent to having a special kind of capability – a personal identity capability that individuals can develop more or less successfully to manage their multiple self-representations.

8.4.1 A Second-order Capability

Livet treats the choices that individuals make in developing their capabilities as not only mapping out pathways of action but as also involving a process of continual self-evaluation. As in self-concept analysis, one decides what one wishes to do in light of one's various self-representations. As we have many interrelated self-representations, however, changes in our courses of action can be accompanied by a change in how these self-representations are structured. This is especially clear when we think about how people make choices that reverse past courses of action. A reversal of a course of action displaces the self-representation that previous course of action presupposed and substitutes another self-representation that the new course of action implies. That people can move back and forth across capability pathways thus means that they operate with a structure of self-representations that is dynamic and revisable. Livet explains the self-evaluation side of this in capability terms as a matter of exercising a reflexive "second-order capability," or a "capability of reorganising our paths of choice and the evaluation of our steps of action" (Livet 2006, 340). Our first-order capabilities are what Sen treats as our achieved functionings. We always begin our analysis, then, with "the set of functionings" that individuals recognize they possess together with their "preferences or priorities over these functionings" that capture the self-representations appropriate to them (ibid., 331), and we go on to ask how the individual's choices change this combination. Let us consider one possible case.

Choice reversals that return us to earlier courses of action that had been abandoned – "reversals of reversals" – are particularly interesting for Livet. He distinguishes two sorts: ones that involve arbitrary choices and ones that involve nonarbitrary choices. Arbitrary choices are those in which individuals essentially ignore the fact that they are returning to a past course of action. Self-evaluation is absent. Nonarbitrary choices, in contrast, are those in which individuals are specifically prepared to accept the consequences of the revisions they impose on their lives. They are choices in which I am prepared to make "a reverse revision ... to come back to my previous choices" (ibid., 329). Nonarbitrary choices, that is, are those in which the individual is engaged in an active process of self-evaluation. It is this that Livet associates with having a personal identity in dynamic terms. If one is able to reject a past reversal and return to a previous course of action, then one is able to judge the rejected change from the perspective of the direction of development one had earlier undertaken. In terms of the working self-concept idea, one is able to use an earlier self-representation as a point of reference in evaluating the self-representation implied by the now rejected alternative pathway. Being able to compare self-representations in this way is the sort of thing that would be at root in having a personal identity.[6]

Can people, then, exercise this special kind of capability? Livet sees a kind of path-dependency problem that has to be addressed to be able to say they do. When we set off on a new course of action, the functionings we choose to develop can "have irreversible effects on the quality of other functionings from which we can choose" (ibid., 330), thus making it difficult for us to compare their attendant self-representations. For each new functioning chosen,

we will have to assess how our commitment to this functioning for a certain time increases or decreases the value of this functioning, and how the inactivation of another functioning during this same time decreases or increases the value of the inactivated functioning. However, the estimation of the value of one functioning in a capability set depends also on the future consequences of the chosen functioning, including the revisions that foreseeable changes of the world and new information will require, and including the possible effect of such revisions on the retrospective evaluation of the functioning previously chosen. For example, if I choose to be a professional sportsman, it will be impossible to be later a prominent researcher in mathematics.... When I reach 40 years old, maybe I will regret my choice and assess negatively my past career of sportsman. (ibid.)

Thus, there is a path-dependency in our selection of courses of action that might prevent individuals from engaging in the sort of self-evaluation that having a working self-concept as a sort of personal identity might allow. To address this, Livet argues people impose two sorts of limitations on themselves regarding electing new functionings.

---

[6]   One can also see simple reversals of courses of action as involving a comparison of self-representations – "I saw myself as doing that, now I am doing this" – but Livet's case is arguably richer, because a reversal of a reversal provides a re-appraisal of the past course of action in light of experience with the first reversal.

8.4.2 Continuity Constraints

Continuity constraints are essentially psychological principles people employ to create "paths of justified revision" for themselves in their selected courses of action (ibid., 331). Livet's view is that people seek to maintain personal identities as coherent accounts of the courses of action they pursue and rely on certain devices (whether consciously or not) that enable them to deal with ambiguous situations, such as the one discussed in the previous section. Thus, continuity constraints are "justified" in practical terms because they serve the goal of maintaining a personal identity in a dynamic manner. In working self-concept terms, they are mechanisms like many others that social psychologists investigate that contribute to the ways in which individuals continually structure and restructure their multiple self-representations. First, then, following Peter Gärdenfors (1988), Livet makes use of the idea of "epistemic entrenchment" to account for individuals' concern with consistency in their beliefs and expectations. Because the choice of a new functioning changes a person's situation, and because this change can generate expectations at odds with past expectations, individuals need a method for revising their expectations. The idea behind "epistemic entrenchment" is that they tend to remove their least entrenched beliefs as one continuity constraint they place on themselves. Second, because people place value on their commitments to different sets of functionings, they are also "emotionally linked to any functioning-evolution," so that when "we revise our beliefs, we also have to revise our affective evaluations of the situation" (Livet 2006, 332). This second continuity constraint concerns justified revision of our preferences and priorities.

Thus, in terms of the previous example, these two continuity constraints guide a sequential process of decision making whereby the individual assesses each new functionings choice according to whether it can be regarded as justified. "Our overall comparison between the two paths cannot be done except if: we imagine the successive steps of actions, including the required revisions, namely first the epistemic and then the affective one, stage by stage for each step, qualify each step as a step of a justified path of revisions or not, and revise retrospectively from the point of view of the final step the latest evaluation (ibid., 339). People, then, are able to maintain personal identities more or less successfully according to their skill in employing these two continuity constraints. Of course, one could respond to Livet that he has assumed people are indeed motivated to maintain personal identities and has worked out his analysis to produce that result. However, he has a strong argument for saying that people are indeed so motivated, which adds to what social psychologists have argued regarding our working self-concepts. Maintaining a personal identity – or at least seeking to maintain one – for him cannot be separated from being able to make free choices in life. "Autonomy implies not only being able to choose between different activities but also being able to commit oneself to act in accordance with the values and goals that have led one to choose an activity" (ibid., 327). That is, one can only "commit oneself to act in accordance with [one's] values and goals" when there is a basis for one's commitments in some understanding one has of oneself.

Much of this self-understanding may well be implicit and unconscious, as social psychologists argue is the case with respect to the varying degrees of accessibility of our different self-representations. If we are to suppose people behave as agents, then it seems fair to say that they do so by maintaining accounts of themselves that function as dynamic personal identities. Individuals as developing collections of capabilities then essentially have a special personal identity capability. The question this leaves us with is: How might they develop such a capability? Having a personal identity can be said to be a human functioning, but being able to exercise it involves successfully developing it as a capability. To better understand what this successful exercise entails, I return to the topic of self-narratives.

8.5 Personal Identity and Dynamic Self-narratives

Self-narratives, as studied in the field of narrative psychology, are discursive accounts people keep of themselves. Among their motivations, the one especially relevant to economic life is the need for coherent choice and action in continually changing interaction with others. How one acts in a particular situation depends on one's capabilities, but because on an evolutionary or dynamic view of the individual one's capabilities develop and change, one's account of oneself also evolves and changes. It is a working self-narrative that the individual needs to be able to constantly revise and develop as her capabilities and view of what they allow changes. Essentially the individual's working self-accounts thus function as a means of indexing and organizing new experiences.

What exactly a personal identity self-narrative might involve in economic life, however, has not been much of a focus in economics in which the reflexive dimensions of individual behavior and the concept of personal identity have gone largely ignored (though cf. Aguiar et al. 2010). Here I only seek to further extend the idea of self-narratives through summary remarks of ideas shared by two quite different philosophers' ways of understanding them, and I do so in the context of the role they play in connection with action and choice motivation. That role emphasizes keeping straight for oneself how one wants to act in interaction with others as one's capabilities develop. A self-narrative in this sense is one's own personal identity narrative.[7]

8.5.1 Schechtman: Constituting the Self

Schechtman (1996) argues that personal identity should be understood in terms of how people develop autobiographical narratives. She rejects the traditional approach to personal identity in philosophy that seeks to provide necessary and sufficient conditions for showing "how a person identified at one time [is] the same person as a person identified at another" (Noonan 1991, 2), and which understands this reidentification strictly in terms of individuals having one unchanging set of psychological characteristics or as psychological continuity. The question that is paramount, she believes, is not how we reidentify individuals, but how we characterize them as persons in terms of their actions, experiences, and characteristics. To the extent that we can talk about reidentifying individuals, it is because we are able to say who they are as persons. The idea of being a "person," she then argues, ought not be approached in a logical-metaphysical way in terms of what would have to be the case for the different "time-slices" of a person to belong to one person, but in a more historical-epistemological way in terms of how we attribute personal identity to people according to our understanding of what a person is. For Schechtman, that understanding involves four main things: survival, moral responsibility, self-interested concern, and compensatory fairness (ibid., 14–15).

An autobiographical narrative, then, is a self-constitution narrative, and these four things are the respects in which individuals constitute themselves as persons. Approaching identity from this perspective begins from the assumption that "not all sentient creatures are persons" and proceeds from "the assertion that individuals constitute themselves as persons by coming to think of themselves as persisting subjects who have had experiences in the past and will continue to have experience in the future, taking certain experiences as theirs" (ibid., 94). Thus, when people successfully develop coherent accounts of themselves, "a person's *identity* … is constituted by

---

[7] Economics as narrative per se has been extensively discussed by Deirdre McCloskey (1990, 1994). Though related, my focus is on economic agents' narratives about themselves, that is, their self-narratives. Of course economists are agents, and so much of what McCloskey has to say about explanations made by economists bears on the topic of self-narratives.

the content of her self-narrative" (ibid.). To say when a self-narrative is "coherent," Schechtman (like Livet) places constraints on what that self-narrative must do, specifically that people can articulate their self-narratives and that those narratives are broadly consistent with reality. Minus these requirements, people fail to self-constitute themselves as persons. Essentially, then, a successful narrative is just what we think of when we describe a "story" as a conventional, linear narrative. Here, Schechtman draws on Jerome Bruner's definition:[8]

A narrative is composed of a unique sequence of events, mental states, happenings involving human beings as characters or actors. These are its constituents. But these constituents do not, as it were, have a life or meaning of their own. Their meaning is given by their place in the overall configuration of the sequence as a whole – its plot or *fabula* (Bruner 1990, 43–4; quoted in Schechtman 1996, 96).

Schechtman recognizes there are other types of alternative or "nonstandard" narratives but rejects these as a basis for self-narratives on the grounds that they do not produce well-defined characters according to standard expectations in our culture regarding the nature of stories. In this respect, her view is like Ross's view of how individuals' interaction with one another unifies them as single individuals. One's self-narrative account is not held together by principles of internal coherence alone, but is fit to an inherited set of principles operating in human society regarding what makes it an acceptable story. Lacking this, it fails to constitute the individual as a person and create an identity for that person that is recognizable to others.

At the same time, individuals' construction of their autobiographical narratives need not proceed self-consciously. The first constraint that Schechtman imposes on self-narratives is that people can "locally" articulate them. "This means that the narrator should be able to explain why he does what he does, believes what he believes, and feels what he feels" (Schechtman 1996, 114). This is not to say that people who create self-narratives are always able to explain themselves, but we must nonetheless have some evidence that they are engaged in doing so. Essentially this requirement comes down to people being able to give reasons for what they do that link up to their view of who they are – allowing also that their reasoning may often not be especially good. For Schechtman, these reasons are structured by the four ways in which we characterize persons (survival, moral responsibility, self-interested concern, and compensatory fairness).

---

[8]   Bruner's view, among others, is also employed in the social psychology literature on self-concepts, particularly when it addresses the issue of personal identity (Markus and Wurf 1987).

There is much one might debate regarding these four social structural principles, but the main point here seems correct. These socially recognized
kinds of principles guide people in giving reasons for what they do, and so
underlie the process of constructing self-narratives. Schechtman's general
argument is that one should look upon personal identity as something constructed by individuals, but that this self-construction does not occur in a
vacuum. Somehow the materials people employ in creating their stories are
socially given, and so the stories they tell must be consistent with the nature
of those materials.

The second constraint that Schechtman imposes on self-narratives – the
reality constraint – is more difficult. Once we move to an idea of personal
identity as a story, reality can no longer have the meaning typically ascribed
to it in science. How, then, does "reality" now reconfigured as that of a coherent story act as a constraint on self-narratives? The issue comes up even in
connection with the articulation constraint in connection with self-deception. Sometimes "a person's *explicit* self-narrative diverges from his *implicit*
self-narrative" (ibid., 115, also cf. 129). To make this judgment, others need
to weigh in on the accuracy of an individual's story. However, this creates questions about where the boundary lies between the individual's and
others' command of the story. The reality constraint per se for Schechtman
is that there should be "[f]undamental agreement on the most basic features
of reality" (ibid., 119). People can be in error about certain facts about the
world – an issue of inaccuracy – but they cannot be wrong about the main
features of their stories according to how we understand the world and history. This position, I think, will be perceived as wanting by many. Realism
is a difficult enough view to explain from the perspective of science; what
constitutes realism in narrative cannot but be more difficult to determine.
There is a way, however, that we might take another look at Schechtman's
reality constraint in light of what Dennett says about individuals as fictional
characters.

8.5.2 Dennett's Fictional Characters

In Chapter 6, I briefly explained Dennett's intentional stance view. Agents of
all kinds, whether human or not, relate to the world just as if they had wants,
beliefs, and expectations. On this view, agents are like characters in stories
and occupy roles appropriate to the parts they play in whatever intentional
setting they find themselves (Dennett 1991; cf. Ross 2005, 279–86). As a
character in a story, a person is not just "able to explain why he does what
he does, believes what he believes, and feels what he feels" (Schechtman

1996, 114). What one does, believes, and feels is determined by the nature of the part one plays. At the same time, in an evolutionary world the story is always unfinished. Thus, a person not only plays a role as a certain type of character, but is also constantly engaged in rewriting the story and the parts being played. For Dennett, individuals are thus authors of themselves, and whereas there is no playwright on whom they can depend for all their lines and cues, they do have coauthors, other people who know the sorts of stories that are getting told, and others who are equally busy writing and rewriting different parts of them from the perspective of the roles they see themselves playing. These multiple authors writing and rewriting their respective parts then produce interlocking stories about certain types of characters.

This clearly puts Schechtman's reality constraint on autobiographical narratives in a different light. She seems right to say that people's self-narratives are constrained to be realistic, but her standard of realism is not clear. Dennett's approach, however, puts the question of realism on an altogether different foundation. On the one hand, his emphasis on people's stories having fictional characters makes the individual's self-narrative a shared product of many coauthor storytellers, all of whom are working with story types reflecting a long history of human storytelling. Human life narratives are thus ancient endeavors in the telling of which people continue to participate whatever their own histories, whether these stories are cast as fables or games.[9] Thus, a story or individual self-narrative is realistic according to whether it fits one of many models of stories whose structure has been refined and tested over many years and across many civilizations and societies. I don't say that this gives us a highly determinate standard by which we might judge the realism of a given self-narrative. Rather, just as the telling and retelling of stories is a process, so their evaluation is a process in which judgments are debated, revised, and often left unsettled. That is, on this evolutionary way of looking at things, realism in narratives is not a question with a one-off answer but a framework of questions subject to continual investigation. Dennett's view of selves as authors with coauthors does, then, give us more to say about the nature of the reality constraint on autobiographical personal identity narratives.

Reinforcing this for Dennett is his view of human language as a superstructural scaffolding supporting individual storytelling. Stories, of course, are communicated in a linguistic medium that has a long history of public

---

[9]   Thus, Ross interprets Dennett's view that individuals have coauthors in their self-narratives in game-theoretic terms (Ross 2005, 290). Indeed, game theory has always investigated a proto-typical set of "classic" games (prisoner's dilemma, battle of the sexes, etc.), and in important respects is just the study of classic human stories.

institutionalization. Here, his view recalls Andy Clark's idea that historically human cognition increasingly relies on various forms of "external
scaffolding" that are employed to regiment and strengthen many of our
natural cognitive abilities, whose natural processing is too clumsy or defi-
cient for human goals (Clark 1998). A key thing about how human beings
scaffold their cognitive life is the building of enduring structures in the
world, which secures and preserves past knowledge through its coding and
materialization for those structures. Not only, then, do we tell certain types
of shared stories, but the telling of those stories is also likely to respect rules
for how people can be represented that are embedded in the many institutions of human communication (books, films, documentation practices,
legal systems, academic research programs, archival systems, etc.). Whether
autobiographical narratives are coherent, then, is a less open question than
may appear on first consideration, because the development of language
as a system of communication embeds constraints on self-representation
in a variety of external structures in the world. It follows that the accounts
people keep of themselves as methods of self-organization are likely more
substantial than many might believe. They depend on long-established
practices regarding how individuals report on and explain their experiences
and values that are learned as part of their ordinary learning about how to
live in a human world. One measure of this is that children from quite early
in life can produce understandable self-narratives, indeed well before they
learn mathematics.

Dennett together with Schechtman, then, give us a fairly full picture of
how people produce autobiographical accounts of themselves that make
sense to others and themselves. This makes personal identity something
that is jointly and socially produced, though with the primary responsibility falling on individuals who go about constructing their stories to keep
account of themselves. I will provide a further rationale for this last conclusion in the following chapter, but I conclude this one by taking stock of the
capabilities conception of the individual developed in this chapter.

8.6 Capability Development and Human Heterogeneity

The conception of the individual understood as a collection of capabilities
developed in this chapter is anchored in the idea of the individual having one
special capability, a personal identity capability, interpreted as a capability
for maintaining and developing an account of oneself in changing interaction with others. The capability framework comes from Sen. I have built on
it by arguing that it is reasonable to suppose that people have this particular

capability on the grounds that social psychology explains individual behavior in terms of the operation of working self-concepts, on Livet's grounds that it is reasonable to suppose people employ certain constraints on the capability development paths they follow, and on the grounds of what we may say about the nature of individuals' working self-concepts as types of autobiographical narratives. Sen's capability approach does not make this special capability explicit, but I claim it is implied by the idea of human capability development as always moving the individual toward having a more heterogeneous set of complex capabilities. That is, as people develop an increasing range of different complex capabilities, they individually become less and less like others, and so more and more reliant on ways of keeping track of their particular development pathways through life. Their accounts of themselves as self-narratives are their means for doing this, though they develop their self-narratives with the assistance of others in a shared language and a medium of established institutions and culture. Their development of a special capability for giving autobiographical accounts of themselves for themselves thus goes hand in hand with their tendency to develop more complex capabilities. Ironically, then, whereas people become more unlike one another as they develop, their principle common bond increasingly becomes the fact of being different. Sen says: "Human beings are thoroughly diverse" (Sen 1992, 1). Thus, people are not alike in virtue of some common set of characteristics; their common bond lies in being diverse and different from one another.

This conclusion might be argued to be reflected in economics' own historical development. In the earlier "pre-modern" stage of history in which complex capability development was less widespread, slowly rising individual diversity was not widely apparent and was thus not seen as central to explaining the economic process. Indeed, most people (and indeed many people still throughout the world today in impoverished settings) were only concerned with elementary capability development. In effect, the human division of labor was not very much extended by comparison with what it has become today and promises to become in the future. It should come as no surprise, consequently, that the classical economists saw individuals as basically the same, and that many of them sought to make this central to economic explanation, as in the treatment of prices in terms of labor values understood as an essential human capacity to expend so much labor effort in a given period of time. By the end of the nineteenth century and beginning of the twentieth in Europe, however, the diversity in individual motives in economic behavior had become more prevalent and could no longer be overlooked. The neoclassical economists thus abandoned human homogeneity, and they made differences in individuals via differences in tastes the basis for price. Industrialization had produced a greater diversity of markets, because people were increasingly different, leading to a greater social division of labor. Differences in taste were a first way this might be captured. However, differences between people at a point in time are not the same thing as differences in their pathways of development. Neoclassicism's *Homo economicus* remains a static being and thus cannot tell us very much about what rising human heterogeneity means for economic life. In my view, then, economics will need to say much more about the increasingly complex character of individuality if it is to explain the evolving nature of economic life. This is one thing the capabilities approach is meant to achieve in its attention to human diversity.

This chapter began with the problem that people understood as collections of capabilities might be collections of multiple selves and not unified beings in virtue of their having multiple social identities. The response to this problem the chapter offered was to explain individuals as self-organizing in terms of having a special personal identity capability. However, whereas in principle this seems a reasonable way to address this problem, little was nonetheless said about how people have, adopt, and give up social identities. This recurring issue – one that has made its way into economics via Akerlof and Kranton and Bachrach's analyses – arguably needs more careful attention at this point if the general view advanced in this chapter is to be persuasive. Thus, the following chapter turns to the topic of social identity, or the "economics of identity" as this subject has been recently labeled, and argues that treating personal identity as a capability to keep a self-narrative provides a way of understanding how individuals manage their many often conflicting social identities.

NINE

The Identity of Individuals
and the Economics of Identity

Individuals construct their own identity, but they do not construct their identity just as they please; they do not construct it under circumstances chosen by themselves, but under circumstances encountered, given and transmitted from the past.

(Darity, Mason, and Stewart 2006, 290)

Identity can't be compartmentalized. You can't divide it up into halves or thirds or any other separate segments. I haven't got several identities: I've got just one, made up of many components in a mixture that is unique of me, just as other people's identity is unique to them as individuals.

(Maalouf 1998 [2000], 2)

9.1 The Economics of Identity

What is the "economics of identity?" In fact, the meaning of that expression is ambiguous and contested (Kirman and Teschl 2004; Fine 2009). Many nonetheless associate it with Akerlof and Kranton's (2000) proposal to introduce the concept of social identity into economics by expanding the traditional *Homo economicus* utility function to include a set of self-images associated with the individual's different social identities. On that view, people gain or lose utility according to how their social identity self-images are affected by their interaction with others. However, this does not explain the role that individuals have in determining which social identities they wish to have. That would entail having some account of how individuals choose certain social identities and also some explanation of the extent to which they are influential in determining what social identities they have. That is, it would entail having some understanding of the relationship between who they are, or what their personal identity involves, and their many social identities. Akerlof and Kranton, though they do not refer to personal identity, implicitly equate it with the individual's utility function.

However, because the utility function only tells us how people are affected by their social identities, it does not allow us to say how they influence their determination, thus making it the choice of the economic modeler to say what social identities individuals have. That is, with no real account of personal identity, they are unable to explain the relationship between personal identity and social identity.

I argued in the previous chapter that on a capabilities conception of the individual people's development of their capabilities goes hand in hand with their development of a special personal identity capability that allows them to keep narrative accounts of themselves. If one capability they develop, then, is of being able to elect particular social identities, how they keep narrative accounts of themselves constitutes a way of explaining the relationship between personal identity and social identity. Yet it would be a mistake to say that their doing this gives people complete freedom to determine what social identities they will have. Recall from Chapter 3, then, that in contrast to the psychology's social identity approach and Turner's self-categorization theory (Turner 1985) that Akerlof and Kranton draw on, the sociological approach to identity assumes that individuals and social groups mutually influence one another. On this view, the personal and social identities of individuals and also the identities of social groups are all mutually determined. On the one hand, the social construction and assignment of social categories to individuals influences what social groups they belong to and thus what social identities they elect. This in turn influences their personal identities. On the other hand, the social groups individuals belong to and the social identities they elect influences the formation of social groups and the construction of social categories used to represent those social groups. This frames the evolutionary-relational side of the individual conception developed previously in much broader terms that allow us to begin to capture the more indirect social influences that operate on individuality. In effect, what we try to do here, then, is locate that individual conception in an "identity dynamics" (Potts 2008) that operates across individuals and groups.

This chapter thus takes up the "economics of identity" from a point of view alternative to the conventional one. It begins in Section 9.2 by examining how we might understand a process of endogenous interaction between individuals and groups that produces identities for each. I first look at the stochastic evolutionary model developed by Ulrich Horst, Alan Kirman, and Miriam Teschl that shows how individuals joining and leaving social groups explains both the emergence of groups and their identities and tells us something about the nature of individuals' personal identities. Section 9.3 examines another strategy for endogenizing identity, one that shows how an identity dynamics involves norms, conventions, and social rules that influence individuals' choices and identities. In this case, I look at the evolutionary game-theoretic model of William Darity Jr., Patrick Mason, and James Stewart that shows how racial identity norms emerge and persist as a result of the way individuals interact with social groups. Section 9.4 then discusses social identity more generally and looks at individuals' social identities as an entire structure of interconnected and competing social claims that I argue are both imposed on and embraced in different degrees by individuals. I distinguish two kinds of social identities psychologists have said individuals have – relational and collective – and explain how the differences between them provide a way of explaining how individuals relate to their social identities as a whole. Section 9.5 then returns to self-narratives as a special kind of second-order capability and argues that individuals use discursive self-narratives (unlike conventional narratives) as a means of simultaneously looking backward and forward to manage their social identities as they develop their capabilities. Section 9.6 concludes with brief comments on how the capabilities conception treats individuals as socially embedded, and then raises the issue of what normative recommendations follow from this view of individuals.

9.2 Endogenizing Personal Identity

Horst, Kirman, and Teschl's (2007) model of endogenous identity determination of individuals and groups contributes to a recent "interactionist" literature in complexity economics that aims to explain how the behavior of populations of individuals evolves stochastically when they engage in direct interaction with one another rather than indirectly through the intermediation of the price system (cf., Brock and Durlauf 2001). The innovation Horst, Kirman, and Teschl bring to this literature is to suppose that, among the many things that concern people when they interact with others, their personal identities are a foremost concern. They capture this with the idea that people have a personal identity self-image that they desire to attain. With this self-image in mind, they then join those particular social groups that they believe have characteristics that match (some subset of) their desired personal identity self-images in an effort to "realize" those personal identity self-images. In effect, people choose some social groups over others, because they perceive there to be a better match between their desired personal identities and the social identities of those groups. However, entry to and exit from social groups is open, so their composition and characteristics change as their membership changes.[1] If this upsets the match individuals perceive exists between their desired self-image and the characteristics of the groups they have joined, they may exit those groups. As they do this, however, they change the characteristics of the groups they leave and also change their own self-images and characteristics that reflect the array of groups to which they belong. As this goes on across many individuals and groups, it produces an identity dynamic involving "endogenous personal identity formation and an endogenous formation of social groups" (Horst, Kirman, and Teschl 2007, 5).

What Horst, Kirman, and Teschl's formal model adds to this general description of the process of endogenous identity determination is an analysis of equilibrium conditions in which the evolution of groups "settles down" in the long run such that there comes to exist a given number of social groups with unchanging characteristics, individuals move back and forth across these different groups, and the proportions of individuals belonging to each group remains constant (ibid.).[2] They thus essentially put to the side how group identity is endogenized – groups in the long run are referred to as "types" that individuals choose from (ibid., 14) – to focus on the implications of their analysis for thinking about personal identity when it is seen as being highly endogenized. Roughly speaking, their rationale is that social group identities tend to stabilize over time or at least vary at a slower rate than individuals' personal identities. Of course, formally the argument could be inverted, and it could be also argued that the evolution of individuals' personal identities "settles down" in the long run to a given number of types with different vectors of unchanging characteristics. However, Horst, Kirman, and Teschl essentially say that social group identities stabilize faster than individuals' personal identities, and there may indeed be good historical reasons for adopting this stylized fact and seeing group identities as more stable, as I will suggest later in this chapter. Traded off against this, however, are the conclusions they are led to make about the nature of personal identity.

---

[1] "A social group will be represented by a vector of the members' 'typical', predominant or average characteristics" (ibid., 13).

[2] Their key assumptions, following other social interaction models, places two conditions on the character of interaction. One, "moderate social interaction," means agents have low dependency on current groups; the second, "moderate individual interaction," means they have a low dependency in their choices on the individual's current state (Horst, Kirman, and Teschl 2007, 11).

What their analysis in this regard allows them to do, then, is focus on what they characterize as the degree of "connectedness" of a person's choices over time as a measure of personal identity. Their conclusion is that

People's choices are relatively *unconnected* from one moment to the next, that is, they are sufficiently independent of people's personal history and social backgrounds. Paradoxically, perhaps, this can be thought of as saying that the personal identity of individuals is relatively weak. (ibid., 23)

People's probabilities of being in any one social group, that is, do not depend very much on the social groups they have belonged to in the past. In effect, they adapt quite easily to a continual change in their desired self-images and personal characteristics, and therefore move readily across different types of social groups. In this sense, they conclude, individuals are simply collections of "multiple selves" (ibid.), and indeed it seems difficult to say that they even have personal identities in any enduring sense of the term. Horst, Kirman, and Teschl fully embrace this conclusion and emphasize that one of the aims of their analysis was "to show that social interaction does not always consist in conformity or in aligning behaviour to particular reference groups as previous social interaction papers have often assumed, but that individuals can also be seen as relatively 'autonomous' and 'independent' beings, despite being members of a particular social structure" (ibid., 24). Thus, they distance themselves quite clearly from Akerlof and Kranton's static equilibrium view.

In fact, their view might be thought closer to Livet's (whose work they acknowledge), who we saw in the previous chapter similarly sees a tension between freedom of choice and having a single personal identity. However, there is an important difference. Livet uses Sen's capability approach to explain individuals' choices in terms of how they seek to develop their capabilities, so his view of personal identity has quite different foundations. An important dimension of this concerns how individuals reflexively evaluate themselves exercising what we saw he calls a "second-order capability" (Livet 2006, 340). Being able to exercise this capability involves taking into account a variety of considerations regarding possible alternative choice pathways in life, such as assessing how a commitment to a particular functioning increases or decreases its value, how developing one functioning affects other functionings not pursued, how future consequences of the pathway chosen figure into one's evaluations of all one's possible functionings (including how one's information about the world may change), and how one's chosen paths may affect one's retrospective evaluations of paths not chosen (ibid., 330). Livet offers a complicated picture of how people reflexively evaluate their choices, one reflecting his treatment of them as having many capabilities.

In contrast, Horst, Kirman, and Teschl use a fairly simple behavioral framework drawn from self-concept psychology – in particular, E. Tory Higgins' "self-discrepancy" theory (Higgins 1987). The key idea is that there is a difference between the individual's ideal self and the individual's actual self that individuals work to eliminate in their interaction with others. This theory is quite like the psychological or psychodynamic view that Akerlof and Kranton employ when they argue that individuals seek to reduce cognitive dissonance or the "*anxiety* that a person experiences when she violates her internalized rules" (Akerlof and Kranton 2000, 728). Indeed, in both cases choice behavior has a monocausal, all-encompassing basis: to minimize a single difference value. I don't say that people do not have motivations of this sort, but it seems Livet's view that people make choices employing a variety of motivations is more realistic (albeit more complicated and difficult to model). We might say that individuals self-evaluate themselves and their choices according to multiple considerations because the consequences of their choices have many dimensions. Livet (and Sen) thus emphasize that people deliberate. Those engaged in equilibrium modeling of course seek a more determinate form of analysis, and they are likely to argue that an emphasis on deliberation does not tell us enough about behavior. However, simplifying the explanation of choice to a succession of one-off self-discrepancy decisions may also not be enough to explain identity choice and, worse, may compel us to draw only one type of conclusion about the nature of personal identity.

Note, then, that Horst, Kirman, and Teschl employ a standard social interaction model random utility function in which the "noise" term "reflects all the other factors not necessarily listed in the basic characteristics of an individual which may influence this individual's choices as well as identity" (Horst, Kirman, and Teschl 2007, 10). Though this makes their analysis stochastic and dynamic, nonetheless, as in Akerlof and Kranton's analysis, individuals can only react to discrepancies between their desired selves and actual selves. They have no "cushion," as it were, in the form of the larger deliberative space Livet describes in which many factors come into play in individual decision making, and might be traded off against one another, and which taken together explain some sort of general continuity in personal identity. Thus, it should not come as a surprise that for Horst, Kirman, and Teschl individuals' "choices are relatively *unconnected* from one moment to the next" and are independent of their "personal history and social backgrounds," because the role these sorts of things can play as factors giving individuals some sort of continuity in their lives has been cut out of their modeling. Nor should it come as a surprise that Horst, Kirman, and Teschl reproduce Akerlof and Kranton's multiple selves result now in a dynamic terms. In effect, their approach, valuable as it is in its recognition of the need to endogenize identity, is too constrained by the mathematics of equilibrium theorizing to generate sufficient behavioral structure to produce any other account of personal identity but the one they anticipate.

I will further argue in this chapter that deliberation and self-narrative provide more behavioral structure in identity determination than commonly supposed, but I also argue that social structures play an important role vis-à-vis individuals' self-narratives. To introduce this latter side of the matter, I turn to a second dynamic model of endogenous identity determination: Darity, Mason, and Stewart's analysis of racial identity norms.

9.3 The Persistence of Racial Identity Norms

Darity, Mason, and Stewart (2006) develop an evolutionary game theory model to endogenously explain individuals' identities in terms of the choices they make between joining and not joining exclusionary social groups, specifically racial groups. When individuals join a racial group – for example, "White" or "Black" in the American context – their personal identities are said to effectively collapse to their racial social identities in the sense that their behavior then involves being altruistic toward ingroup individuals and antagonistic toward outgroup individuals. That is, their choices are then strictly those appropriate to typical members of their social group, and they are accordingly called "racialists," whether they are White or Black. In contrast, people who are neutral in their social interactions with others are called "individualists," and their personal identities and choice behavior are independent of their social identities, even though they may be distinguishable by skin color. The question Darity, Mason, and Stewart address is: What is the distribution between racialists and individualists likely to be in a world in which racial identity norms are emergent on social behavior and there exist certain wealth structures? If racialists tend to dominate, then this would get expressed in persistent racial identity norms that reinforce the differences between ingroup and outgroup interaction and sustain the dominance of racialists. In new and unfamiliar decision-making situations, people would generally fall back on these norms of behavior. The model is one in which racial identity is socially constructed according to an identity dynamic that operates in a specific historical context, namely, one in which there is an inherited inequality of wealth across racial groups.[3] In contrast to Horst, Kirman, and Teschl, people get locked into racial group social identities rather than move back and forth across them in a relatively unconnected way.

Darity, Mason, and Stewart's model works as an evolutionary game in which people are distinguished by skin color ("Africans" and "Europeans") and randomly interact in pairs across ingroup, outgroup individual encounters. Though "[t]he proportional division of the population between African and European is exogenous and fixed over time ... [w]ithin each social group, the division between individualists and racialists evolves endogenously" (ibid., 285), thus influencing who matches with whom and accordingly individuals' average economic payoffs (in terms of enhancing productive potential). This dynamic also influences the kinds of games people play. Thus at one extreme, when matching is only within groups, Africans and Africans and Europeans and Europeans each play their own respective ingroup coordination games, and there are significant payoffs to racialist behavior. At the other extreme, when matching is only between groups, Africans and Europeans play a prisoner's dilemma game, and racialism dominates for individuals in both groups (though they would be better off playing as individualists). What types of games, payoffs, and identity behavior result depend crucially, however, on parameter values established for average payoffs and initial conditions. These in turn are determined according to historical context in which, in the American case, wealth differences between Africans and Europeans are significant.

Darity, Mason, and Stewart employ a more sociological ingroup/ outgroup type of psychology compared to the self-discrepancy psychology of Horst, Kirman, and Teschl. Social group racial identities and the norms they generate determine what kinds of games people on average play, the overall social distribution of racialists and individualists distributes altruism and antagonism across people, and this tells us what characteristics and personal identities people must have. Even being an individualist, which is not having a racial group identity as one's personal identity, is a social outcome in the sense that some people will find their payoffs in interaction with others to be such that this is the identity that they adopt. That is, a particular "person's decision to accept or reject a racialized identity

---

[3]   "The [1994] median wealth of African American families was US$ 10,329, while the median for White American households was US$ 76,519. Thus, the median White family had a net worth near the 84th percentile of the Black wealth distribution (US$ 79,048)" (Darity, Mason, and Stewart 2006, 284). Ingroup altruism and outgroup antagonism are well established in the experimental social psychological literature (cf. Tajfel et al. 1971).

depends on the extent to which others accept or reject a racialized identity" (ibid., 286). Clearly we are again considerably removed from Akerlof and Kranton's static world in which individuals' social identities are given. For Darity, Mason, and Stewart, it is the evolutionary dynamic, together with inherited conditions, that does the identity assigning.

Yet at the same time one cannot but feel that something is missing in Darity, Mason, and Stewart's characterization of "individualism" especially because it is basically defined as a failure to adopt a racialized identity and omits any sort of individual motivation that is not tied to the single issue of orientation toward groups. Their reason for adopting this characterization is that they believe "macrolevel social processes define the choice set and constrain the social and economic implications of individual identity choices" (ibid., 289); certainly it is hard to disagree with this. However, "constraining" is also not the same thing as "determining," which is what we are concerned with in connection with identity determination. Consider, then, what would be required in the case of there being a pure racialist economy: "racialism will emerge as a social norm if the cost of altruism [directed towards insiders] is not sufficiently large for each group," or if "when the cost of altruism is sufficiently large ... the within-group effect is dominated by the between-group effect" (ibid., 297). There is no question here regarding the logic of the model. It nicely implements social psychology's theory of ingroup/outgroup behavior. The question is whether costs of the sort described are sufficient to explain individual behavior. Is deliberation only a matter of costs, however conceived? My argument in the previous section was that individual behavior does not have a monocausal basis, particularly where complex personal identity choices are at issue. However, what we have here is also a monocausal theory of individual behavior.

At the very least, then, it seems we need to enlarge Darity, Mason, and Stewart's behavioral account of individualism. This might not seriously affect their macrolevel conclusions about racial identity norms, which reflect important facts about racial wealth distribution and which likely do much to explain average individual behavior. However, a theory of what social identity means to individuals ought to also go beyond average behavior. How, then, are we to go about broadening our account of how individuals address their social identities? In the section that follows, I begin to answer this question by further focusing on the social identity side of the story by describing social identity as an entire structure of different kinds of interrelated social identities that generates competing and crosscutting claims on individuals that they need to order and address. Individuals do not encounter one social identity at a time, but rather many simultane-ously. Then in the section following this one, I turn back to the individual to argue that, although people are constrained by how their social identities are defined and assigned to them by others, they also exercise first-person power over what social identities they wish to embrace. How they do this – and how they self-organize themselves and develop their capabilities – is a matter of working out their self-narratives about their identities.

9.4 Social Identity as a Complex Structure

To understand social identity as an entire structure, it is helpful to think about the interconnectedness of social groups. Individuals' different social identities derive from the different social groups to which they belong. However, many social groups share members, and are accordingly inter-connected with one another. For example, language groups typically correspond to particular national and regional social groups, religious social groups and ethnic social groups often coincide, and gender is often tied to specific occupational social groups. Consequently, many of the social identities individuals have are also interconnected. This suggests that one way of understanding how individuals relate to their social identi-ties is to begin by looking at clusters of social identities they possess and ask how individuals relate to these clusters as individuals. Thus, feminist "intersectionality identity theory," which is concerned primarily with race, gender, and class, seeks to explain how individuals sustain an autonomy – a "relational autonomy" – vis-à-vis sets of interlocked demands that their different but related social identities may make on them (Crenshaw 1989; Meyers 1989, 2000; MacKenzie and Stoljar 2000). These demands can be especially difficult to address, because the social groups from which they derive are central to individuals' lives and because the demands they place on individuals frequently conflict. Why, then, might individuals thus under-stood be nonetheless thought to be autonomous? The main reason is that, because these conflicting demands arise out of individuals' strongest social identities, none can easily be dismissed (as often can the demands arising out of their relatively less important social identities), and this motivates individuals to prioritize and organize the relationships between their social identities, or at least attempt to do so. Thus, they behave autonomously in a self-organizing way precisely because their social identities exist as an entire structure that continually generates conflicting demands on them.

This view resembles self-discrepancy theory and ingroup/outgroup discrimination in the sense that it attributes to people a psychological motivation to resolve tensions they encounter in their social relationships. However, it is also quite different in that in this case individuals simultaneously face multiple conflicts, not a clean sequence of one-off conflicts, and these multiple conflicts are likely to be interrelated and at the same time noncomparable in important respects. The multiple social claims on a poor woman of color come all at once and cannot be traded off against one another according to any simple substitution logic. This means individuals have few generalizable guidelines regarding how to proceed in life, and they accordingly have little alternative but to continually devise and revise rules or strategies to make choices as each new situation requires. However, they may succeed in pursuing coherent capability development pathways if they can keep an account of the choices they make and their contexts, constantly evaluating new states of affairs by the experience of the past. To get a better sense of what this involves, let us turn to current social identity theory to distinguish two main types of social identities and then how individuals are constrained and free to order their social identities.

9.4.1 Two Types of Social Identities

Chapter 4 discussed the current state of social identity theory in connection with the debate in the social psychology literature between two main approaches: a psychology-based approach called social identity theory and the sociology-based symbolic interactionist approach called identity theory (cf. Hogg, Terry, and White 1995; also Brown 2000). The two approaches involve different strategies of analysis, but social psychologists have also combined them to produce an overall view of social identity by making a "distinction between two levels of social selves – (i) those that derive from interpersonal relationships and interdependence with specific others and (ii) those that derive from membership in larger, more impersonal collectives or social categories" (Brewer and Gardner 1996; cf. Brewer 2001). That is, individuals have social identities that are "identifications of the self *as* a certain kind of person" – a role-based identity – and they also have social identities involving "identifications of the self *with* a group or category as a whole" – a collective identity (Thoits and Virshup 1997, 106). Another way of understanding this is to say that people's social identities can be seen as *relational* or *categorical*. They are relational when a person occupies a position in a "relational web" (family, friendship, patron-client, team member, etc.) and socially identifies with another person or set of people to whom they are connected in a specific kind of way. They are categorical in regard to their "sharing some categorical attribute" with other like people (race,

Table 9.1. *Two forms of social identity*

Object of identification	Social identity concept	Basis for identification
Social roles	Relational social identity	Differences from others
Social groups	Collective social identity	Commonalities with others

ethnicity, gender, age, disability, language, class, nationality, sexual orientation, etc.), and one then socially identifies with another person as representative of that shared category (Brubaker and Cooper 2000, 15–17).

Psychology's social identity theory, then, better addresses individuals' collective social identities based on their identification with social groups represented by social categories assigned to them, whereas sociology's symbolic interactionist identity theory better addresses individuals' relational role identities based on their identification with specific others with whom people regularly interact. Important to this distinction between kinds of social identities is a difference in how individuals compare to those with whom they identify. In the case of relational social identities, individuals identify with others based on *differences* between them, such as in the case of different social roles in families or positions in workplaces. In contrast, in the case of collective identities, individuals identify with others based on *commonalities* they share in virtue of all being members of the same religion, nationality, gender, class, and so forth.[4] This basic distinction between two kinds of social identity can be refined to include further gradations within each and mixed cases that blur the line between them, but for simplicity I use this distinction to represent consensus thinking in social identity theory. In Table 9.1, the top row captures the main thrust of symbolic interactionist identity theory, whereas the bottom row captures that of social identity theory.

This framework also has an historical dimension. Relational social identity is the historically older form, because people had and recognized their relational social identities in the earliest stages of human life. However, collective social identity is a relatively modern phenomenon emergent on the development of large-scale human social organization as made possible by higher levels of economic production. One of the distinguishing

---

[4] This can be put in terms of informational conditions. Thus, "if two objects x and y belong to the same *isoinformation set I*, then they must be treated in the same way J.... Such an invariance requirement is specified in a particular context, involving (among other things) the characterization of 'objects' (x, y, etc.) and that of being treated 'in the same way' (J)" (Sen 1985b, 170).

characteristics of modern society, it seems fair to say then, is the explosive development of new and ever more elaborate systems for social classification combined with the development of increasingly sophisticated statistical techniques and tools for drawing inferences about relationships between social categories. If several hundred years ago really very little information about human beings existed, today governments, private organizations, scientists and researchers, public media, and experts of all kinds are all involved in a vast "collective social identity information revolution," compiling, classifying, and organizing an exponentially expanding body of category-based information about people. Of course, there were methods of social classification and inference in older societies, even ancient ones, particularly in connection with armies and census and tax systems, but they were quite primitive by comparison with the profusion of forms, methods, and technologies for classifying and characterizing people today. Among the reasons for these contemporary classification systems, then, are: legal responsibility, tax obligations, rights protection, market contract compliance, managing social conflict, pension and social services delivery, criminal prosecution, medical treatment, immigration management, education and training, insurance, creditworthiness, census, birth and death verification, archival records, and scientific investigation. Supporting these classification systems are a variety of different social statistical technologies for tracking individuals in these different domains over time, such as: names, number assignments, biometric measures (photographs, fingerprints, DNA identification, medical and dental records, brain scans, and iris scans), personalized records and identifiers of all kinds, resumes, family trees, surveillance, and incarceration or institutionalization. These tracking technologies are "external scaffolding" for these social classification systems, in Clark's (1997) sense of the term. They increase the efficiency of the systems they implement by embedding them in material structures that are long-lasting and secure vis-à-vis the ongoing social processes those systems are meant to describe. They effectively give these classification systems a life of their own in human society.

Because most of these social identification systems did not exist until relatively recently, it follows that categorical or collective social identity has historically played a comparatively smaller part in people's lives than relational social identity. This has now changed dramatically, however, and categorical or collective social identity clearly plays a very important part in the experience of most people. This means many now tend to associate "having a social identity" strictly with the concept of collective social identity, whose basis is the idea that people share certain commonalities when they are said to share membership in social groups. This idea of commonality, in turn, arguably also elevates the idea of an individual even having something called an "identity" – a characteristically modern concern[5] – if the idea of identity is first introduced via the thinking that all individuals who are members of some category get assigned one shared "identifying" characteristic. Then personal identity also tends to get defined in a way derivative of this understanding of identity as some single characteristic people must have through time (cf. Schechtman 1996, 7–12). In contrast, when we think in more relational social identity terms, the idea of having something called an identity is less prominent, because then people are characterized by their roles, relational circumstances, and person-specific ties to others, which are typically not framed in the language of identity. Nonetheless, it does not follow from this that individuals' relational social identities are less important than their collective social identities. Quite the contrary, I will argue that their relational social identities constitute a principle gateway by which they make sense of all their social identities and determine how they manage their often conflicting demands.

9.4.2 Individuals' Social Identity Structures

To argue this, I set out here one way of understanding how individuals' social identities constitute an interconnected structure of relational and collective social identities. Note, then, that when it comes to defining and characterizing social identity, there is an important difference between relational and collective social identities that reflects the types of representations they involve. Collective social identities are essentially what I called – originally back in Chapter 6 in connection with the discussion of the "normal human" individual brainset – third-person representations that use the language of "he," "she," "it," and "they" to refer to those to whom the general categories they involve apply. For example, the category and collective social identity "unemployed" used by government and academic economists refers to any person – "he" or "she" – who fulfills officially established requirements of being unemployed. It is a general or abstract category because it makes no reference to any particular individuals who might be unemployed. On the other hand, relational social identities, whereas they include third-person representations and socially

---

[5]   The concept of having a "personal" identity really only makes its first significant appearance in the form it now has in philosophy at the end of the seventeenth century in the thinking of John Locke (Locke 1975[1694]; cf. Noonan 1991).

Table 9.2. *Individuals' social identity structures*

| | | Individuals identify with | |
		Specific others	Groups
Nature of Influence	Individuals	Co-construct relational social identities	Interpret socially constructed collective social identities
	Third Parties	Co-construct relational social identities	Construct collective social identities

constructed categories, also derive their meaning from reflexive first-person representations that use the language of "I" and "me" to apply those categories. For example, "employee" and "employer" are collective social identities, but they also refer to linked social roles and thus involve relational social identities. They must accordingly still be represented in third-person terms, but they take on further meaning as relational social identities for anyone who is an "employee" or "employer" through how they interpret and apply the third-person representation of "employee" and "employer" on the occasion of their interaction with one another. In effect, the meaning of "employee" and "employer" is not complete until the people occupying these roles ask themselves – and thereby use first-person representations – what their roles entail for them when they interact with one another as "employee" or "employer."

Individuals, then, influence the interpretation of their relational social identities – they "co-construct" them – but only third parties construct the collective social identities on which they are based. The direct interaction people have with one another involves them in determining the meaning of the former, but the social category construction process occurs away from the sites of interaction that social categories are used to describe. That is, people's influence on their social identities is local and relational, at least in the short run. Table 9.2 summarizes all this and shows the influence that individuals and third parties each have in determining what social identities individuals have. The top row shows the influence that individuals have. Individuals co-construct their relational social identities, but their influence on what collective social identities they have (I will argue) is limited to interpreting those they employ in co-constructing their relational social identities. The bottom row of the table shows the influence that third parties have on determining individuals' relational and collective social identities. Third parties co-construct individuals' relational social identities and fully construct their collective social identities.

In the long run, how individuals behave surely influences the construction of their collective social identities, because the third parties who construct the abstract social categories on which they are based continually revise and redevelop them in light of what is learned about social behavior. Social classification systems and the categories they generate evolve over time to reflect what gets learned about social interaction and how it evolves as well; but in the short run, people are limited in their influence on what their collective social identities are to how they apply and interpret these abstract categories.

How, then, do individuals navigate their social identity structures, and what does this explain about the nature of the competing demands that their different social identities make on them? On the view here, people first determine what relational social identities they have via their social roles. They then determine what collective social identities apply to them according to what relational social identities they have, interpreting these collective social identities according to how their own understanding of their social roles relates to third parties' construction of the social categories involved in those social identities. For example, for the collective social identity "employee" a person draws on the associated "employee"/"employer" relational social identity, and interprets being an "employee" according to first-person representations of what her social role requires ("what I should do") in comparison with standard third-person representations of what it means to be an "employee" ("what people typically should do"). This makes two points about how a person navigates the whole of all her relational and collective social identities. First, it says that the individual's access to all her social identities is via her relational social identities, and indeed that she has many ways of accessing that structure in virtue of having many possible social group roles. Second, it tells us that from these many points of entry the person's whole structure of social identities expands outward to include *only* those collective social identities as are associated with the different social categories used to characterize the individual's relational social identities. For example, the culture from which a person comes might have certain practices the person finds objectionable, but if the person's particular social roles and attendant relational identities do not include these practices, then any collective cultural social identity constructed by third parties to include those practices is irrelevant to this person, even though others may claim it applies to her. Thus, the person's own structure of social identities is tailored, as it were, to her own life experience.

This, then, allows us to distinguish two ways in which individuals are relatively autonomous with respect to the claims made on them in the name of collective social identities others assign them. One such source of autonomy is that the set of such claims is limited to those collective social identities implied by their own relational social identities. This is the freedom to deny others' social identity assignments. A second source of autonomy lies in individuals' interpretation of the abstract social categories appropriate to their relational identities from the perspective of their first-person representations of their social roles. Of course, a person can say that "what I ought to do" is "what people typically should do." However, the point is that first-person representations are different from third-person ones, and so people have the discretion to use the former to determine how and whether they will observe the latter. Moreover, on the assumption that individuals' central collective social identities often make competing demands on them, they have motivational grounds for reinterpreting the meaning and force of claims on them regarding "what people typically should do." This is the freedom to reason and deliberate about the meaning of one's social identities.[6]

What autonomy might people have to manage their social roles and relational social identities? On a capabilities conception of individuals, people develop their capabilities in interaction with others. If we now look at this from the perspective of their relational social identities, then people develop their capabilities in interaction with one another across the spectrum of different social roles they have that structure their interaction with one another. Indeed, as the social roles individuals have change over the course of their lives, the capabilities they develop change as well, and so it seems better to say that people continually develop a range of capabilities that operate in conjunction with the corresponding sets of social roles they adopt to exercise these capabilities. Thus, while at any one time people may accordingly be locked in to one set of social roles and their associated relational identities, their nature as beings that develop their capabilities creates continuing choices for them regarding their future social roles and relational identities. Whether this is a matter of "deepening" their existing capabilities or "broadening" their capability sets, their social roles are likely

---

[6]   The freedom to deny social identity assignments is discussed at length by Sen (2006), and the freedom to deliberate using first-person representations is what his frequent emphasis on self-scrutiny involves. Korsgaard (1996) explains the latter as follows:

From a third-person point of view, outside of the deliberative standpoint, it may look as if what happens when someone makes a choice is that the strongest of his conflicting desires wins. But that isn't the way it is *for you* when you deliberate. When you deliberate, it is as if there were something over and above all of your desires, something which is *you*, and which *chooses* which desire to act on. (Korsgaard 1996, 100)

to change as individuals develop new capabilities. They thus also have a relative autonomy with respect to their relational identities, though in this case this autonomy has its basis in the nature of the individual as a self-organizing being developing capabilities; whereas in the case of collective social identities, the emphasis lies on how individuals respond to and interpret the social categories involved.

Individuals, then, navigate their relational and collective social identities as a complex structure that constrains their choices but also allows them to influence what social identities they have as they seek to develop their capabilities. Their social identities, then, are not simply given, as in the conventional "economics of identity" framework; and their personal and social identities, when seen as mutually influencing, do not evolve along clear equilibrium pathways, as in the two endogenous identity models discussed previously. Where do these conclusions then leave us, especially with respect to the concept of personal identity? In the section that follows I return to the individual and offer an answer to this question that builds on the previous chapter's treatment of personal identity as a second-order capability and argues that people develop personal identities as a particular kind of evolving self-narrative they produce when they navigate all their relational and social identities seen now as a structure that evolves.

9.5 Personal Identity as an Evolving Narrative

In Horst, Teschl, and Kirman's analysis, social groups change in nature as individuals with different characteristics enter and exit them. In Darity, Mason, and Stewart's model, social groups evolve in terms of ingroup bias as individuals sort themselves across them. When individuals and social groups are mutually influencing, then, individuals' social identities should be seen to evolve just as their personal identities evolve. Moreover, as an individual's different social identities are likely to evolve in different ways, the entire structure of an individual's interrelated relational and social identities should be expected to evolve as well. This seems to imply that there is not much we can say about the nature of either in the long run. Perhaps this is not much an issue with respect to social identity, but it is particularly a problem when it comes to the concept of personal identity, because it seems to undermine the very idea of having a personal identity. How can someone be said to have a personal identity if what that involves continually changes? Indeed, this is essentially the conclusion of Horst, Teschl, and Kirman, who say that "the personal identity of individuals is relatively weak" (Horst,

Kirman, and Teschl 2007, 23). For them, people really don't have personal identities when we think of them endogenously.

Against this, I have argued that individuals are enduring beings when seen as self-organizing, and that this can be understood in terms of their having a second-order personal capability associated with being able to produce narratives about themselves. What are these self-narratives then? If they also evolve over individuals' lives, why should they be thought to provide a basis for individuals having enduring personal identities? Here I try to bring together the idea of individuals as self-organizing and their constructing self-narratives by saying more about what self-narratives are. The main argument is that a self-narrative is not a single unchanging story given in at least its main outline from early in life. Indeed, self-narratives are quite unlike conventional narratives in virtue of their dynamic character. Rather, they are better seen as the way individuals track and organize personal identity accounts of themselves at any one point in the process of developing their capabilities.

9.5.1 Conventional Narratives Versus Self-narratives

There are two important differences between conventional narratives and self-narratives. First, the conventional view of narrative treats narratives in a nonevolutionary way as having a close-ended quality in which, even if all that is narrated is not resolved, nonetheless the story comes to some kind of end. Stories can of course be repeated and retold in different ways, but they are still oriented toward some type of resolution and do not function as stories unless they have some measure of completeness. In contrast, self-narratives, seen as a special kind of capability, are evolutionary, open-ended, and generally do not get resolved, because people are continually engaged in developing their capabilities, and this continually creates new possibilities for how their narratives will proceed. Basically, as people themselves are open-ended in terms of their capability development, so are their self-narratives. Thus, self-narratives are really not quite like autobiographies or life stories that have an after-the-fact quality in telling the story of an entire life. Rather, they are more like active means employed to solve a continuing sequence of problems in progress, namely, how one finds ways to develop one's capabilities in a world in which one is constantly negotiating many competing and changing social identities.

Second, self-narratives are also not like conventional narratives in that the latter generally maintain some degree of stability in characters and accounts of their interaction, whereas the former revolve around changing casts of characters and changing ways people interact. The identity dynamics of people's lives are simply too variable for conventional narratives, which correspond at best to the short-run analysis of how individuals manage a given set of interrelated social identities. In the long run, however, the way people's social groups and social identities change upsets this normal storytelling. There is not the kind of continuity in people's lives that standard narratives depend on, which requires a certain amount of stability and predictability to achieve their intended dramatic effect. Of course people's lives are often dramatic, and people sometimes behave dramatically. However, their self-narratives, understood in terms of capability development, are not organized around achieving dramatic effect. They are not continuity stories.

If self-narratives, then, are not really like stories in the conventional sense, how are they narratives at all? They are narratives in a sense more basic than stories in simply being discursive accounts that impose an order of some kind on a variety of different sorts of phenomena. Histories have this quality in a backward-looking way; the strategies and plans people produce for dealing with an unknown future have it in a forward-looking way. Both are discursive means of ordering disparate phenomena, and indeed both are also subject to constant, sometimes fundamental revision, unlike stories. Taking personal identity self-narratives, then, to involve a special capability that individuals exercise in developing all the rest of their capabilities, I suggest that they continually combine personal histories and strategies for action as the person's own understanding of how she sees herself developing her capabilities. That is, people develop their capabilities retrospectively in light of past capability development and prospectively with an eye to what this past development makes possible in the future. This makes self-narrative an account that integrates and balances the individual's two temporal perspectives always at the point of decision. Forward-looking self-representations depend at any one moment on a particular set of backward-looking self-representations; backward-looking self-representations at any given time are framed in terms of a particular set of forward-looking self-representations. The two temporal perspectives are thus constantly being linked by individuals in their changing self-narratives. Self-narratives are consequently like a moving window through which the individual simultaneously looks in two directions as their circumstances evolve and change.

It is important to note one criticism of self-narratives as a view of how the individual maintains personal identity that particularly applies here. People might be said to only produce self-narratives that copy other people's self-narratives, and so self-narratives cannot generate personal identities (Strawson 2004). Indeed, when it comes to capabilities, it is true that people's patterns of capability development often follow pathways already pursued by others, and so it is true that they might appear to only need to tell standard stories. I argue, however, that this point is only relevant – and then only partially so – in connection with the development of elementary capabilities, in which many choices people make are shared in at least a general way. However, human history goes much beyond elementary capability development, and in fact complex capability development has become increasingly characteristic of human life. By comparison, complex capability development typically follows highly anomalous pathways reflective of growing number of ways in which people can build new sets of capabilities on past ones. If, as was argued in the previous chapter, we see the collections of capabilities that make people up as becoming increasingly heterogeneous over time, we consequently ought to expect their self-narratives to be increasingly individualized and increasingly different from one another. This would also imply that individuals should place great weight on having such narratives, because standard accounts of what they should do in developing their capabilities would offer only general-purpose benchmarks. What do individuals then put in the place of such benchmarks? Here again, psychologists have something valuable to tell us about how individuals actually go about producing self-narratives.

9.5.2 Tracking and Managing Personal Capability Development

Consider how the retrospective/prospective link works in capability development. People develop their future capabilities in light of their past capability development, and this means that how one remembers what one can do is important in determining what one might be able to do. Regarding memory, then, psychologists are generally in agreement that people's memories take on propositional form, meaning that they take the form of statements and therefore need to be articulated in a shared language as declarative knowledge, or "knowledge that" something is the case (Anderson 1976, 1983). Even people's procedural knowledge, or "knowledge how" to do something, they believe, must at least be capable of being expressed in propositional terms for people to be able to say they know how to do something ("I know *that* this is *how* you do *x*"). That is, how we remember procedural knowledge is embedded in how we remember declarative knowledge. This especially applies to how we remember our capabilities, which combines procedural knowledge about how we are able to do certain things with declarative knowledge about what we know about the world. Of course, people often do things and are unable to say how they were able to do them. Indeed, psychologists recognize that people do many things more or less unconsciously. The issue here rather concerns what is involved in explicitly using memory as a tool for producing a knowledge of past experience. On this score, the consensus view is that memory is propositional in nature.

This is relevant, then, for how we think about individuals using self-narratives to develop their capabilities in that it implies that those self-narratives are articulated in a shared language as declarative knowledge. Thus, the intrapersonal judgments people make regarding what their past capability experience permits in the way of developing future capabilities are always framed in interpersonal terms according to the existing state of declarative knowledge in the social discourse on capabilities. Or, self-narratives about capabilities are part of public narratives about capabilities. Notice that this sort of framing is different from that which is associated with nonpropositional perceptual cues in choice behavior, as in Kahneman and Tversky's prospect theory reference-point analysis. Reference points are perceptual, are not propositional anchors, are largely unconscious, and therefore do not play a role in memory formation and knowledge. They are private phenomena, and are accordingly associated with the isolated individual framework. When we operate with a social conception of the individual, however, and think of individuals as collections of capabilities, the cues people use to interpret their past experience in developing their capabilities are drawn from public discourse about capability development. In setting out their own capability pathways, then, people do not simply imitate and follow capability development pathways already pursued by others, but draw on the existing state of social knowledge about capability development.

That social knowledge about human capability development is complex, many-sided, and constantly evolving. As propositional in nature, it continually gets "scaffolded" in Clark's sense of how human cognitive processes are offloaded into material structures and institutionalized. Thus today, in addition to schools and training programs of many kinds, there are many well-established measures, descriptions, international evidence, and theories about human capability development, as for example is involved in the Human Development Index and the other related indices maintained by the United Nations Development Programme. This is not to say that people thinking about their own choices regarding how they might develop their own capabilities always consult or are even necessarily familiar with the state of social discourse about human capability development. The influence that the state of knowledge about capabilities has on particular individuals is far more indirect. However, their self-narratives about how they themselves look upon their choices trade in the language and meanings of this social discourse and cannot be understood apart from it. The anchoring it provides, then, does not tell people how they ought to invariably proceed but provides only a broad understanding of the possibilities they face. From this perspective, self-narratives are both highly individualized and highly institutionalized accounts people produce to track how they see their own capability development pathways. They are the means individuals employ to track and organize how they interpret their choices with respect to the general human problem of how one develops one's capabilities.

9.6 Socially Embedded Individuals

This and the previous chapter have treated the capabilities conception of the individual as a conception of socially embedded individuals. In standard "economics of identity," individuals are lightly socially embedded in that they have social identities that influence their choices, but their preferences nonetheless remain exogenous and socially uninfluenced. Their personal identities in the form of their utility functions are unaccountably asocial. In the alternative "economics of identity" framework discussed in this chapter, individuals are more deeply socially embedded in that their personal and social identities are mutually influencing. Thus, they are socially embedded in two ways. Who they are is socially influenced, while at the same time they are a part of the social world because they influence it as well. This view entails we go beyond representing individuals in a static way with a given nature to rather represent them dynamically as beings that change. The first strategy secures individuality by an assumption that does not stand up to reasonable scrutiny. The second strategy derives individuality dynamically via the idea of the person as self-organizing. If, then, on the first strategy what people are made up of must be unchanging, on the second strategy what they are made of must be seen as always changing. Conventionally understood preferences are fixed and unchanging. People's capabilities are always changing, are socially mediated and influenced, and yet always belong to those who exercise them.

The standard view of the individual provides a well-known basis for normative policy recommendation in economics. Pareto efficiency recommendations tell us, not only how we ought to produce improvements in the economy given individuals' preferences, but also that the character of the normative gain we make is to be understood in terms of increased preference satisfaction. Yet when we look at the economy in an evolutionary way, and understand individuals as always developing their capabilities, this framework becomes irrelevant if not meaningless. Consequently, a capabilities conception of individuals requires a new normative basis to make new types of policy recommendations. I turn to this in the final chapter as a conclusion to both Part 3 and the book.

TEN

Economic Policy, Democracy, and Justice

Human good is heterogeneous because the aims of the self are heterogeneous.
(Rawls 1971, 554)

Disagreement does not necessarily have to be overcome ... [and] may remain an important and constitutive feature of our relations to others.
(Williams 1985, 133)

10.1 Relinking the Normative to the Positive in Economics

Most economists believe that economics is basically a positive value-free science, and that because there is a clear difference between the language of description ("is" statements) and the language of prescription ("ought" statements), there is strong separation between positive economics and normative economics. This view reflects a number of methodological errors and misconceptions about the nature of language and science (cf. Blaug 1998; Mongin 2006; Boumans and Davis 2010), and what should rather be said is that economists' explanatory frameworks, which are value-laden in many different ways, largely determine how they formulate economic policy. This is especially the case with respect to the explanation of the individual one employs. Indeed, policy's impact is ultimately on people, and so its formulation depends first and foremost on how they are explained. Thus, the standard form of policy recommendation in economics, Pareto efficiency judgments, rules out making interpersonal comparisons, only because the utility function conception of the individual defines people as collections of subjective preferences, which are supposed to be incomparable. Of course, restricting economic policy recommendations to Pareto recommendations significantly limits the space of policy evaluation and eliminates a whole range of fundamental normative concerns – fairness, rights, justice, equality, and so forth – from the domain of economic policy. That is, the standard "description" of the individual determines what is allowed and not allowed in policy "prescription." Most economists overlook this evident bias, because they are committed to some form of the preference conception of the individual, and suppose it to be value-free. This has had odd effects on recent efforts to reintroduce some of these missing normative concerns into economics through the "back door" by way of social preference analysis of such things as fairness and equality. It's a "back door" strategy because introducing a concern with fairness and equality as arguments in utility functions means they are not valuable per se, but only as a means to increased preference satisfaction. What is wrong with this is that such things as fairness and equality have normative value irrespective of whether they increase preference satisfaction. They constitute fundamental normative concerns people have that are independent of the question of preference satisfaction. Therefore, they ought to also be objects of economic policy, because they also concern the well-being of individuals; and to act as if they are not, or are subsidiary to preference satisfaction, simply biases economic policy – hardly what one would expect from a "positive value-free science."

Thus, far from there being a strong separation between positive and normative economics, the connection, especially with respect to how individuals are explained, is really quite close. An alternative way to understand the relationship between explanation and recommendation in economics, then, is to accept this link and see economic policy as being designed to help individuals achieve what they seek to do, however they are conceived. Pareto recommendations aim at preference satisfaction, because it is assumed that individuals should be understood as collections of preferences who aim at preference satisfaction. The form of economic policy, that is, derives from the underlying view of what the individual seeks to achieve. If individuals, however, are rather seen as being constantly engaged in developing themselves as collections of capabilities, economic policy should accordingly be reformulated so as to make it possible for them to achieve this aim. However, given the differences between the preference conception and the capabilities conception, that would involve departing from Pareto framework. What, therefore, does the capabilities conception of the individual entail regarding economic policy? This chapter first takes up this question. It distinguishes three key ideas involved in that conception, links them to fundamental normative concerns, and discusses policy recommendation in these terms.

The chapter then goes on to discuss how economic policy is framed, not just by the individual conception one employs, but also socially by democratic political systems and by the ambition democratic political systems have to promote justice. The reason for this is that once we reinterpret economic policy as being concerned with a range of normative values rather than just one, and give up viewing it in Pareto terms as a domain of narrow technical expertise, the larger social space in which those normative values operate becomes part of how we understand their application in the domain of economic policy. That is, one cannot really explain how such values as fairness and equality should play a role in economic policy until one has considered the meaning and role of these values in the larger domain of democratic social policy. Economists have long insulated their policy recommendation process from this larger social value space by remaining steadfast in their commitment to an asocial conception of the individual. As that individual conception and its single normative value focus does not stand up to reasonable scrutiny, economic policy and its wider array of normative concerns then needs to be seen in a social-political context. I regard this larger context as that of democratic, just societies, because they genuinely aspire to produce the good of individuals, however complex and multidimensional that objective may be.

Section 10.2 argues that three relatively distinct and important normative value concerns are associated with the capabilities conception – (i) human rights, (ii) commitment, trust, and responsibility, and (iii) individual dignity – and ought to therefore be objects of economic policy. The section concludes that as economic policy needs to be open to the diversity of prospects individuals face, it needs to address how people come to determine their agreed upon goals of economic policy. Section 10.3 then turns to the nature of democratic political systems and argues that they need to be understood in terms of not just outcomes but also the processes by which individuals collectively deliberate over social outcomes. Here, I draw on Fabienne Peter's account of democratic legitimacy, because it emphasizes the nature of democracy in societies characterized by value pluralism and then argues that this view is central to thinking of individuals as collections of capabilities. Section 10.4 ends the chapter's discussion of values, policy, and democracy by addressing Sen's recent view of how democratic systems approach the problem of justice. The argument here is that our conception of what justice we can achieve also needs to correspond to our conception of what a person is. Section 10.5 concludes with summary remarks on how Part 3 closes the argument of the book.

10.2 The Normative Implications of the Capabilities Conception

The capabilities conception of individuals laid out in the preceding two chapters treats three ideas as central to understanding what a person is. Individuals continually evolve as they interact with others and develop their capabilities, they actively self-organize themselves, and they are becoming increasingly heterogeneous and different from one another as they more and more develop different complex capabilities. Thus, in comparison to the preferences conception that reduces the person to the single idea of being a preference-satisfier, the capabilities conception is multidimensional in that its characterization of the person depends on three relatively distinct ideas. This implies that an economic policy designed to help individuals develop their capabilities ought to also be seen as multidimensional in virtue of combining the different normative values associated with these ideas. It also follows that, in contrast to Pareto recommendations, which are highly determinate in nature – either a given state of affairs is a Pareto improvement or it is not – policy recommendations appropriate to the capabilities conception are many-sided, because they involve multiple normative values that may be integrated in different ways. Economic policy understood in this way thus ultimately depends on how people deliberate over the relationships between these different values as well as the social conditions under which this process of deliberation occurs. Rather than a disadvantage, however, this seems to be an advantage, because moral life in fact exhibits many normative values, and Pareto-based recommendations have too long given a misleadingly simple and one-sided view of the nature of economic policy. At the same time, this reverses conventional wisdom regarding the relationship between economics and ethics. Rather than ethics being the unwanted companion to economics, ethics now emerges as an especially important form of analysis whose subject in this instance is the integration of different normative values in social economic policy. What, then, are the three distinct normative values associated with the three key ideas in the capabilities conception? In what follows, I emphasize one value in connection with each idea, though there are cross-connections and alternative linkages one might also defend.

10.2.1 Human Rights

The capabilities conception treats individuals as continually developing their capabilities in interaction with others. However, if individuals are continually changing, how are they objects of moral regard? If we are to preserve the view that people are morally important, and at the same time accept that as always changing they are never just one thing to which we can refer, then their moral value as persons must be abstract – something we choose to attribute to them per se as human beings and which we say is intrinsic to their being persons. I suggest that this is what is involved in the most basic understanding of individuals having human rights. Human rights are a set of protections people have purely in virtue of being human beings. To go beyond this basic idea, human rights have been further justified in a number of more specific ways: as what is presupposed in the idea of purposeful human action (Gewirth 1996), as what is minimally required to be a person (Shue 1996), as a condition for human autonomy (Copp 1992), and as the freedoms and opportunities that allow individuals to determine which sets of functionings they wish to develop (Sen 2005). Each of these justifications has merit, but Sen's view also has the merit of explicitly portraying the individual as developing and clearly departs from a static conception of the individual. What specifically, then, is the connection between being in a state of continual development and human rights?

Sen argues that freedoms and opportunities that human rights secure are not a matter of being in a certain state (for example, "*being* well-nourished or in good health"), but are a matter of "the extent to which the person is *able to choose* particular combinations of functionings" (ibid., 334; his emphasis). That is, for him human rights only need secure to individuals the opportunity to pursue (or not pursue) possible paths of personal development, and should not aim to secure any set of actual outcomes, as for example might be enumerated in some list of basic functionings that individuals need to achieve regardless of their goals. Why not focus on actual outcomes, particularly in a world in which many do not have the minimum requirements for life? Focusing on actual outcomes runs the risk of freezing the number and kinds of things that can fall within the scope of individuals' rights. No doubt we can often say what people's basic needs are and thus what economic rights they should have to achieve these needs (cf. Hertel and Minkler 2007). Sen's conceptual basis for human rights, however, is different. It is not about securing a list of things that people may be and do but about securing the human possibility for a person to become any number of things. If we take it to be characteristic of human beings that they continually develop their capabilities, then seeing this as a right makes it a distinctively human right. Yet why should this be a right, however human it may be? The answer is that people develop their capabilities in interaction with others. If there were only a set number of basic needs and people only developed elementary capabilities, in principle, given the world's resources as we understand them, they might all be compatibly addressed without conflict. However, it is hard to see how a capability development that increasingly emphasizes complex capabilities can be free of conflict. Thus, to preserve capability development as a fundamental human aim, it must be regarded as a right, that is, a human right.

This argument is not meant to diminish other justifications for human rights. It is rather meant to show an important normative implication of seeing individuals as continually developing their capabilities in interaction with others. At the same time, this particular justification of human rights gives these rights a different meaning than other justifications in virtue of not representing individuals in static terms. This raises the interesting question of whether static individual conceptions can provide adequate defenses of human rights, a question I do not pursue here. The point is rather that when we look upon individuals as continually developing, we need to consider what they require per se as dynamic beings. Human rights from this perspective simply secure this property to people on principle.

10.2.2 Commitment, Trust, and Responsibility

The capabilities conception as I have explained it also treats individuals as actively self-organizing themselves. That is, they do not just change as they develop their capabilities, but they develop them in such a way as to continually individualize themselves. They do this by retrospectively and prospectively building on their past capability development when they adopt new pathways that distinguish their own from pathways that others pursue. This is a reflexive or self-regarding sort of activity that depends on being able to engage in a process of self-evaluation. Psychologists, we saw, argue that individuals do this by relying on multidimensional self-concepts that they continually reorder and rebuild as they experience the results of their past capability development strategies. Philosophers explain this from the perspective of the whole individual in terms of the concept of integrity (e.g., McFall 1987). Specifically, people have personal integrity when they have coherent views of themselves, such as when they consistently exercise higher-order desires to regulate their first-order desires (Frankfurt 1971). Bernard Williams (1973, 1981) links personal integrity to moral integrity, arguing that when people interact they often make (personal) "identity-conferring commitments" to one another regarding what they will do and not do in the future. An identity-conferring commitment has a dual quality in that it commits oneself to doing and being something at the same time that it makes a commitment to another person. For Williams, then, identity-conferring commitments produce personal integrity by way of moral integrity.

People of course make commitments to one another all the time, no less in economic life than in other domains in connection with market transactions. Market transactions are open-ended in that not all the terms of performance can be fully specified. This is especially the case with agreements that have long-term dimensions. On the conventional view of the individual, such agreements need to be structured so that parties to them find it in their interest or have incentives to comply with their terms, such as in principal-agency relationships (Jensen and Meckling 1976). However, for this view to be descriptively adequate, the conditions and circumstances surrounding most market relationships would need to be more stable and transparent than they are. Too much is unforeseen because the world changes to suppose interest alone explains market relationships. Moreover, why should we ignore the considerable evidence that people often act on principles that go beyond interest, and that this is related to their sense of personal integrity (Minkler 2008)?[1]

On a capabilities conception of the individual, we can argue that one way people acquire the personal histories they use in developing their capabilities is through a succession of identity-conferring commitments they make to others. That is, their commitments to others, whether in personal or market connections, are a part of how they continually self-organize themselves over time. A person's history of capability development is then also a history of that person's commitments to others. This is not to say, of course, that people never violate their commitments nor redirect their histories! Psychologists treat individuals' working self-concepts as being made up of many self-conceptions that are continually being reorganized. Williams argues that when people's commitments conflict, the stronger ones dominate. Which ones are the strongest can be different from one time to another. Nor does an emphasis on commitment mean that individuals never interact with others in an instrumentally rational way. Commitment indeed involves a deontological kind of choice in which people act on a principle irrespective of payoff (Minkler 2008; Sen 1977, 1985b; Peter and Schmid 2007). It constitutes an additional motive people exercise that cannot be explained

---

[1]   To explain the principles people act on, Minkler makes a distinction between preference-integrity and commitment-integrity, in which the former is a strongly-held overriding preference or disposition (say, to be honest or keep agreements one makes) and the latter lies in reflective deliberation on the principles one chooses to abide by. The latter is associated with moral judgments, and, as in Williams' analysis, is identity-conferring.

in terms of instrumentally rational behavior, as explained in terms of the preferences conception of the individual.

Commitment is associated with the concepts of trust and responsibility. Trust is essentially the obverse of commitment in that the latter is the orientation the individual takes toward others, whereas trust is the orientation others take toward those who make commitments to them. The companion concept to trust, responsibility, is then the posture the individual takes when trusted by others. These concepts have normative force when the parties involved believe that commitments that have been made ought to be honored. That, in turn, depends on whether they share a belief that a commitment was made and what the shared expectations were when it was made. Not all commitments have normative significance, but many do. The capabilities conception of the individual, when explained in connection with identity-conferring commitments, allows us to consider this a dimension of economic policy.

10.2.3 Individual Dignity

The third aspect of the capabilities individual conception I have emphasized is that, as developing complex capabilities more and more dominates human capability development, individuals' are increasingly heterogeneous and different from one another. This idea is not inherent in the idea of people as dynamic beings or self-organizing; it rather represents a claim about the changing nature of the human capability space. The argument is that, as the global social division of labor advances to produce an ever greater variety of types of human activities, individuals' developmental pathways are increasingly disparate. Their human experience may be broadly similar, yet their choices regarding how they individually develop their capabilities are increasingly specific to their particular life pathways. Thus paradoxically, the way in which people are generally alike is that they are becoming more diverse and more heterogeneous from one another. Note that there is a parallel between this view and the standard preferences view of the individual, in which people are all different from one another in virtue of each having their own preferences (even where their preferences are identical). The difference between the two accounts of human heterogeneity is that the foundation of the preference conception lies in privacy and subjectivity – a circular and unsupportable basis for individuality – whereas the foundation for heterogeneity in the capabilities conception lies in interaction in a public world and intersubjectivity – a supportable basis, though one that puts a burden for its defense on social policy, as I will argue in the next section.

What normative values are we concerned with, then, when individuals' common bond is difference? Consider how people go about developing their capabilities when their pathways seem to be theirs alone. They may be impelled to develop their capabilities as they choose, as this is what their lives require of them, but whether, additionally, they value how they go about doing so when they may share little with others about how to do this requires that they also esteem what they do, or have pride and self-esteem in their efforts. Avishai Margalit gets at what this involves when he explains the character of the concept of human dignity as two-sided in combining self-esteem and self-respect.

Dignity is similar to pride. Pride is the expression of self-esteem; dignity is the expression of the feeling of respect persons feel toward themselves as human beings. Dignity constitutes the external aspect of self-respect. Self-respect is the attitude persons have to the fact of their being human. (Margalit 1996, 51)

People may feel self-esteem in their choices without the respect of others, but when they believe they have that respect, they then have self-respect, the external aspect of which is dignity. Margalit's view is that self-esteem becomes self-respect when a person believes it is merited in the eyes of others. This is what invests a person with dignity, seen as the key normative value underlying individuality. For him, "self-esteem is a ranking concept [that] relies on the beliefs people have about their own achievements," whereas self-respect is a matter of "belonging" that one has in virtue of social membership (ibid., 46–7). Individuals consequently have dignity when they not only pursue but also value their own developmental pathways in the confidence that others respect what they do.

Thus, dignity is a central normative value when we focus on the individualizing nature of personal capability development. It might seem odd to say that this value needs to be emphasized in economic policy, because Pareto recommendations assume individuals are (subjectively) distinct, and this would appear to value individuals in themselves. However, Pareto reasoning is a species of utilitarian thinking, and thus, as John Rawls pointed out, "does not take seriously the distinction between persons" (Rawls 1971, 27). This is not just a matter of the familiar charge that utilitarian thinking ignores the distribution of utility across people, a charge that applies equally in its ordinal formulation and to the Pareto principle. What Rawls was rather referring to was the "separateness" of persons, as influenced by

Immanuel Kant's view of people as ends in themselves. In this sense, then, human dignity is a quite different sort of normative value – one I suggest anchors the normative interpretation of the capabilities conception.[2]

10.2.4 Economic Policy Recommendation

When operating with a capabilities conception of individuals, then, economic policy recommendation ought to promote human rights, trust and responsibility, and individual dignity. To be sure, these normative goals do not exclude others, particularly ones formulated in terms of the promotion of aggregate social well-being. When, for example, we consider changes in the organization of markets and the nature of economic institutions, and identify strategies meant to increase net economic output, economic policies that aim to promote these strategies simply have their basis in the goal of promoting the well-being of individuals on average or in general. What these latter policies do not do is promote the well-being of individuals one-by-one, and indeed, as Rawls suggests, they may neglect it altogether. In part, this seems to be because their traditional basis in Pareto efficiency recommendations does not capture the forward-looking character of individuals, who continually need to project futures that are only vaguely understood. Public policy operates in a highly uncertain environment complicated by continuous institutional change in which reasons for action run from an imagined future back to the present, but the Pareto principle is built around today's preferences and sets aside institutional change (cf. esp. Bromley 2006). To ask whether proposed policy changes respect individuals as well as promote well-being in general requires making judgments about how particular individuals might fare were those policies adopted. Pareto-based policy recommendations do not do this. Of course, policy invariably concerns many people in often very different circumstances, so there can be no simple way to proceed in formulating policy. Different people will inevitably have different views about desirable public policy. What this tells us, however, is that formulating policy, economic or otherwise, involves the difficult task of establishing "sufficient reason" for courses of collective action that get undertaken (ibid.). Policy does not get established in a technocratic way apart from public discussion. It has to have its basis in

---

[2] The term "separateness" of persons comes from Robert Nozick (1974, 32–33), who was similarly influenced by Kant. Thomas Nagel and Joshua Cohen have argued that Rawls' view of the inherent value of persons was rooted in his religious thinking (cf. Rawls 2009).

broad public reason regarding people in general. In the following section, I explain this in terms of how democratic political systems develop public policy, though not necessarily according to one interpretation of this, the idea of forming a shared consensus.

10.3 The Democratic Framework

10.3.1 Deliberative Democracy

Economic policy is socially framed by political systems and framed in democratic societies in particular to achieve the goals of individuals. However, as Peter (2009) makes clear, there are different ways in which democracy can be understood that have distinct implications for how democracy frames economic policy. Note, then, that there are two main paradigms in contemporary political theory with respect to the nature of democracy: "deliberative democracy" and "aggregative democracy." Aggregative democracy builds on the traditional understanding of democracy as government by voting. Economists' interpretation of this is generally referred to as the "economic theory of democracy," which follows social choice theory initiated by Kenneth Arrow (1963 [1951]) as an account of how, or whether, individual preferences can be aggregated to produce a consistent social preference ordering of different possible social states. For Arrow, voting is just like a market in that it aggregates individual preferences to produce collective outcomes. Preferences, moreover, are revealed preferences, so they can have any motivation, self-regarding or other-regarding (as in social preference analysis), and rely on any underlying normative values people might have. Thus, how people vote reveals their values, and voting outcomes are therefore seen as democratic in translating individuals' preferences into voters' collective social choices. The conditions Arrow imposed on this analysis, of course, generated his famous "impossibility theorem" result, which implied that the only collective social choice possible involved the dictatorship of one person's preferences. However, this result has been taken by many social choice theorists not as a reason for abandoning Arrow's approach so much as an invitation to reconsider and revise his conditions in order to explain democracy as a reflection of individual preferences.[3]

---

[3] This, for example, is Sen's view. Most impossibility-type results, he argues, can be "largely resolved by making the social decision procedures more informationally sensitive," for example, by adding "[i]nformation on interpersonal comparisons of well-being and relative advantages" (Sen 2009, 93). Arrow's four conditions are unrestricted domain, independence of irrelevant alternatives, the (weak) Pareto principle, and nondictatorship.

In contrast, the deliberative democracy paradigm accepts that voting is important to democratic decision making, but expands our view of how we get to the point of voting, as well as what voting means, by emphasizing the variety of ways in which people discuss, debate, and deliberate about their prospective choices prior to and after voting. That is, it explains democracy in terms of a public reasoning process rather than in terms of episodic acts of voting (Cohen 1997). This is a departure from the aggregative democracy idea in two ways. First, it makes democracy a dynamic social process rather than simply a periodically invoked mechanism for tallying votes. Second, because a process of deliberation involves the consideration and exchange of reasons for different possible courses of action, it replaces preferences over action with reasons for action. People may indeed have their preferences, but what counts are the reasons they give for the views they adopt. Together, then, these two departures make for a much more complicated view of democratic systems because there are many ways in which such a process can be explained. One interpretation of a democratic deliberative process, then, is that the exchange and debate it involves must ultimately move toward a resolution understood as a shared consensus over the issues debated (e.g., ibid., 75). However, Peter argues that this view overlooks "value pluralism," and that "differences over what constitutes the best social choice on a certain issue will always remain" even when social decisions are made (Peter 2009, 34). The fact that voting results are only majority results confirms this view. Despite debate and exchange, despite social action, people continue to disagree. This then seems to be the right way to understand public deliberation, and indeed it brings out its character as a process. A process that is ongoing is arguably driven by the dynamic that sustains it. The notion that it includes forces that dampen debate and converge to an equilibrium consensus seems contrary to this. Peter's claim, however, rests on her understanding of value pluralism. What, then, does this involve?

Essentially her view is that the differences between people related to gender, race, sexuality, national origin, religion, class, and so forth, are deep, that these differences give rise to their having often quite different social values, and that there is no particular reason to think that these differences will be erased in social exchange. Yet at the same time, value pluralism does not imply that meaningful debate and public deliberation is impossible. Indeed, it is possible and realistic to expect, Peter argues following the later Rawls (1993), when we think of people in a pluralistic way as reasonable rather rational individuals.

Persons are reasonable insofar as they recognize that, though they have good reasons to hold their own conception of the good, there are good reasons for other citizens to hold their own conceptions of the good. Reasonable citizens accept that their society will always contain a plurality of conceptions of the good. (Peter 2009, 39–40)

This view directly underlies the idea that democracy involves a deliberative social process in that it explains why people have grounds for debate and exchange. They do because they differ in their values and yet are tolerant toward others – indeed feel a kind of empathy towards them – in accepting that this difference is what is inescapably involved in a democratic political system. Value pluralism, from this perspective, is actually constitutive of the democratic process because it explains why deliberation occurs. This crucially assumes, of course, that people are reasonable in supposing that all people's views count and that society is made up of a citizenry of politically equal individuals, all of whom are entitled to participate in the democratic process.

However, this latter condition – political equality – raises difficult issues when we go beyond simply relying on aggregative democracy's standard "one person one vote" measure to emphasize equal opportunity to participate in the political process. This is a key focus of Peter's understanding of public reasoning and democratic legitimacy, a view she develops as an account of "epistemic democracy" in which "democratic decision-making processes are valued at least in part for their knowledge-producing potential" (Peter 2009, 110). What she sees as important in this view is that it explains how in a democratic process "the normative and empirical premises of policy proposals," for example, those underlying economic policy recommendations, are "subjected to the scrutiny of an inclusive process of public deliberation prior to voting" (ibid., 3). I do not go into her discussion of this here,[4] but turn to what it implies about the nature of individuals and argue that understanding democracy in this way places special emphasis on the three normative goals distinguished previously that are inherent in a capabilities conception of the individual. That is, I argue that the capabilities conception of individuals and its normative content expressed in terms of these values, together with the deliberative view of democracy, jointly frame economic policy formulation – individually and socially, as it were – in a society based on value pluralism.

10.3.2 The Capabilities Conception in a Democratic Society

What, then, does social deliberation in democratic societies, seen specifically as a process of exchange and debate over public policy initiatives, actually

---

[4] Though see the discussion in Emami and Davis (2009).

require of individuals? When we assume value pluralism, we suppose that people's value differences are not eliminated by exchange and debate, and that in varying degrees they even remain in disagreement with policies that ultimately get adopted. At the same time, as Peter emphasizes, democratic societies not only succeed in adopting collective policies but also generally succeed in making the deliberative process meaningful in the eyes of people themselves – even when they disagree with its outcomes. One way we can understand this difficult balance is to consider how people individually address debate and exchange. On the one hand, they surely revise and change their views as a result of their interaction with one another; on the other hand, given value pluralism, they also preserve differences between themselves and others with respect to values. This does not seem to require that they preserve any particular set of values. Like self-conceptions, people sometimes abandon or revise values that are long-held, though they also often maintain certain values for long periods of time. What it seems to imply they do from the perspective of the capabilities conception is reorder and reorganize their values, changing the ranking and weights given to them and changing the ways in which they see interconnections between them. That is, people are self-organizing with respect to their values just as they are with respect to their capabilities, as we would expect because both develop in interaction with others and people's capabilities and values are no doubt closely associated.

Of course, no one assumes that this kind of combination is easily achieved in the world of actual political systems. Nondemocratic political systems, and arguably many democratic ones that function primarily in an aggregative way, generally work to impose social consensus and often discourage the sort of sustained disagreement over policy decisions that would arise in a society committed to value pluralism. For individuals, this then increases the risk of revising and changing their views and values in a process of debate and exchange with others, because the idea behind an imposed consensus is that disagreement should be eliminated. Thus, if indeed most people's beliefs do not exactly coincide with accepted policies, reflection on one's views may seem, practically speaking, like an invitation to abandon them rather than to revise them. Assuming that people are truly different in their values, the inference individuals would likely then make is that one ought to always avoid compromise and change in order to preserve some degree of value autonomy. Given the link between capabilities and values, this in turn would presumably discourage individuals from pursuing new strategies of personal capability development, because change in one's capabilities likely brings along unexpected change in one's values, and this may be socially risky in a social-political world based on consensus, whether democratic or nondemocratic.

With respect to the three ideas I argue underlie the capabilities conception of the individual, value pluralism clearly corresponds to the principle of human heterogeneity. Because people are different, they have different values. When we think in terms of political systems, then, the other two ideas I have emphasized as being part of that conception – that people continually evolve when they interact with others and develop their capabilities and that they actively self-organize themselves – become consequences of the heterogeneity principle. Whether people are able to act on these behavioral grounds thus depends in important ways on whether human heterogeneity is accepted via a democratic social commitment to value pluralism. Consider, then, what happens when consensus becomes an ideal of social policy. Consensus, when defined as it is here as the goal of eliminating disagreement, removes differences between people as a relevant consideration in thinking about collective choice. That is, it makes what was referred to previously as the "separateness" of persons irrelevant to society's self-conception regarding shared policy. The separateness idea, I suggested, expresses the normative value that all people have an inherent dignity. So whereas the principle of human heterogeneity acts as the entry point for the other two main ideas in the capability conception, the dignity value is also an important avenue by which the values of human rights and trust and responsibility arise. In contrast, in a consensus-driven political system, it is neither clear what rights people have per se to develop themselves and their capabilities nor clear what trust and confidence they should have in others in a social interaction.

I close this discussion with a more summary normative evaluation that reflects Peter's focus on the problem of political equality. Equality with respect to the vote is perhaps one clear measure of equality; but what is the measure of equality with respect to participation? It is tempting, given voting as a model, to look for an equally determinate mechanism that might be institutionalized by a set of constitutional rules that are thought to express ideal qualities of a democratic (and just) political system. However, this way of looking at the matter is more appropriate to the aggregative view of democracy, which employs a conception of individuals as collections of preferences. Given the usual conditions imposed on preferences to make choices "rational," all individuals' "votes" count equally. In contrast, the idea that equality arises out of participation is nonepisodic and points us towards how we understand equality in a social process. Certainly there are many things this can involve, and it consequently seems wrong-headed from the start to try to produce a single set of criteria for this that would apply across all kinds of societies for all time (though this is not to say that anything goes, as there is much debate in contemporary democracies about what equality in participation ought to involve). In this light, were we then to take the conception of individuals as collections of capabilities as essential to framing the goals of social economic policy, equality in participation should be understood in terms of what makes it possible for all individuals to develop their capabilities. That is, equality in participation is tied to equality in capability development.

There is much that is left unexplained in this participatory view of equality. Part of the reason for this is that what we take to be a democratic system based on equality depends on what we specifically regard as a just democratic system. People can be equal in some respects and not in others in a participatory sense no less than in voting, but we cannot say when this should be unless we can assess equalities and inequalities according to our standards of justice. Thus, the section that follows asks how democratic systems approach the problem of justice, particularly when we understand individuals as collections of capabilities.

10.4 Justice and Capabilities

What should we expect of a system of justice when we emphasize value pluralism? Rawls, whose thinking about justice has been the most influential, sometimes suggests value pluralism is important, but nonetheless clearly excludes it from his theory of justice. He tells us that: "Human good is heterogeneous because the aims of the self are heterogeneous" (Rawls 1971, 554). However, when he explains how his famous principles of justice are chosen when people are imagined to be behind a veil of ignorance in the original position, he also tells us that these principles would be their unanimous choice. Consider this argument he makes for this remarkable conclusion:

To begin with, it is clear that since the differences among the parties are unknown to them, and everyone is equally rational and similarly situated, each is convinced by the same arguments. Therefore, we can view the choice in the original position from the standpoint of one person selected at random. If anyone after due reflection prefers a conception of justice to another, then they all do, and a unanimous agreement can be reached. (Rawls 1971, 139)[5]

---

[5] In contrast, Rawls' imagined experimental procedure for how his principles of justice would be selected simply imposes unanimity.

I shall simply take as given a short list of traditional conceptions of justice.... I then assume that the parties are presented with this list and *required to agree unanimously* that one conception is the best among those enumerated. (Rawls 1971, 122; emphasis added)

There are differences between people, but as they cannot know them behind the veil of ignorance, the implied debate and exchange between them regarding the "arguments" for candidate principles of justice treats "everyone [as] equally rational and similarly situated," so that they cannot but reach the same conclusions. That is, the veil of ignorance negates value pluralism and the differences that exist between people, so that it is as if but one (representative) person determines the principles of justice, and ironically the "separateness" of people that Rawls otherwise emphasizes has no significance when it comes to determining the principles of justice. This is similar to Arrow's dictatorship solution to collective social choice, because, though for Arrow individuals have different preferences, only those of the dictator count. It is also similar in that what really goes on behind the veil of ignorance is not exchange and debate over the reasons regarding "arguments" that might be advanced for one set of principles versus another, but simply a registering of preference. People are imagined as being asked: What principles of justice do they prefer? That is, Rawls unanimous vote is really just a unanimous preference, so that, at least with respect to his treatment of how the principles of justice are selected, he similarly operates with an aggregative view of the foundations of justice.

Suppose, however, that we rather make value pluralism central to our understanding of the principles of justice. Unanimity and consensus would then cease to be foundational, and our "system" of justice would need to admit rival principles whose application could generate conflicting recommendations. In his *The Idea of Justice*, Sen's parable-like example of three children contesting who ought to have a flute is an illustration. One makes a case based on knowing how to play it; another's case is based on being the poorest; the third's case is based on having made the flute (Sen 2009, 13). Three conflicting principles of justice are thus in play. Who is right? In fact, none of the claims can be summarily dismissed. At the same time, Sen emphasizes, this does not imply that there is no just resolution of the children's claims. A just resolution of conflicting legitimate claims, however, does not come about through some sort of abstract argument in which one principle trumps all others that can be applied in all circumstances. That is precisely what is missing here. Rather, it comes through a reasoned evaluation of how the process of debate between people with different values ought to ultimately reach conclusions. Suppose for the moment, then, that the debate does come to an end, the flute is allocated, and the three children accept the result as just. If we maintain value pluralism, and accordingly see them as each still believing that their respective principles of justice are appropriate with respect to who should get the flute, we can only infer that they have a more complicated view of what is involved in a just resolution of their dispute. Key to this is their having an awareness that disputes such as this one regularly recur and that conflicts over what is just are a normal part of a continuing process of social interaction. That is, people judge a particular resolution of a conflict as just if they perceive that the process leading up to it plus the resolution are just – what Sen calls a "comprehensive outcome" (ibid., 215).

Sen thus argues that we need to understand justice, not in terms of ideal time-independent systems of perfect principles – an approach he labels transcendental institutionalism – but in terms of the practice of achieving "agreement, based on public reasoning, on rankings of alternatives that can be realized" – an approach he contrasts as one emphasizing realization-focused comparisons (ibid., 7, 17). His argument for this proposed redirection goes back to and extends his early "partial orderings" approach to social choice theory that explains choice in connection with two important forms of incompleteness: unbridgeable gaps in information and judgmental unresolvability (Sen 1970; 2009, 103).

Thus, for reasons both of incomplete individual evaluations and of incomplete congruence between different individuals' assessments, persistent incompleteness may be a hardy feature of judgements of social justice. This can be problematic for the identification of a just society, and make transcendental conclusions difficult to derive. And yet, such incompleteness would not prevent making comparative judgements about justice in a great many cases – where there might be fair agreement on particular pairwise rankings – about how to enhance justice and reduce injustice. (ibid., 105)

For him, then, transcendental approaches to justice, such as he finds in Rawls and in the contractarian tradition generally, are neither sufficient nor necessary to explain just decision making: not sufficient, because falling short of an ideal standard of justice tells us little about concrete choices we must make regarding just outcomes; not necessary, because we often make comparative judgments about what is just quite successfully without appealing to standards of ideal justice (ibid., 98ff.).

What an emphasis on realization-focused comparisons accordingly involves is a view of justice as a social process that continually operates on a case-by-case basis, comparing circumstances *a* and *b* to determine which course of action would be judged just. A key condition for justice to be pursued in this way is that any determination of what actions ought to be pursued should result from a vigorous, transparent process of public reasoning. If ideal principles of justice are too removed from the concrete world of conflict and rival views of justice to tell us how to practice justice, then we have no alternative but to construct a process of public reasoning that allows us to make the best possible judgments we can. Democratic societies, particularly when seen as being deliberative in nature, offer the best chance of achieving this. Democratic public reasoning alone is not enough, however. What more is needed, Sen argues (ibid., 13ff.), is a widespread conviction that the process of public reasoning is fair and impartial, as Rawls had originally argued in characterizing justice as fairness (Rawls 1958), and as he argues Adam Smith captured even more effectively in his *Theory of Moral Sentiments* with his idea of an impartial spectator open to seeing things from any point of view (Smith 1759 [1976]). It is ultimately people's sense of impartiality that allows them to accept outcomes that are not in their favor and that fail to employ the principles and values they believe correct.

Much of Sen's *Idea of Justice* is devoted to the myriad considerations that impinge on people's perceptions of fairness and impartiality (e.g., Sen 2009, chap. 5 and 6). Smith is an inspiration for much of this thinking, but Sen's argument is ultimately one based on a more modern commitment to cosmopolitanism and a critique of all forms of parochialism (ibid., 403ff.). However, what basis is there for this perspective, as widely shared as it may be today? Cosmopolitanism is in many respects simply a plea for tolerance toward all peoples irrespective of their cultures and histories. Many of the arguments for it, for example prudentialist ones emphasizing the payoffs to cooperation, typically depend on the view that value pluralism and human heterogeneity are themselves of great benefit. But this gives those arguments a highly contingent status. My argument in this chapter has been that policy conceptions, as well as their framing in democratic political systems and by the interpretations of justice appropriate to those systems, are ultimately anchored in underlying views of what it is that individuals seek to achieve. That is, we pursue policies and develop just political systems just because we think they are ultimately conducive to the well-being of individuals. Thus, the ultimate defense of the value pluralism perspective is that individuals are collections of capabilities who are increasingly different from one another in their personal capability pathways. Thus, I argue that the broad goals of social economic policy, the understanding of democracy as deliberative, and the view that justice depends on fair processes, are all built around an understanding of individuals as open-ended, different, and self-organizing.

10.5 Embedding Individuals

I take this last section to comment briefly on how the argument of Part 3 closes the argument of the book. Part 3 advanced a capabilities conception of individuals as socially embedded on the grounds that we cannot really understand individual capabilities except in a social world in which we see how they are exercised. However, the focus on capabilities was also the result of an extension of the evolutionary arguments about individuals advanced at the end of Part 2. There, I argued that in an evolutionary world seeing individuals as self-organizing depends on assuming that they have certain fundamental capacities – learning and empathy – but I then argued that to fully understand these capacities we need to explain how people develop them in social interaction in the form of whole collections of capabilities that then make them up. That is as I see it, the capabilities conception relies on an evolutionary-relational thinking about individuals, which involves an agenda for explaining individual behavior quite different from that involved in revised preferences conceptions of the individual, which were the focus of Part 1. Preferences conceptions, of course, are static, point-in-time conceptions, which by nature cannot capture the dynamic, agency character of individuals. Indeed, one of the conclusions of Part 1 was that increasing the psychological realism of the preference conception, as in connection with the recognition of time-inconsistent behavior, shows the inherent limitation of static conceptions in their inability to say why individuals do not dissolve into multiple selves. The other main conclusion of Part 1 concerned the asocial character of preference conceptions. The social preferences strategy seeks to overcome this in a clever way by embedding sociality in individuals rather than by embedding individuals in a social world. What this strategy ultimately fails to do, however, is go beyond largely ad hoc and vague explanations about the nature of behavioral motivation and say why essentially asocial individuals should be thought to have social motivations. Understanding social motivations, Part 2 argued, depends on having a fuller explanation of how social interaction affects individuals, which in turn cannot be separated from an understanding of how individuals and the forms of interaction evolve together. The arguments of the second half of the book were intended to show how these barriers can be overcome in a conception of socially embedded individuals seen as enduring and developing.

Chapter 1 began with two criteria necessary for explaining individuals – individuation and reidentification – and used them to define the space in which single-individual explanations need to be set out in terms of the sub-personal and supra-personal bounds that operate on those explanations. Adequate conceptions of individuals need to be able to explain how they are individuated or hold together as single beings and how they can be reidentified through change and do not disappear into social aggregates. As I argued that the individual conceptions discussed in Part 1 fail to successfully address the sub-personal bound, and that there is mixed success in addressing the supra-personal bound in the conceptions discussed in Part 2, the implication was that the evolutionary capabilities conception advanced in Part 3 would satisfy both the individuation and reidentification criteria and explain individuals vis-à-vis both bounds. The case for saying that individuals do not dissolve into multiple selves and can be individuated as single individuals rests on the argument that individuals can exercise a second-order personal identity capability that produces self-narratives they use to organize their lives. The case for saying that individuals do not disappear into social aggregates and can be reidentified as enduring social beings rests on the argument that individuals' social identities come structured in first-person and third-person terms, so that the social construction of individual identity goes hand in hand with individuals' management of their constructed identities. My view is that this framework offers a successful conception of the individual, but this does not imply that individuals thus understood are themselves successful in maintaining personal identities and living out their lives as single enduring beings. On the one hand, there is the question of what they actually do themselves; on the other hand, there is the question of how societies operate and whether how they are organized and function is conducive to sustaining individuality in the world. These questions mark where the argument of this book leaves off.

Of course, the capabilities conception of the individual developed here possesses many ambiguities and problematic aspects, as one would expect of any examination of individuals and identity. However, if my discussion has often not been persuasive, I hope to at least have convinced readers of the seriousness of the issue and its fundamental importance. It seems the history we have inherited could well have told us that individuals do not count in this world and that only "higher" causes matter. This book presupposes just the opposite conclusion and asks that it be taken as central to economics and economic life.

References

Abbott, Andrew (1988) *The System of Professions: An Essay on the Division of Expert Labor*, Chicago: University of Chicago Press.

Abrams, Dominic and Michael Hogg (1999) *Social Identity and Social Cognition*, Oxford: Blackwell.

Aguiar, Fernando, Pablo Brañas-Garza, Maria Paz Espinosa, and Luis Miller (2010) "Personal Identity: A Theoretical and Experimental Analysis," *Journal of Economic Methodology* 17: 4.

Ainslie, George (1992) *Picoeconomics: The Strategic Interaction of Successive Motivational States within the Person*, Cambridge: Cambridge University Press.

(2001) *Breakdown of the Will*, Cambridge: Cambridge University Press.

Akerlof, George and Rachel Kranton (2000) "Economics and Identity," *Quarterly Journal of Economics* 115: 715–53.

(2002) "Identity and Schooling: Some Lessons for the Economics of Education," *Journal of Economic Literature* 40 (4): 1167–201.

(2005) "Identity and the Economics of Organizations," *Journal of Economic Perspectives* 19 (1): 9–32.

(2010) *Identity Economics: How Our Identities Shape Our Work, Wages, and Well-Being*, Princeton, NJ: Princeton University Press.

Alač, Morana (2004) "Negotiating Pictures of Numbers," *Social Epistemology* 18 (2–3): 199–214.

Anderson, John R. (1976) *Language, Memory, and Thought*, Hillsdale, NJ: Erlbaum.

(1983) *The Architecture of Cognition*, Hillsdale, NJ: Erlbaum.

Andreoni, James (1989a) "Giving with Impure Altruism: Applications to Charity and Ricardian Equivalence," *Journal of Political Economy* 97: 1447–58.

(1989b) "Impure Altruism and Donations to Public Goods: A Theory of Warm-Glow Giving," *Economic Journal* 100: 464–77.

Angner, Erik and George Loewenstein (forthcoming) "Behavioral Economics," in U. Mäki, eds., *Philosophy of Economics*, vol. 13, Dov Gabbay, Paul Thagard, and John Woods, eds., *Handbook of the Philosophy of Science*, Amsterdam: Elsevier.

Ariely, Dan, George Loewenstein, and Drazen Prelec (2003) "Coherent arbitrariness: Stable Demand Curves without Stable Preferences," *Quarterly Journal of Economics* 118: 73–105.

(2006) "Tom Sawyer and the Myth of Fundamental Value," *Journal of Economic Behavior & Organization* 60: 1–10.

Aristotle (1924) *Metaphysics*, rev. with an introduction and commentary by W. D. Ross, Oxford: Clarendon Press.

Arrow, Kenneth (1963 [1951]) *Social Choice and Individual Values*, 2nd ed., New Haven and London: Yale University Press.

(1982) "Risk Perception in Psychology and Economics," *Economic Inquiry* 20: 1–9.

Arthur, W. Brian (1994) "Inductive Behavior and Bounded Rationality," *American Economic Review* 84: 406–11.

(1995) "Complexity in Economic and Financial Markets," *Complexity* 1 (1): 20–5.

Arthur, W. Brian, Steven Durlauf, and David Lane (1997) "Introduction," in Arthur, Durlauf, and Lane, eds., *The Economy as an Evolving Complex System II*, Proceedings, Volume XVII, Reading, MA: Addison-Wesley: 1–14.

Ashby, W. Ross (1947) "Principles of the Self-Organizing Dynamic System," *Journal of General Psychology* 37: 125–8.

Aumann, Robert (1976) "Agreeing to Disagree," *Annals of Statistics* 4: 1236–9.

(1985) "What is Game Theory Trying to Accomplish?" in K. Arrow and S. Honkapohja, eds., *Frontiers of Economics*, Oxford: Blackwell: 909–24.

(1987) "Correlated Equilibrium as an Expression of Bayesian Rationality," *Econometrica*, 55: 1–18.

(1989) "Game theory," in J. Eatwell, M. Milgate, and P. Newman, eds., *The New Palgrave: A Dictionary of Economics*, Vol. 2 London: Macmillan: 460–82.

Aumann, Robert and Adam Brandenburger (1995) "Epistemic Conditions for Nash Equilibrium," *Econometrica* 64:1161–80.

Axelrod, Robert (1980a) "Effective Choice in the Prisoner's Dilemma," *Journal of Conflict Resolution* 24: 3–25.

(1980b) "More Effective Choice in the Prisoner's Dilemma," *Journal of Conflict Resolution* 24: 379–403.

(1981) "The Emergence of Cooperation among Egoists," *American Political Science Review* 75: 306–18.

(1984) *The Evolution of Cooperation*, New York: Basic Books.

(1997), *The Complexity of Cooperation: Agent-Based Models of Competition and Collaboration*, Princeton: Princeton University Press.

Bacharach, Michael (2006) *Beyond Individual Choice: Teams and Frames in Game Theory*, N. Gold and R. Sugden, eds., Princeton: Princeton University Press.

Banaji, Mahzarin and Deborah Prentice (1994) "The Self in Social Contexts," *Annual Review of Psychology* 45: 297–332.

Bandura, Albert (1977) "Self-efficacy: Toward a Unifying Theory of Behavioral Change," *Psychological Review* 84: 191–215.

(1997) *Self-efficacy: The Exercise of Self-control*, New York: Freeman.

Bardsley, Nicholas (2005) "Experimental Economics and the Artificiality of Alternation," *Journal of Economic Methodology* 12 (2): 239–51.

Battaglini, Marco, Roland Bénabou, and Jean Tirole (2005) "Self-Control in Peer Groups," *Journal of Economic Theory* 112 (4): 848–87.

Becker, Gary (1971 [1957]) *The Economics of Discrimination*, 2nd ed., Chicago: University of Chicago Press.

(1996) *Accounting for Tastes*, Cambridge, MA: Harvard University Press.

Bénabou, Roland and Jean Tirole (2002) "Self-Confidence and Personal Motivation," *Quarterly Journal of Economics* 117 (3): 871–915.

(2003a) "Intrinsic and Extrinsic Motivation," *Review of Economic Studies* 70: 489–520.

(2003b) "Self-Knowledge and Self-Regulation: An Economic Approach," in I. Brocas and Juan Carrillo, eds., *The Psychology of Economic Decisions: Volume One: Rationality and Well-Being*, Oxford University Press: 137–67.

(2004) "Willpower and Personal Rules," *Journal of Political Economy* 112 (4): 848–86.

Bennett, Max and Peter Hacker (2003) *Philosophical Foundations of Neuroscience*, Oxford: Blackwell.

Bettman, James R. (1979) *An Information Processing Theory of Consumer Choice*, Reading, MA: Addison-Wesley.

Bicchieri, Cristina (2002) "Covenants without Swords: Group Identity, Norms, and Communication in Social Dilemmas," *Rationality and Society* 14 (2): 192–228.

Binmore, Ken (1994) *Game Theory and the Social Contract. Volume 1: Playing Fair*, Cambridge: MIT Press.

(1998) *Game Theory and the Social Contract. Volume 2: Just Playing*, Cambridge: MIT Press.

(1999) "Why Experiment in Economics?" *Economic Journal* 109: F16–24.

(2005a) "Economic Man – or Straw Man?" *Behavioral and Brain Science* 28: 817–18.

(2005b) *Natural Justice*, New York: Oxford University Press.

(2006) "Why Do People Cooperate?" *Politics, Philosophy & Economics* 5 (1): 81–96.

Binmore, Ken and Avner Shaked (2010) "Experimental Economics: Where Next?" *Journal of Economic Behavior & Organization* 73: 87–100.

Blaug, Mark (1998) "The Positive-Normative Distinction," in John Davis, Wade Hands, and Uskali Mäki, eds., *The Handbook of Economic Methodology*, Cheltenham: Edward Elgar Publishing, 370–4.

Bodner, Ronit and Drazen Prelec (2003) "Self-Signaling and Diagnostic Utility in Everyday Decision Making," in I. Brocas and Juan Carrillo, eds., *The Psychology of Economic Decisions: Volume One: Rationality and Well-Being*, Oxford University Press: 105–23.

Boumans, Marcel and John Davis (2010) *Economic Methodology: Understanding Economics as a Science*, London: Palgrave.

Bourdieu, Pierre (1988) *Homo Academicus*, trans. P. Collier, Palo Alto: Stanford University Press.

Bowker, Geoffrey and Susan Starr (1999) *Sorting Things Out: Classification and Its Consequences*, Cambridge, MA: MIT Press.

Brewer, Marilyn (2001) "The Many Faces of Social Identity: Implications for Political Psychology," *Political Psychology* 22: 115–25.

Brewer, Marilyn and Wendy Gardner (1996) "Who Is This 'We'? Levels of Collective Identity and Self-Representations," *Journal of Personal and Social Psychology*, 71: 83–93.

Brock, William and Steven Durlauf (2001) "Discrete Choice with Social Interactions," *Review of Economics Studies* 68: 235–60.

Bromley, Daniel (2006) *Sufficient Reason: Volitional Pragmatism and the Meaning of Economic Institutions*, Princeton, NJ: Princeton University Press.

Broome, John (1978) "Choice and Value in Economics," *Oxford Economic Papers* 30 (1): 313–33.

Brown, Rupert (2000) "Social Identity Theory: Past Achievements, Current Problems and Future Challenges," *European Journal of Social Psychology* 30: 745–78.

Brubaker, Rogers and Frederick Cooper (2000) "Beyond 'identity,'" *Theory and Society* 29: 1–47.

Bruner, Jerome (1990) *Acts of Meaning*, Cambridge: Harvard University Press.

(2002) *Making Stories: Law, Literature, Life*, New York: Farrar, Straus and Giroux.

Camerer, Colin (2006) "Behavioral Economics," in R. Blundell, W. Newey, and T. Persson, eds., *Advances in Economics and Econometrics*, Cambridge: Cambridge University Press: 181–214.

(2008) "The Potential of Neuroeconomics," *Economics and Philosophy* 24: 369–79.

Camerer, Colin and George Loewenstein (2003) "Behavioural Economics: Past, Present, Future," in C. Camerer, G. Loewenstein, and M. Rabin, eds., *Advances in Behavioral Economics*, New York: Russell Sage Foundation Press and Princeton: Princeton University Press: 3–52.

Camerer, Colin, George Loewenstein, and Drazen Prelec (2005) "Neuroeconomics: How Neuroscience Can Inform Economics," *Journal of Economic Literature* 43: 9–64.

Camerer, Colin, George Loewenstein, and Matthew Rabin, eds. (2003) *Advances in Behavioral Economics*, New York: Russell Sage Foundation Press and Princeton: Princeton University Press.

Carrillo, Juan and Thomas Mariotti (2000) "Strategic Ignorance as a Self-Disciplining Device," *Review of Economic Studies* 67: 529–44.

Cartwright, Nancy (1999) *The Dappled World: A Study of the Boundaries of Science*, Cambridge: Cambridge University Press.

Casajus, Andre (2001) *Focal Points in Framed Games: Breaking the Symmetry*, Berlin: Springer-Verlag.

Chang, Ruth, ed. (1997) *Incommensurability, Incomparability and Practical Reason*, Cambridge: Cambridge University Press.

Charness, Gary and Matthew Rabin (2002) "Understanding Social Preferences with Simple Tests," *Quarterly Journal of Economics* 117: 817–69.

Clark, Andy (1997) *Being There*, Cambridge: MIT Press.

Coase, Ronald (1937) "The Nature of the Firm," *Economica* 4 (16): 386–405.

Cohen, Joshua (1997) "Deliberation and Democratic Legitimacy," in J. Bohman and W. Rehg, eds., *Deliberative Democracy*, Cambridge, MA: MIT Press: 67–91.

Colander, David, Hans Föllmer, Armin Haas, Michael Goldberg, Katarina Juselius, Alan Kirman, Thomas Lux, and Brigitte Sloth (2009) "The Financial Crisis and the Systemic Failure of Academic Economics," Kiel Institute for the World Economy working paper no 1489 (February).

Colander, David, Ric Holt, and Barkley Rosser (2004) *The Changing Face of Economics*, Ann Arbor, MI: University of Michigan Press.

Collins, Randall (1998) *The Sociology of Philosophies: A Global Theory of Intellectual Changes*, Cambridge, MA: Harvard University Press.

Cooley, Charles (1902) *Human Nature and the Social Order*, New York: Scribner's.

Copp, David (1992) "The Right to an Adequate Standard of Living: Justice, Autonomy, and Basic Needs," *Social Philosophy and Society* 9: 231–61.

Cot, Annie (2009) "Inventing Experimental Economics: The Harvard 'Fatigue Laboratory' and the Hawthorne Effect," paper presented at the History of Economics Society annual meeting (June 29).

Crenshaw, Kimberlé (1989) "Demarginalizing the Intersection of Race and Sex: A Black Feminist Critique of Antidiscrimination Doctrine, Feminist Theory, and Antiracist Politics," *University of Chicago Legal Forum*, 139–67.

Crespo, Ricardo (2008) "On Sen and Aristotle," Universidad Austral, working paper.

Cubitt, Robin, Chris Starmer, and Robert Sugden (2001) "Discovered preferences and the experimental evidence of violations of expected utility theory," *Journal of Economic Methodology* 8 (3): 385–414.

Darity, William Jr., Patrick Mason, and James Stewart (2006) "The Economics of Identity: The origin and persistence of racial identity norms," *Journal of Economic Behavior and Organization* 60: 283–305.

Davis, John (1995) "Personal Identity and Standard Economic Theory," *Journal of Economic Methodology* 2: 35–52.

(2002) "Collective intentionality and individual behavior," in E. Fullbrook, ed., *Intersubjectivity in Economics*, London: Routledge.

(2003) *The Theory of the Individual in Economics: Identity and Value*, London: Routledge.

(2007a) "Akerlof and Kranton on Identity in Economics: Inverting the Analysis," *Cambridge Journal of Economics* 31 (May): 349–62.

(2007b) "Identity and Commitment: Sen's Fourth Aspect of the Self," in Bernhard Schmid and Fabienne Peters, eds., *Rationality and Commitment*, Oxford: Oxford University Press: 313–35.

(2007c) "Review: Economic Theory and Cognitive Science, by Don Ross," *Economics and Philosophy* 23 (July 2007): 245–52.

(2008a) "Complex Individuals: The Individual in Non-Euclidian Space," *Advancements in Evolutionary Institutional Economics: Evolutionary Mechanisms, Non-Knowledge, and Strategy*, Hardy Hanappi and Wolfram Elsner, eds., Cheltenham: Elgar: 129–47.

(2008b) "The Individual in Recent Economics: Internalist and Externalist Conceptions," *Storia del pensiero economico*, n.s., 5 (gennaio/giugno 2008): 5–24.

(2008c) "The Turn in Recent Economics and Return of Orthodoxy," *Cambridge Journal of Economics* 32 (May 2008): 349–66.

(2009a) "Competing Conceptions of the Individual in Recent Economics," in Harold Kincaid and Don Ross, eds., *The Oxford Handbook of the Philosophy of Economic Science*, Oxford University Press: 223–44.

(2009b) "Identity and Individual Economic Agents: A Narrative Approach," *Review of Social Economy* 67: 71–94; reprinted in *Ethics and Economics: New Perspectives*, Mark White and Irene van Staveren, eds., London: Routledge, 2009.

(2009c) "The Capabilities Conception of the Individual," *Review of Social Economy* 67 (December): 413–29.

(2009d) "Two Relational Conceptions of Individuals: Teams and Neuroeconomics," in *Research in the History of Economic Thought and Methodology*, vol. 27: 1–21.

Dawes, Robyn, Alphons van de Kragt, and John Orbell (1990) "Cooperation for the Benefit of Us, Not Me, or My Conscience," in J. Mansbridge, ed., *Beyond Self-Interest*, Chicago: University of Chicago Press: 97–110.

De Boer, Jelle (2008) "Collective Intention, Social Identity, and Rational Choice," *Journal of Economic Methodology* 15: 169–84.

Debreu, Gerard (1986) "Theoretical Models: Mathematical Form and Economic Content," *Econometrica* 54 (6): 1259–70.

Dennett, Daniel (1987) *The Intentional Stance*, Cambridge: MIT Press.

(1991) *Consciousness Explained*, Boston: Little Brown.

Dumit, Joseph (2004) *Picturing Personhood: Brain Scans and Biomedical Identity*, Princeton: Princeton University Press.

Dutta, Prajit and Roy Radner (1999) "Profit Maximization and the Market Selection Hypothesis," *Review of Economic Studies* 66: 769–98.

Eakin, John (2007) "The Economy of Narrative Identity," E. Weintraub and E. Forget, eds., *Economists' Lives and Autobiography in the History of Economics*, Durham: Duke University Press: 117–33.

Edwards, Ward (1954) "The Theory of Decision Making," *Psychological Bulletin* 41: 380–417.

(1961) "Behavioral Decision Theory," *Annual Review of Psychology* 12: 473–98.

Edwards, Ward, Harold Lindman, and Leonard J. Savage (1963) "Bayesian Statistical Inference for Psychological Research," *Psychological Review* 70: 193–242.

Edwards, Ward, Ralph Miles, and Detlof von Winterfeldt (2007) *Advances in Decision Analysis: From Foundations to Applications*, Cambridge: Cambridge University Press.

Elster, Jon (1983) *Sour Grapes: Studies in the Subversion of Rationality*, Cambridge: Cambridge University Press.

Emami, Zohreh and John Davis (2009) "Democracy, Education, and Economics," *International Journal of Pluralism and Economics Education* May.

Epstein, Seymour (1973) "The Self-concept Revisited," *American Psychologist* 28: 404–12.

Fehr, Ernst and Urs Fischbacher (2002) "Why Social Preferences Matter – The Impact of Non-Selfish Motives on Competition, Cooperation and Incentives," *Economic Journal* 112 (March): C1–C33.

Fehr, Ernst, Urs Fischbacher, and Simon Gächter (2002) "Strong Reciprocity, Human Cooperation, and the Enforcement of Social Norms," *Human Nature*, 13 (1): 1–25.

Fehr, Ernst and Simon Gächter (2000a) "Cooperation and Punishment in Public Goods Experiments," *American Economic Review* 90: 980–94.

(2000b) "Fairness and Reciprocity," *Journal of Economic Perspectives*, 14 (3): 159–81.

Fehr, Ernst and Klaus M. Schmidt (1999) "A Theory of Fairness, Competition, and Cooperation," *Quarterly Journal of Economics* 114: 817–68.

Fine, Ben (2009) "The Economics of Identity and the Identity of Economics?" *Cambridge Journal of Economics* 33: 175–91.

Fine, Ben and Dimitris Milonakis (2009) *From Economics Imperialism to Freakonomics: The Shifting Boundaries Between Economics and Other Social Sciences*, London; New York: Routledge.

Folbre, Nancy (1994) *Who Pays for the Kids? Gender and the Structures of Constraint*, London: Routledge.

Foster, John (2005) "From Simplistic to Complex Systems in Economics," *Cambridge Journal of Economics* 29: 873–92.

Frankfurt, Henri (1971) "Freedom of the Will and the Concept of a Person," *Journal of Philosophy* 68: 5–20.

Frederick, Shane, George Loewenstein, and Ted O'Donoghue (2002) "Time Discounting and Time Preference: A Critical Review," *Journal of Economic Literature* 40 (2): 351–401.

Friedman, Milton (1953) The Methodology of Positive Economics, in *Essays in Positive Economics*, Chicago and London: University of Chicago Press: 3–43.

Fudenberg, Drew and Jean Tirole (1989) "Non-cooperative game theory for industrial organisation: An Introduction and Overview," in R. Schmalensee and R. Willig, eds., *Handbook of Industrial Organization*, Amsterdam: North Holland: 259–327.

Fryback, Dennis (2005) "Ward Edwards: Father of Behavioral Decision Theory," *Medical Decision Making* 25: 468–70.

Galison, Peter and David Stump (1996) *The Disunity of Science: Boundaries, Contexts, and Power*, Stanford, CA: Stanford University Press.

Gärdenfors, Peter (1988) *Knowledge in Flux*, Cambridge, MA: MIT Press.

Garner, Marvin (1970) "Mathematical Games," *Scientific American* October: 120–123.

Gewirth, Alan (1996) *The Community of Rights*, Chicago: University of Chicago Press.

Gieryn, Thomas (1993) "Boundaries of Science," in *Handbook of Science and Technology Studies*, S. Jasanoff, G. Markle, J. Petersen, and T. Pinch, eds., Thousand Oaks, CA: Sage: 393–443.

  (1999) *Cultural Boundaries of Science: Credibility on the Line*, Chicago: University of Chicago Press.

Gigerenzer, Gerd (2001) "The Adaptive Toolbox," in G. Gigerenzer and R. Selten, eds., *Bounded Rationality: The Adaptive Toolbox*, Cambridge: MIT Press: 37–50.

Gigerenzer, Gerd and Reinhard Selten, eds. (2001) *Bounded Rationality: The Adaptive Toolbox*, Cambridge: MIT Press.

Gigerenzer, Gerd, Peter Todd, and the ABC Research Group (1999) *Simple Heuristics That Make Us Smart*, New York: Oxford.

Gilbert, Margaret (1989) *On Social Facts*, London: Routledge.

  (2008) "Two Approaches to Shared Intention," *Analyse & Kritik* 30: 483–514.

Gilovich, Thomas and Dale Griffin (2002) "Introduction – Heuristics and Biases: Then and Now," in Gilovich, Griffin, and Kahneman, eds., *Heuristics and Biases: The Psychology of Intuitive Judgment*, Princeton: Princeton University Press: 1–18.

Gilovich, Thomas, Dale Griffin, and Daniel Kahneman, eds. (2002) *Heuristics and Biases: The Psychology of Intuitive Judgment*, Princeton: Princeton University Press.

Giocoli, Nicola (2003a) "Fixing the Point: The Contribution of Early Game Theory to the Tool-Box of Modern Economics," *Journal of Economic Methodology* 10 (1): 1–39.

  (2003b) *Modeling Rational Agents: From Interwar Economics to Early Modern Game Theory*, Cheltenham: Edward Elgar.

Glaeser, Edward (2004) "Psychology and the Market," *American Economic Review*, 94 (2): 408–13.

Gleason, Philip (1983) "Identifying Identity: A Semantic History," *The Journal of American History* 69 (4): 910–31.

Glimcher, Paul, Joseph Kable, and Kenway Louie (2007) "Neuroeconomic Studies of Impulsivity: Now or Just as Soon as Possible?" *American Economic Review* 97 (2): 142–7.

Gold, Natalie and Robert Sugden (2006) "Conclusion," in N. Gold and R. Sugden, eds., *Beyond Individual Choice: Teams and Frames in Game Theory*, Princeton: Princeton University Press: 155–201.

(2007) "Theories of Team Agency," in F. Peter and H. Schmid, eds., *Rationality and Commitment*, Oxford: Oxford University Press: 286–312.

Grether, David and Charles Plott (1979) "Economic Theory of Choice and the Preference Reversal Phenomenon," *American Economic Review* 69 (4): 537–57.

(1982) "Economic Theory of Choice and the Preference Reversal Phenomenon: Reply," *American Economic Review* 72 (3): 575.

Guala, Francesco (2002) "On the Scope of Experiments in Economics: Comments on Siakanaris," *Cambridge Journal of Economics* 26: 261–7.

(2005) *The Methodology of Experimental Economics*, New York: Cambridge University Press.

Guth, Werner, R. Schmittberger, and B. Schwarze (1982) "An Experimental Analysis of Ultimatum Bargaining," *Journal of Economic Behavior and Organization* 3 (4): 367–88.

Hakakian, Roya (2004) *Journey from the Land of No*, New York: Three Rivers Press.

Hands, Wade (2006) "Individual Psychology, Rational Choice, and Demand: Some Remarks on Three Recent Studies," *Revue de Philosophie Economique* 13: 3–48.

Hargreaves Heap, Shaun and Yanis Varoufakis (2004 [1995]) *Game Theory: A Critical Introduction*, 2nd ed., London: Routledge.

Harrison, Glen (1994) "Expected Utility and the Experimentalists," *Empirical Economics* 19: 223–53.

Harsanyi, John (1967/1968) Games with Incomplete Information Played by Bayesian Players," *Management Science* 14: 159–82, 320–34, 486–502.

(1973) "Games with Randomly Disturbed Payoffs: A New Rationale for Mixed Strategy Equilibrium Points," *International Journal of Game Theory* 2 (1): 1–23.

(1982) "Morality and the Theory of Rational Behavior," in A. Sen and B. Williams, eds., *Utilitarianism and Beyond*, Cambridge: Cambridge University Press: 39–62.

(1995) "Games with Incomplete Information," *American Economic Review* 85 (3): 291–303.

(1997) "Utilities, Preferences and Substantive Goods," *Social Choice and Welfare* 14 (1): 129–45.

Hausman, Daniel (2005) "Sympathy, Commitment, and Preference," *Economics and Philosophy* 21 (1): 33–50.

Hayek, Friedrich (1945) "The Uses of Knowledge in Society," *American Economic Review* 35: 519–30.

Helfat, Constance, Sydney Finkelstein, Will Mitchel, Margaret Peteraf, Harbir Singh, David Teece, and Sydney Winter (2007) *Dynamic Capabilities: Understanding Strategic Change in Organizations*, Oxford: Basil Blackwell.

Henrich, Joseph (2006) "Cooperation, Punishment, and the Evolution of Human Institutions," *Science* 312: 60–1.

Henrich, Joseph, Robert Boyd, Samuel Bowles, Colin Camerer, Ernst Fehr, and Herbert Gintis, eds. (2004) *Foundations of Human Sociality: Economic Experiments and Ethnographic Evidence from Fifteen Small-Scale Societies*, Oxford: Oxford University Press.

Henrich, Joseph, Robert Boyd, Samuel Bowles, Colin Camerer, Ernst Fehr, Herbert Gintis, Richard McElreath, Michael Alvard, Abigail Barr, Jean Ensminger, Natalie Smith Henrich, Kim Hill, Francisco Gil-White, Michael Gurven, Frank W. Marlowe, John Q. Patton, and David Tracer (2005) "Models of Decision-Making and the Coevolution of Social Preferences," *Behavioral and Brain Sciences* 28 (6):838–55.

Herman, David, Manfred Jahn, and Marie-Laure Ryan, eds. (2005) *Routledge Encyclopedia of Narrative Theory*, London: Routledge.

Hertel, Shareen and Lanse Minkler (2007) "Economic Rights: The Terrain," in Hertel and Minkler, eds., *Economic Rights: Conceptual, Measurement, and Policy Issues*, Cambridge: Cambridge University Press.

Heukelom, Floris (2009) "Kahneman and Tversky and the Making of Behavioral Economics," University of Amsterdam PhD Thesis.

Higgins, E. Tory (1987) "Self-Discrepancy: A Theory Relation Self and Affect," *Psychological Review* 94 (3): 219–340.

Higgins, E. Tory, Gillian King, and Gregory Mavin (1982) "Individual Construct Accessibility and Subjective Impressions and Recall," *Journal of Personality and Social Psychology* 43: 35–47.

Hodgson, Geoffrey (2007) "Meanings of Methodological Individualism," *Journal of Economic Methodology* 14 (2): 211–26.

Hodgson, Geoffrey and Thorbjørn Knudsen (2006) "Why We Need a Generalized Darwinism, and Why Generalized Darwinism Is not Enough," *Journal of Economic Behavior and Organization* 61:1–19.

(2008) "In Search of General Evolutionary Principles: Why Darwinism Is Too Important to Be Left to the Biologists," *Journal of Bioeconomics* 10 (1, April): 51–69.

Hogg, Michael (2001) "Self-categorization and Subjective Uncertainty Resolution: Cognitive and Motivational Facets of Social Identity and Group Membership," in J. Forgas, K. Williams, and L. Wheeler, eds., *The Social Mind: Cognitive and Motivational Aspects of Interpersonal Behavior*, New York: Cambridge: 323–49.

Hogg, Michael, Deborah Terry, and Katherine White (1995) "A Tale of Two Theories: A Critical Comparison of Identity Theory with Social Identity Theory," *Social Psychology Quarterly* 58: 255–69.

Holland, John (1975) *Adaptation in Natural and Artificial Systems: An Introductory Analysis with Applications to Biology, Control, and Artificial Intelligence*, Ann Arbor, MI: University of Michigan Press.

(1995) *Hidden Order: How Adaptation Builds Complexity*, Reading, MA: Addison-Wesley.

Hollis, Martin (1998) *Trust within Reason*, Cambridge: Cambridge University Press.

Horst, Ulrich, Alan Kirman, and Miriam Teschl (2007) "Changing Identity: The Emergence of Social Groups," Princeton, NJ: Institute for Advanced Study, School of Social Science, Economics Working Papers: 1–30.

Janssen, Maarten (2001) "Rationalizing Focal Points," *Theory and Decision* 50: 119–48.

Jensen, Michael and William Meckling (1976) "Theory of the Firm: Managerial Behavior, Agency Costs and Ownership Structure," *Journal of Financial Economics* 3 (4): 305–60.

Kahneman, Daniel (2000) "Experienced Utility and Objective Happiness: A Moment-Based Approach," in D. Kahneman and A. Tversky, eds., *Choices, Values, and Frames*, New York: Cambridge University Press: 673–92.

(2003) "Autobiography," in T. Frängsmyr, ed., *Les Prix Nobel/Nobel Lectures*, Stockholm: Nobel Foundation.

Kahneman, Daniel, Jack L. Knetsch, and Richard Thaler (1986a) "Fairness and the Assumptions of Economics," *Journal of Business* 59: S285–S300.

(1986b) "Fairness as a Constraint on Profit Seeking: Entitlements in the Market," *American Economic Review* 76: 728–41.

Kahneman, Daniel, Paul Slovic, and Amos Tversky, eds. (1982) *Judgment Under Uncertainty: Heuristics and Biases*, New York: Cambridge University Press.

Kahneman, Daniel and Amos Tversky (1979) "Prospect Theory: An Analysis of Decision Under Risk," *Econometrica* 47: 263–91.

Kahneman, Daniel and Amos Tversky, eds. (2000) *Choices, Values, and Frames*, New York: Russell Sage Foundation Press and Cambridge: Cambridge University Press.

Kirman, Alan and Miriam Teschl (2004) "On the Emergence of Economic Identity," *Revue de Philosophie économique* 9 (1): 59–86.

Klein, Judy (1998) "Controlling Gunfire, Inventory and Expectations with the Exponentially Weighted Moving Average," paper presented to the annual meeting of the History of Economics Society, Montreal.

(1999) "Economic Stabilization Policies and the Military Art of Control Engineering," paper presented to the Economists at War conference, Erasmus University, Rotterdam.

Korsgaard, Christine (1996) *The Sources of Normativity*, Cambridge: Cambridge University Press.

Lamont, M. and V. Molnár (2002) "The Study of Boundaries in the Social Sciences," *Annual Review of Sociology* 28: 167–95.

Lazear, Edward (2000) "Economic Imperialism," *Quarterly Journal of Economics* 115 (1): 99–146.

Lee, Kyu Sang (2004) "Rationality, Minds, and Machines in the Laboratory: A Thematic History of Vernon Smith's Experimental Economics," University of Notre Dame PhD Thesis.

Lichtenstein, Sarah and Paul Slovic (1971) "Reversals of Preference between Bids and Choices in Gambling Decisions," *Journal of Experimental Psychology* 101: 46–55.

(2006) "The Construction of Preference," in S. Lichtenstein and P. Slovic, eds., *The Construction of Preference*, Cambridge: Cambridge University Press: 1–40.

Livet, Pierre (2004) "La pluralité cohérente des notions d'identité personnelle," *Revue de Philosophie Economique* 9: 29–57.

(2006) "Identities, Capabilities, and Revisions," *Journal of Economic Methodology* 13 (3): 327–48.

Lloyd, Dan (2007) "Civil Schizophrenia," in Don Ross, David Spurrett, Harold Kincaid, and G., Lynn Stephens, eds., *Distributed Cognition and the Will*, Cambridge, MA: MIT Press: 323–48.

Locke, John (1975 [1694]) *An Essay Concerning Human Understanding*, ed. P.H. Nidditch, Oxford: Clarendon Press.

Loewenstein, George (1996) "Out of Control: Visceral Influences in Behavior," *Organizational Behavior and Human Decision Processes* 65 (3): 272–92.

(1999) "Experimental Economics from the Vantage-Point of Behavioral Economics," *Economic Journal* 109 (February): F25–F34.

Loewenstein, George and Drazen Prelec (1992) "Anomalies in Intertemporal Choice: Evidence and an Interpretation," *Quarterly Journal of Economics* 107 (2): 573–97.

Loomes, Graham (1991) "Experimental Methods in Economics," in D. Greenaway, M. Bleaney, and I. Stewart, eds., *Companion to Contemporary Economic Thought*, London: Routledge: 593–613.

Luce, R. Duncan and Howard Raiffa (1957) *Games and Decisions*, New York: Wiley.

Luhmann, Niklas (1984) *Soziale Systeme: Grundriß einer allgemeinen Theorie*, Frankfurt: Suhrkamp; trans. as *Social Systems*, Stanford: Stanford University Press, 1995.

Maalouf, Amin (1998 [2000]) *Les Identités Meurtrières* [In the Name of Identity]. Trans. Barbara Bray, 2000. Paris: Grasset.

MacIntryre, Alasdair (1981) *After Virtue: A Study in Moral Theory*, Notre Dame, IN: University of Notre Dame Press.

Mackenzie, Catriona and Natalie Stoljar (2000) "Introduction: Autonomy Refigured," in C. Mackenzie and N. Stoljar, eds., *Relational Autonomy: Feminist Perspectives on Autonomy, Agency, and the Social Self*, Oxford: Oxford University Press: 3–31.

Madrian, Brigitte and Dennis Shea (2001) "The Power of Suggestion: Inertia in 401(k) Participation and Savings Behavior, *Quarterly Journal of Economics* 116 (4): 1149–87.

March, James (1978) "Bounded Rationality, Ambiguity, and the Engineering of Choice," *Bell Journal of Economics* 9 (2): 587–608.

Margalit, Avishai (1996) *The Decent Society*, Cambridge, MA: Harvard.

Markus, Hazel and Elissa Wurf, (1987) "The Dynamic Self-concept: A Social Psychological Perspective," *Annual Review of Psychology* 38: 299–337.

Maynard Smith, John (1982) *Evolution and the Theory of Games*, Cambridge: Cambridge University Press.

Mayr, Ernst (1961) "Cause and Effect in Biology," *Science* 134: 1501–6.

McCabe, Kevin, Daniel Houser, Lee Ryan, Vernon Smith, and Theodore Trouard (2001) "A Functional Imaging Study of Cooperation in Two-Person Reciprocal Exchange," *Proceedings of the National Academy of Sciences of the United States of America* 98 (20): 11832–35.

McCabe, Kevin and Vernon Smith (2001) "Goodwill Accounting and the Process of Exchange," in G. Gigerenzer and R. Selten, eds., *Bounded Rationality: The Adaptive Toolbox*, Cambridge: MIT Press: 319–42.

McCall, George and J. L. Simmons (1978) *Identities and Interactions*, New York: Free Press.

McCloskey, Deirdre (1990) *If You're So Smart: The Narrative of Economic Expertise*, Chicago: University of Chicago Press.

(1994) *Knowledge and Persuasion in Economics*, Cambridge: Cambridge University Press.

McFall, Lynne (1987) "Integrity," *Ethics* 98: 5–20.

Mead, George (1934) *Mind, Self, and Society*, Chicago: University of Chicago.

Merton, Robert and Alice Kitt (1950) "Contributions to the Theory of Reference Group Behavior," in R. Merton and P. Lazarsfeld, eds., *Continuities in Social Research: Studies in the Scope and Method of "The American Soldier,"* Glencoe: Free Press: 40–105.

Meyers, Diana (1989) *Self, Society, and Personal Choice*, New York: Columbia University Press.

(2000) "Intersectional Identity and the Authentic Self?" in C. Mackenzie and N. Stoljar, eds., *Relational Autonomy: Feminist Perspectives on Autonomy, Agency, and the Social Self*, Oxford: Oxford University Press: 151–80.

Minkler, Lanse (2008) *Integrity and Agreement: When Principle Also Matter*, Ann Arbor: MI: University of Michigan Press.

Mirowski, Philip (2002) *Machine Dreams: Economics Becomes a Cyborg Science*, Cambridge: Cambridge University Press.

Mischel, W. (1973) "Toward a Cognitive Social Learning Reconceptualization of Personality," *Psychological Review* 80: 252–84.

Mongin, Philippe (2006) "Value Judgments and Value Neutrality in Economics," *Economica* 72: 257–86.

Nagel, Thomas (1970) *The Possibility of Altruism*, Oxford: Oxford University Press.
   (1986) *The View from Nowhere*, Oxford: Oxford University Press.

Nelson, Richard and Sidney Winter (1982) *An Evolutionary theory of Economic Change*, Cambridge, MA: Harvard University Press.

Noonan, Harold (1991) *Personal Identity*, London: Routledge.

North, Douglass (2006) "On Kenneth Binmore's *Natural Justice*," *Analyse & Kritik* 28: 102–3.

Nozick, Robert (1974) *Anarchy, State, and Utopia*, New York: Basic Books.

Nussbaum, Martha (1988) "Nature, Function, and Capability: Aristotle on Political Distribution," *Oxford Studies in Ancient Philosophy*, suppl. : 145–84.

Orbell, John, Alphons van de Kragt, and Robyn Dawes (1988) "Explaining Discussion-Induced Cooperation," *Journal of Personality and Social Psychology* 54: 811–19.

Payne, John and James Bettman (1992) "Behavioral Decision Research: A Constructive Processing Approach," *Annual Review of Psychology* 43: 87–131.

Payne, John, James Bettman, and Eric Johnson (1993) *The Adaptive Decision Maker*, New York: Cambridge University Press.

Peter, Fabienne (2009) *Democratic Legitimacy*, London: Routledge.

Peter, Fabienne, and Hans Bernhard Schmid, eds. (2007) *Rationality and Commitment*, Oxford: Oxford University Press.

Phillips, Lawrence and Detlof von Winterfeldt (2007) "Reflections on the Contributions of Ward Evans to Decision Analysis and Behavioral Research," in W. Edwards, R. Miles, and D. von Winterfeldt, eds., *Advances in Decision Analysis: From Foundations to Applications*, Cambridge: Cambridge University Press: 71–80.

Plott, Charles (1991) "Will Economics Become an Experimental Science?" *Southern Economic Journal* 57: 901–19.
   (1996) "Rational Individual Behavior in Markets and Social Choice Processes," in K. Arrow, E. Colombatto, M. Perlman, and C. Schmidt, eds., *The Rational Foundations of Economic Behavior*, Basingstoke: Macmillan: 225–50.

Plott, Charles and Vernon Smith, eds. (2008) *Handbook of Experimental Economics Results, Volume 1*, Amsterdam: Elsevier.

Pokinghome, Donald (1998) *Narrative Knowing and the Human Sciences*, Albany, NY: State University of New York Press.

Potts, Jason (2008) "Economic Evolution, Identity Dynamics and Cultural Science," *Cultural Science* 1: 2.

Poundstone, William (1992) *Prisoner's Dilemma*, New York: Anchor.

Quine, Willard (1969) *Ontological Relativity and other Essays*, New York: Columbia University Press.

Rabin, Matthew (1993) "Incorporating Fairness into Game Theory and Economics," *American Economic Review* 83 (5): 1281–1302.
   (1996) "Daniel Kahneman and Amos Tversky," in W. Samuels, ed., *American Economists of the Late Twentieth Century*, Cheltenham: Edward Elgar: 111–37.
   (1998) "Psychology and Economics," *Journal of Economic Literature* 36: 11–46.

Radden, Jennifer (1996) *Divided Minds and Successive Selves*, Cambridge, MA: MIT Press.

Radner, Roy (1997) "Economic Survival," in D. Jacobs, E. Kalai, and M. Kamien, eds., *Frontiers of Research in Economic Theory: The Nancy L. Schwartz Memorial Lectures, 1983-1997*, Cambridge: Cambridge University Press: 183–209.

Rawls, John (1958) "Justice as Fairness," *Philosophical Review* 67 (2): 164–94.

(1971) *A Theory of Justice*, Cambridge, MA: Belknap Press of Harvard University Press, rev. ed. 1999.

(1993) *Political Liberalism*, New York: Columbia University Press.

(2009) *A Brief Inquiry in the Meaning of Sin and Faith, With "On My Religion,"* T. Nagel, ed., with commentaries by Thomas Nagel and Joshua Cohen, and by Robert Merrihew Adams, Cambridge, MA: Harvard University Press.

Ricouer, Paul (1988) *Time and Narrative*, K. McLaughlin and D. Pellauer, trans., vol. 3, Chicago: University of Chicago Press.

(1992) *Oneself as Another*, K. Blamey, trans., Chicago: University of Chicago Press.

Rizvi, S. Abu Turab (1994) "Game Theory to the Rescue?" *Contributions to Political Economy* 13: 1–28.

Ross, Don (2005) *Economic Theory and Cognitive Science: Microexplanation*, Cambridge: MIT Press.

(2006) "The Economic and Evolutionary Basis of Selves," *Cognitive Systems Research* 7: 246–58.

(2007) "*H. sapiens* as Ecologically Special: What Does Language Contribute?" *Language Sciences* 29.5: 710–31.

(2008) "Two Styles of Neuroeconomics," *Economics and Philosophy* 24: 373–83.

Ross, Don, Carla Sharp, Rudy E. Vuchinich, and David Spurrett (2008) *Midbrain Mutiny: The Picoeconomics and Neuroeconomics of Disordered Gambling*, Cambridge, MA: MIT Press.

Ross, Don, David Spurrett, Harold Kincaid, and G. Lynn Stephens (2007) *Distributed Cognition and the Will: Individual Volition and the Will*, Cambridge, MA: MIT Press.

Ross, W. D. (1923) *Aristotle*, London: Methuen.

Rosser, J. Barkley, ed. (2009) *Handbook of Complexity Research*, Cheltenham: Elgar.

Roth, Alvin (1995) "Bargaining Experiments," in J. H. Kagel and A. E. Roth, eds., *Handbook of Experimental Economics*, Princeton: Princeton University Press: 253–348.

Rubinstein, Ariel (1979) "Equilibrium in Supergames with the Overtaking Criterion," *Journal of Economic Theory* 21:1–9.

Samuelson, Paul (1937) "A Note on Measurement of Utility," *The Review of Economic Studies* 4 (2): 155–61.

(1938) "A Note on the Pure Theory of Consumer Behavior," *Economica* 5: 61–71.

Samuelson, William and Richard Zeckhauser (1988) "Status Quo Bias in Decision Making," *Journal of Risk and Uncertainty* 1 (1): 186–91.

Santos, Ana Cordeiro (2010) *The Social Epistemology of Experimental Economics*, London: Routledge.

Sarbin, Theodore, ed. (1986) *Narrative Psychology: The Storied Nature of Human Conduct*, Westport, CT: Praeger.

Savage, Leonard (1954) *The Foundations of Statistics*, New York: John Wiley.

Schechtman, Marya (1996) *The Constitution of Selves*, Ithaca: Cornell University Press.

Schelling, Thomas (1960) *The Strategy of Conflict*, Cambridge: Harvard University Press.

(1969) "Models of Segregation," *American Economic Review* 59 (2): 488–93.

(1971) "Dynamic Models of Segregation," *Journal of Mathematical Sociology* 1: 143–86.

Schram, Arthur (2005) "Artificiality: The Tension between Internal and External Validity in Economic Experiments," *Journal of Economic Methodology* 12 (2) 225–37.

Schumpeter, Joseph (1942) *Capitalism, Socialism and Democracy*, London: George Allen and Unwin.

Searle, John (1990) "Collective Intentions and Actions," in P. Cohen, J. Morgan, and M. Pollack, eds., *Intentions in Communication*, Cambridge: MIT Press: 401–15.

Selten, Reinhard (1998) "Aspiration Adaptation Theory," *Journal of Mathematical Psychology* 42: 191–214.

Selten, Reinhard and Rolf Stoecker (1986) "End Behavior in Sequences of Finite Prisoner's Dilemma Supergames," *Journal of Economic Behavior and Organization* 7: 47–70.

Sen, Amartya (1970) *Collective Choice and Social Welfare*, San Francisco: Holden-Day.

(1977) "Rational Fools: A Critique of the Behavioral Foundations of Economic Theory," *Philosophy and Public Affairs* 6: 317–44.

(1985a) "Goals, Commitment, and Identity," *Journal of Law, Economics and Organization* 1 (2): 341–55.

(1985b) "Well-Being, Agency and Freedom: The Dewey Lectures 1984," *Journal of Philosophy* 82 (4): 169–221.

(1992) *Inequality Reexamined*, Harvard University Press, Cambridge.

(1993) "Capability and Well-Being," in M. Nussbaum and A. Sen, eds., *The Quality of Life*, Oxford: Clarendon Press: 30–53.

(1997) "Maximization and the Act of Choice," *Econometrica* 65: 745–79.

(1999a) *Development as Freedom*, New York: Alfred A. Knopf.

(1999b) *Reason before Identity*, New Delhi: Oxford University Press.

(2002) *Rationality and Freedom*, Cambridge, MA: Belknap Press.

(2005) "Human Rights and Capabilities," *Journal of Human Development* 6 (2): 151–66.

(2006) *Identity and Violence: The Illusion of Destiny*, New York: Norton.

(2007) "Why Exactly is Commitment Important for Rationality?" in F. Peter and H. Schmid, eds., *Rationality and Commitment*, Oxford: Oxford University Press: 17–27.

(2009) *The Idea of Justice*, Cambridge, MA: Belknap Press of Harvard University Press.

Sent, Esther-Mirjam (2004) "Behavioral Economics: How psychology Made its (Limited) Way Back into Economics," *History of Political Economy* 36: 735–60.

Shue, Henry (1996) *Basic Rights: Subsistence, Affluence, and U.S. Foreign Policy*, 2nd ed., Princeton: Princeton University Press.

Siakantaris, Nikos (2000) "Experimental Economics under the Microscope," *Cambridge Journal of Economics* 24: 267–81.

Simon, Herbert (1947) *Administrative Behavior: A Study of Decision-Making Processes in Administrative Organizations*, New York: Macmillan.

(1955) "A Behavioral Model of Rational Choice," *Quarterly Journal of Economics* 69: 99–118.

(1956) "Rational Choice and the Structure of the Environment," *Psychological Review* 63: 129–38.

(1962) "The Architecture of Complexity," *Proceedings of the American Philosophical Society* 106 (6): 467–82.

(1981/1996) *The Sciences of the Artificial*, 3rd ed., Cambridge: MIT Press.

Simon, Herbert and Albert Ando (1961) "Aggregation of Variables in Dynamic Systems," *Econometrica* 29: 111–38.

Slovic, Paul (1995) "The Construction of Preference," *American Psychologist* 50: 364–71.

Smith, Adam (1759 [1976]) *The Theory of Moral Sentiments*, rev. ed. 1790; republished, Oxford: Clarendon.

Smith, Vernon (1976) "Experimental Economics: Induced Value Theory," *American Economic Review* 66: 274–9.

(1982) "Microeconomic Systems as an Experimental Science," *American Economic Review* 72: 923–55.

(1989) "Theory, Experiment and Economics," *Journal of Economic Perspectives* 3 (1): 151–69.

(1992) "Game Theory and Experimental Economics: Beginnings and Early Influences," *History of Political Economy* 24 (supplement): 241–82.

(2002) "Constructivist and Ecological Rationality in Economics," Nobel Foundation, http://nobelprize.org/nobel_prizes/economics/laureates/2002/smith-lecture.pdf.

(2008) *Rationality in Economics: Constructivist and Ecological Forms*, Cambridge: Cambridge University Press.

Sobel, Joel (2005) "Interdependent Preferences and Reciprocity," *Journal of Economic Literature* 43 (June): 392–436.

Starmer, Chris (1999) "Experiments in Economics: Should We Trust the Dismal Scientists in White Coats?" *Journal of Economic Methodology*, 6: 1–30.

(2000) "Developments in Non-Expected Utility Theory: The Hunt for a Descriptive Theory of Choice under Risk," *Journal of Economic Literature* 38: 332–82.

Stets, Jan and Peter Burke (2000) "Identity Theory and Social Identity Theory," *Social Psychological Quarterly* 63: 283–95.

Stevens, Richard, ed. (1996) *Understanding the Self*, Thousand Oaks: Sage.

Stigler, George and Gary Becker (1977) "De gustibus non est disputandum," *American Economic Review* 67: 76–90.

Strawson, Galen (2004) "Against Narrativity," *Ratio* 17: 428–52.

Stryker, Sheldon (1980) *Symbolic Interactionism: A Social Structural Version*, Menlo Park, CA: Benjamin/Cummings.

Sugden, Robert (1991) "Rational Choice: A Survey of Contributions from Economics and Psychology," *Economic Journal* 101: 751–785.

(1995) "A Theory of Focal Points," *Economic Journal* 105: 533–50.

(2000) "Team Preferences," *Economics and Philosophy* 16: 175–204.

(2005) "Correspondence of Sentiments: An Explanation of the Pleasure of Social Interaction," in Bruni, Luigino and Pier Luigi Porta, eds. (2005) *Economics and Happiness: Framing the Analysis*, Oxford: Oxford University Press: 91–115.

Sunstein, Cass and Richard Thaler (2003) "Libertarian Paternalism Is Not an Oxymoron," *The University of Chicago Law Review* 70: 1159–1202.

Tajfel, Henri (1972) "Social Categorization," in S. Moscovici, ed., *Introduction à la psychologie sociale*, Vol. 1, Paris: Larousse: 272–302.

(1973) "The Roots of Prejudice: Cognitive Aspects," in P. Watson, ed., *Psychology and Race*, Chicago: Aldine: 76–95.

Tajfel, Henri, Michael Billig, Robert Bundy, and Claude Flament (1971) "Social Categorization and Intergroup Behavior," *European Journal of Social Psychology* 1: 149–78.

Tajfel, Henri, Jos Jaspars, and Colin Fraser (1984) "The Social Dimension in European Social Psychology," in H. Tajfel, ed., *The Social Dimension: European Developments in Social Psychology*, Vol. 1, Cambridge: Cambridge: 1–5.

Taylor, Charles (1989) *Sources of the Self: The Making of the Modern Identity*, Cambridge, MA: Harvard.

Tesfatsion, Leigh (2006) "Agent-Based Computational Economics: A Constructive Approach to Economic Theory," in L. Tesfatsion and K. Judd, eds., *Handbook of Computational Economics, Vol. 2: Agent-Based Computational Economics*, Amsterdam, Netherlands: North-Holland/Elsevier: 831–80.

Thaler, Richard (1985) "Mental Accounting and Consumer Choice," *Marketing Science* 4: 199–214.

(2000) "From Homo Economics to Homo Sapiens," *Journal of Economic Perspectives* 14 (1): 133–41.

Thaler, Richard and Cass Sunstein (2003) "Libertarian Paternalism," *American Economic Review* 93 (2): 175–79.

(2008) *Nudge: Improving Decisions about Health, Wealth, and Happiness*, rev. ed., New Haven: Yale University Press.

Thoits, Peggy and Lauren Virshup (1997) "Me's and We's: Forms and Functions of Social Identities," in R. Ashmore and L. Jussim, eds., *Self and Identity: Fundamental Issues*, Vol. 1, Oxford: Oxford University Press: 106–33.

Thomas, Kerry (1996) "The Defensive Self: A Psychodynamic Perspective," in R. Stevens, ed., *Understanding the Self*, Thousand Oaks, CA: Sage: 281–337.

Tuomela, Raimo and Kaarlo Miller (1988) "We-intentions," *Philosophical Studies* 53: 367–89.

Turner, John (1985) "Social Categorization and the Self-Concept: A Social Cognitive Theory of Group Behavior," in E. Lawler, ed., *Advances in Group Processes: Theory and Research*, Vol. 2, Greenwich, CT: JAI: 77–122.

Turner, John, Michael Hogg, Penelope Oakes, Stephen Reicher, and Margaret Wetherell (1987) *Rediscovering the Social Group: A Self-Categorization Theory*, Oxford: Blackwell.

Tversky, Amos and Daniel Kahneman (1981) "The Framing of Decisions and the Psychology of Choice," *Science* 211: 453–8.

(1986) "Rational Choice and the Framing of Decisions," *Journal of Business* 59 (4) pt. 2: s251–78.

(1991) "Loss Aversion in Riskless Choice: A Reference-Dependent Model," *Quarterly Journal of Economics* 106 (4): 1039–61.

(1992) "Advances in Prospect Theory: Cumulative Representation of Uncertainty," *Journal of Risk and Uncertainty* 5 (4): 297–323.

Tversky, Amos, Paul Slovic, and Daniel Kahneman (1990) "The Causes of Preference Reversal," *American Economic Review* 80: 204–17.

United Nations (1948) "Universal Declaration of Human Rights," United Nations, http://www.un.org/en/documents/udhr/; accessed 8 October 2009.

(1966) "International Covenant on Economic, Social, and Cultural Rights," United Nations, http://www2.ohchr.org/english/law/cescr.htm; accessed 8 October 2009.

Urquhart, Robert (2005) *Ordinary Choices: Individuals, Incommensurability, and Democracy*, London: Routledge.

von Neumann, John and Oskar Morgenstern (1944) *The Theory of Games and Economic Behavior*, Princeton, NJ: Princeton University Press.

Vromen, Jack (2004) "Taking Evolution Seriously – What Difference Does it Make for Economics?" In J. B. Davis, A. Marciano & J. Runde, eds., *The Elgar Companion to Economics and Philosophy*, Cheltenham, UK: Edward Elgar: 102–31.

(2009) "Advancing Evolutionary Explanations in Economics: The Limited Usefulness of Tinbergen's Four Questions Classification," in H. Kincaid and D. Ross, eds., *The Oxford Handbook of the Philosophy of Economic Science*, Oxford University Press: 337–67.

Wiener, Norbert (1961) *Cybernetic Systems*, 2nd ed., Cambridge: MIT Press.

Wilcox, Nathaniel (2008) "Against Simplicity and Cognitive Individualism," *Economics and Philosophy* 24: 523–32.

Williams, Bernard (1973) "Integrity," in J. Smart and B. Williams, *Utilitarianism: For and Against*, Cambridge: Cambridge University Press: 108–18.

(1981) *Moral Luck: Philosophical Papers 1973–1980*, Cambridge: Cambridge University Press.

(1985) *Ethics and the Limits of Philosophy*, London: Fontana.

Winter, Sidney (1990) "Survival, Selection, and Inheritance in Evolutionary Theories of Organization," in J. Singh, ed., *Organizational Evolution: New Directions*, Newbury Park, CA: Sage: 269–297.

(2003) "Understanding Dynamic Capabilities," *Strategic Management Journal* 24: 991–5.

Index